THE POLITICAL ECONOMY OF CHINA'S SYSTEMIC TRANSFORMATION

Victoria Mantzopoulos

Probabilities and Statistics (with Xioahui Zhong) (2010)
Fundamentals in Statistics, 2nd edition (2008)
Fundamentals in Statistics (2002)
Statistics for Comparative Politics and Economics (1996)
Statistics for the Social Sciences, Prentice Hall (1995)

Raphael Shen

China's Economic Reform: an Experiment in Pragmatic Socialism (2000)
The Restructuring of Romania's Economy: A Paradigm of Flexibility and Adaptability (1997)
Ukraine's Economic Reform: Obstacles, Errors, Lessons (1995)
Restructuring the Baltic Economies: Disengaging 50 Years of Integration with the U.S.S.R. (1994)
Economic Reform in Poland and Czechoslovakia: Lessons in Systemic Transformation (1993)
The Polish Economy: Legacies from the Past Prospects for The Future (1992)

The Political Economy of China's Systemic Transformation

1979 to the Present

Victoria Mantzopoulos
and Raphael Shen

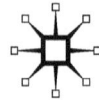

THE POLITICAL ECONOMY OF CHINA'S SYSTEMIC TRANSFORMATION
Copyright © Victoria Mantzopoulos and Raphael Shen, 2011.
Softcover reprint of the hardcover 1st edition 2011 978-0-230-10303-0

All rights reserved.

First published in 2011 by
PALGRAVE MACMILLAN®
in the United States—a division of St. Martin's Press LLC,
175 Fifth Avenue, New York, NY 10010.

Where this book is distributed in the UK, Europe and the rest of the world, this is by Palgrave Macmillan, a division of Macmillan Publishers Limited, registered in England, company number 785998, of Houndmills, Basingstoke, Hampshire RG21 6XS.

Palgrave Macmillan is the global academic imprint of the above companies and has companies and representatives throughout the world.

Palgrave® and Macmillan® are registered trademarks in the United States, the United Kingdom, Europe and other countries.

ISBN 978-1-349-28757-4   ISBN 978-0-230-11934-5 (eBook)
DOI 10.1057/9780230119345

Library of Congress Cataloging-in-Publication Data

Mantzopoulos, Victoria L., 1958–
   The political economy of China's systemic transformation : 1979 to the present / Victoria Mantzopoulos, Raphael Shen.
     p. cm.

   1. China—Economic policy—1976–2000. 2. China—Economic policy—2000– 3. China—Economic conditions—1976–2000. 4. China—Economic conditions—2000– 5. Investments, Foreign—China. I. Shen, Raphael. II. Title.

HC427.92.M3575 2011
330.951—dc22   2010049103

A catalogue record of the book is available from the British Library.

Design by Newgen Imaging Systems (P) Ltd., Chennai, India.

First edition: June 2011
10 9 8 7 6 5 4 3 2 1

Transferred to Digital Printing in 2012

Contents

List of Illustrations	vii
Preface	ix
Acknowledgments	xi
1 Legacies from Mao	1
2 The Political Economy of Reform after Mao	19
3 Reform Approach and Framework	35
4 Foreign Investment	55
5 Foreign Trade Reform	81
6 A Comparative Performance Study	111
7 Successes	141
8 Anomalies and Challenges	163
9 Concluding Observations	189
Notes	205
Bibliography	225
Index	235

Illustrations

Tables

4.1	Foreign Capital Inflow, 1979–2008	68
5.1	China's Foreign Trade, 1978–2008	98
5.2	Major Trading Partners 2005–2008	103
6.1	Correlation Matrix for Selected Variables by Country	127
7.1	Select Macro Indicators, 1979–2008	144
7.2	Select Macro Data for China, Poland, Romania and Ukraine, 1980–2008	157

Figures

6.1	GDP for China, Poland, Romania, and Ukraine	128
6.2	Foreign Direct Investment, Net Inflow	129
6.3	China's Foreign Reserve	130
6.4	Path Analysis Predicting GDP	136

Preface

Sweeping systemic and structural changes have occurred in both former and contemporary communist regimes in recent decades. The respective reform approaches have varied from the "Big Bang" to gradualism strategies. Outcomes have also fluctuated from the impressive to the not nearly so. While economies in Eastern Europe were still in the tight embrace of the command system in the late 1970s, China began experimenting with elements of the market system. There was no prior experience to rely on. There was no historical lesson to learn from. China was indeed the pioneer.

Experiences from the tumultuous decades under Mao Zedong induced the post-Mao era Chinese leaders to insist on stability, whatever the cost. Introducing elements of the market into a fundamentally socialist system had to be orderly, deliberate, and experimental in nature. Only when successes consequent upon experimental reform measures were unmistakable was the scope, pace, and depth of reform policies permitted to advance.

The motto for reform was "enlivening within, opening up without." The sleeping giant of an economy frozen by an inflexible Command system was too cumbersome to awaken. That was particularly true for China's inefficient and wasteful industrial sector. A more active catalyst for change needed to come from without. It was upon "opening up without" that entrepreneurial spirit in nonfarm sectors began stirring.

The cherished motto of "politics in command" was and has been operative throughout the past six decades. As reform began three decades ago, it was still political decisions that defined and promoted reform measures in economic spheres. Parameters of reform policies were clearly delineated and enforced.

Foreseen or not, China's current successes may to a large measure be attributable to its successes in the external sector. More specifically, it has been the phenomenal growth in the export sector over the past three decades that has been the most instrumental in propelling China onto the world stage as an awakened economic giant. Successes in the export sector have in turn been highly dependent on China's successful foreign investment policies. It was social calm and political stability enforced by the regime that assured prospective foreign investors that their ventures in China would be securely protected.

The primary proposition of this study is that tight political controls, especially during early phases of systemic transformation, could be instrumental in securing stable and sustained economic growth. This manuscript first presents some background information on China's political and economic conditions prior to as well as during the early years of reform. Parameters for and successes in foreign investment and foreign trade were then introduced and briefly analyzed in chapters 4 and 5, respectively.

Chapter 6 serves as the "test tube" for the thesis of this manuscript. That is, tight political controls during early phases of systemic transformation could be a significant factor in securing developmental successes. Quantitative performances of four transitional economies—China, Poland, Ukraine, and Romania—were subjected to statistical tests and analyses. To a large measure, results from analyses of macro data from the four economies seem to suggest that there are merits to the proposition of this study. Thereafter, successes, anomalies, and challenges were presented in chapters 7 and 8, respectively. Chapter 9 concludes this study. In the chapter, some of the prerequisites that are fundamental to success are outlined and briefly exemplified with historical instances. The topic of objective value is then raised, with the question as to the future direction of China's reform policies being raised and intimated.

Acknowledgments

We are deeply indebted to Marrina Wenzhe Zhang, our graduate research assistant, for her intellectual acumen, her work ethic, and her professional competence. Her indefatigable readiness and willingness to be of assistance has been a dream come true.

We are also deeply indebted to Samantha Kas-Petrus for her diligent work over the last several years and her meticulous eye for detail. We are also grateful for the contribution of Charles Palermo for his contributions to the project.

Finally, we wish to sincerely thank our friends and family who supported us with great patience as we completed our work. Thank you.

CHAPTER 1

LEGACIES FROM MAO

THE CHINESE COMMUNIST PARTY (CCP) WAS FORMED IN 1921. The initial thrust of the CCP movement in China was centered in urban areas. In 1927, the Nationalist government of Chiang Kai-shek intensified its campaign measures against the nascent CCP. After losing more than 80 percent of its members by late 1927, the 56-member CCP redirected its focus of revolutionary activities from urban to rural regions.

Only a thin demarcation line existed between military and political leaders within the Party's hierarchical structure during early periods of its history. Members of the Politburo also came from the ranks of the field marshals. Though it was Zhou Enlai who led the first armed uprising against the Nationalist government in Nanchang in 1927, it was Mao Ze-Dong (Mao) and field marshal Zhu De who emerged as the most prominent of CCP leaders by 1935.

During the war years—the war against the Japanese (1937–1945) and the subsequent civil war (1945–1949)—it was the military leaders who scored victories in the field and instilled fears among their foes. Mao's successes came more from his being the Party's ideological theoretician and political strategist than from battles in the field. Over time, Mao gradually emerged as the first among equals.

Upon the official founding of the People's Republic of China (PRC) in 1949, it was Mao who declared to the world that "the people of China have stood up." Thenceforward, until his death in 1976, Mao remained the "Great Helmsman" of China. China's history during the years 1949–1976 was thereby inextricably tied to Mao's reading and interpretation of the "objective conditions" prevailing in China at any given time.

Corollary to his vision for China, all major social, economic, and political decisions thereby bore his imprimatur until his demise. By then, the mold had been cast. China's economy remained structurally rigid and functionally inefficient. After more than a quarter century of Mao's development stratagem, China remained among the ranks of the world's underdeveloped nations. To illustrate the need for reform after Mao, a brief review of the political and economic progression during Mao's decades of reign is undertaken.

LAND REFORM

When the CCP moved its focus of revolution from urban to rural regions after 1927, it implemented the land reform policy. During the early years of the civil war, in order to rally broad-based support from the masses in communist-controlled regions, the CCP's land reform policy was to purchase land from the landed gentry for distribution to the peasants. Support for the CCP's cause against the Nationalist government grew. The Party was perceived as the champion for the oppressed. The land reform policy was implemented in an equitable and orderly fashion. However, the policy became brusquer after World War II between 1945 and 1949. The policy changed from land-purchasing to confiscation when the CCP began gaining more and more ground fighting against the Nationalists. Not only the land of landlords but also the land of larger landowners possessing more than the holdings of a typical peasant family was confiscated. In addition, a notable number of landlords were executed without due process, generating fear among landlords, rich peasants, and the moneyed-class in provinces and regions still under the control of the Nationalist government.

By the middle of 1949, forces of the CCP army had gained virtual control of all of China's mainland provinces. A Land Reform Act was promulgated in late 1949, and the wind of seizing land from the landlords swept throughout China, leading to countryside liquidation meetings and swift executions of an untold number of landlords. The landlords were the first of numerous waves of "class enemies" whose lives ended tragically during Mao's reign. On the rural scene, land-to-the-tiller policy stimulated the productive incentives of former tenants and peasants throughout the country. But the land reform program also had laid the foundation for the eventual collectivization and communization of all the rural producing units.

THE "THREE-ANTI" AND THE "FIVE-ANTI" MOVEMENTS

Mao's vision for China was the construction of a socialist state that would progressively evolve into a communist society. Freed from military campaigns against the Nationalist forces in China's mainland, Mao initiated a series of political movements in quick succession. These movements thoroughly impacted not only China's political theaters but also its economic, social, and cultural spheres. While the land reform movement was still in full swing, another political initiative, termed the "Three-Anti" and "Five-Anti" movements, was launched in 1951 and 1952, respectively. The targets of the "Three-Anti" movement were local bureaucrats steeped in past practices, remnant agents from the Nationalist regime, and elements in society deemed undesirable in a socialist state. The "Five-Anti" movement was aimed at "dishonest" businesses, business persons, and their practices. Nominally, the movement was against bribery, tax evasion, dishonest business dealings, economic espionage, and theft from state properties. More realistically, the political movements—under the guise of "class struggle," meaning the proletariat versus nonproletariats—were aimed at the private sector. The underlying effect of the movement as a whole was to bring all elements—whether they were political, administrative, or economic—considered not conducive for the construction of a socialist state into line. Aside from a sizeable number of entrepreneurs committing suicide under the unrelenting and continual pressure from the cadres for their "confessions," many more were given prison terms and sent to labor camps for "reeducation." The seeds of fear and apprehension were sown in the minds of the general public. The lesson was not lost on the masses: adhere to the ordinances and wishes of the Party leadership.

THE CENTRAL PLANNING COMMISSION

Once the consolidation of its military control over mainland territories was complete, the CCP promptly began the process of a systemic transformation, impacting all major spheres of China's social, economic, political, and cultural domains. The model patterned closely after that of the USSR, progressively laying layer after layer of foundations for the formation of a command system. The key mechanism for exercising direct control over all aspects of economic life and economic activities of every citizen was the Central Planning Commission (CPC). Created in 1952, its central function was to expedite the CCP's control over the production, distribution, and consumption of goods and services, not only for the economy as a whole but all the way downward to each and every producing and consuming unit, including all the households throughout China.

Nationalization of all means of production on farms and in other industries was one of the basic tenets of the communist ideology. With progressive centralization of ownership rights in the hand of the state, over time, the role played by the CPC in China's economic life correspondingly expanded. Ultimate decision-making authority supposedly rested with the collective leadership of the CCP's Politburo. However, in China, as in any authoritarian society, the ultimate power over the nation's fate increasingly became centralized in the hands of one person: Mao Zedong. Mao's interpretation of the "correct line of Marxism and Communism" more often than not became the Politburo's starting point for deliberation. And Mao's predilections for China's development path, in most instances, also became the Politburo's decisions and directives to all administrative organizations in China. As handed down by the Politburo to the CPC, targets for economic growth rate, direction, and emphases formed the basis for centralized planning.

The CPC, taking into account historical data on resource consumption, productive potentials, and output performances of each geographic region in the nation, formulates control figures for each of the provincial or regional administrative units. The latter in turn had their respective secondary and successively lower tiers of CPCs. On the basis of consumption and production quotas assigned to them from above, these lower-level administrative units' CPCs in turn worked out a set of control figures for the consuming and producing branches, groups, and entities under their respective jurisdictions. Development objectives were considered fulfilled if the aggregated output from the nation either met or exceeded the assigned quotas.

THE "SOCIALIST TRANSFORMATION"

During the civil war years, prior to 1949, economic activities operated and properties owned by the Nationalist government were taken over by the communist regime as soon as an area came under its control. Properties owned by high-ranking officials of the Nationalist government were confiscated. "Socialist transformation" refers more specifically to the measured process of nationalizing all the means of production after 1949 in nonfarming sectors. Although the nationalization process did include land properties both on farms and in urban centers, "socialist transformation" refers exclusively to the socialization process in nonfarming sectors.

The squeeze on the private sector was relatively slow after 1949. Financial statements from the private sector in urban centers were made mandatory, providing the state with a clear picture of each firm's assets, transaction volumes, and profits. With the state's growing control over the supply of the more scarce resources, smaller business concerns were induced to realize that as individual units in a larger legal organization, they could enjoy easier accesses to the needed inputs. Small business entities in townships and villages were also encouraged to form themselves into larger units to expedite business transactions. The number of production and distribution cooperatives in one form or another in nonfarming regions grew steadily over time, accompanying the growing importance of the state sector in ownership, production, and distribution.

Having accomplished the basic objectives of the "Three-Anti" and "Five-Anti" movements, Mao launched the full-scale "socialist transformation" movement in 1955. The movement spelled the beginning of the end for private economic activities. All private concerns and service units were "encouraged" to enter into a "joint ownership" agreement with the state. Having learned the lessons from the land reform in rural areas and the "Three-Anti" and the "Five-Anti" movements, the capitalists, large and small, more than fully recognized the perils of not joining in the "zeal of socialist transformation" that was sweeping across the nation's landscape. Although business properties were nominally now "jointly owned" by the state and the capitalists, former property owners became de facto state employees. For a brief period, the former asset owners became share holders. In time, they became state employees earning a basic salary. All assets of the private enterprises became the property of the state and all productive activities followed the diktat of the CPC. By then, the "socialist transformation" was complete.

FARM COLLECTIVIZATION AND COMMUNIZATION

Following in the footsteps of the USSR and other socialist governments in Eastern Europe, Mao's emphasis on economic development resided in rapid industrialization. China was a predominantly agriculture-based economy in 1949. The needed capital for investment in industries had to originate from sectors other than the industry itself. Planned and mandated increases in production and productivity from the farm sector provided a ready answer. A deliberate approach to squeezing as much surplus from agriculture as possible was adopted. At the same time, consumer and investment consumption elsewhere was curtailed.

Encouraged by the state from early on, many beneficiaries of the land reform program in rural regions voluntarily pooled their resources in their productive endeavors. Production and distribution cooperatives in the farming sector began emerging. Notable increases in agricultural production and productivity materialized after land reform. Nevertheless, the productivity gains on farms fell short of the planned targets. Intensified investment was planned to come from surpluses arising from rapidly increased productivity on farm. The below-target gains in agriculture caused an unwanted detour on the CPC's map for rapid increases in capital formation. Furthermore, peasants who gained land property during the land reform began manifesting "capitalist tendencies" by withholding back the assigned grain quotas for delivery at state-determined prices.

In order to attain speedier and greater increases in farm productivity and the needed surpluses, Mao saw the solution in farm collectivization and communization. Prior to the completion of the first five-year development plan (FYDP) (1953–1957), Mao envisioned a two-pronged approach to socializing all productive activities by the end of the second five-year plan. Paralleling the "socialist transformation" movement in industry and commerce, existing mutual-aid teams and cooperatives were "voluntarily" herded into collectives.

Collective farms differ from cooperative farms. The former were more rigidly structured, comprising production teams. Members of cooperatives made their own decisions, reaping benefits for themselves. In a collective, individuality vaporized. Production teams had to enter contractual agreements with the respective collectives they belonged to, delivering contracted production quotas at fixed prices. All the means of production that individual households had some control over earlier as cooperatives were now "jointly" owned and managed by collectives. Alternately stated, individual ownership and discretion in decision making dissipated into thin air.

When the "zeal for socialist transformation swept across the country," most of the collectives were further consolidated into agricultural communes within a three-year period between 1955 and 1958.[1] By then, the individual farmers not only became passive players in economic activities, they in effect became faceless individuals living a communal life. Children were "cared for" by commune-based and commune-operated nurseries and schools. Adults worked and had meals together in communal facilities. Frequent meetings to learn the merits of socialism took place in the evenings after long days of hard work. Communal life replaced family life. Peasants became cogs in the huge machine of the "workers paradise."

THE "GREAT LEAP FORWARD"

Both agriculture and industry experienced rapid recovery from ruins of the civil war. Impressive production and productivity increases in both sectors materialized between 1952 and 1956. Impatient with the less-than-phenomenal successes he had dreamed of, Mao initiated yet another nationwide movement termed "the great leap forward" in 1958. The objective on the economic front was fuller utilization of the underemployed and disguised unemployed on farms in support of speedier capital formation and productivity increases in industry. Though unspoken, Mao's tacit objective on the political front at that time was aimed at acclimatizing the masses to mobilize at the Party's bidding, and later on at his bidding, whenever the order was given.

The stated overall objective of "the great leap forward" movement was for China to make a giant leap from "working-toward" to essentially reaching a mature stage of socialism on a drastically accelerated timetable. Members of agricultural communes were pressed into working harder and longer for six to seven days a week. Aside from food production, communes also had to undertake extensive infrastructural construction projects. Such projects included erecting primitive furnaces throughout rural regions for iron production. Communal life had already deprived the farmers of their cherished family life. As if adding insult to injury, they must now also begin producing steel of which they had neither the knowledge nor experience. The glaring productive incentives they were rewarded with shortly after the land reform promptly dissipated.

"The great leap forward" movement turned into a giant step backward. Whatever metal-looking iron the communes managed to produce was mostly useless and unusable for industrial purposes. More catastrophic for China was the fact that disastrous decreases in agricultural production resulted. Severe nationwide famine ensued between 1959 and 1961. Estimates of starvation-induced deaths ranged from 20 million to more than 30 million. Most of the deaths occurred in rural regions. Starvation and malnutrition was experienced nationwide. Neither the knowledge nor the experience, however, could be publicly mentioned. It was only after Mao's demise in 1976 that accounts of cannibalism began surfacing. Official reasons given for the three-year famine was "natural disasters" affecting agricultural production. The farmers knew better; so did the general public.

A document titled "Resolution on Certain Questions in the History of Our Party since the Founding of the People's Republic of China," adopted by the Sixth Plenary Session of the Eleventh Central Committee of the CCP on June 27, 1981, only made cursory and broad mentions of Mao's errors:

> Our Party has made mistakes owing both to its meager experience in leading the cause of socialism and to subjective errors in the party leadership's analysis of the situation and its assessment of China's conditions (at given times)... there were mistakes of exaggerating the scope of class struggle and of impetuosity and rashness in economic construction.[2]

The 1981 Party resolution implicitly identified Mao as the culprit of "subjective error." The CCP's official language censoring Mao for his "subjective errors," however, was not lost on the public.

Preserving Mao on the altar even long after his death, while conveniently overlooking the tens of millions of innocent lives lost, is reflective of Mao's godlike persona while he was still alive. It is clear, therefore, that China's economy immediately prior to the inception of reform in the late 1970s clearly bore the unmistakable imprimatur of China's "great helmsman." It was sorely in need of reform and restructuring.

THE FIVE-YEAR DEVELOPMENT PLANS UNDER MAO

Since the founding of the PRC in 1949 till his demise in September 1976, Mao reigned supreme. Following closely on the footsteps of the USSR,

Mao entered into a wide-ranging set of economic cooperation agreements with its "big brother" to the north. Soviet experts began arriving in China in the early 1950s. One of their principal tasks was providing guidance to China in the formation and implementation of its first five-year development plan.

Unlike the other development plans under Mao, China's first FYDP (1953–1957) began and concluded in a relatively orderly manner. China was an economically backward country in the mid-twentieth century. More than 80 percent of its population still resided in rural regions, engaging almost exclusively in farm-related activities. Industry was still in its nascent stage of development. China's first FYDP was patterned closely after that of the USSR. Though publicly, continually, and repeatedly stressing the imperative of accelerating agricultural development, disproportionate emphasis was given to the development of China's industry, with undue prominence given to heavy industry. Industry—heavy industry in particular—received the top-heavy share of investment expenditures during the first FYDP due to Mao's expectations for rapid industrialization. Between 1953 and 1956, the average annual increases in the total value of industrial and agricultural output were 19.6 and 4.8 percent, respectively. The "successes" of the first FYDP became the showcase of the CCP, "scientifically proving" socialism's superiority to the capitalist system. Mao's penchant for accelerating industrial development at the expense of the rest of the economy thereby fossilized China's structural imbalances and functional inefficiencies for nearly a quarter of a century.

The second FYDP was ready for implementation until Mao supplanted it with his "great leap forward" movement. Agricultural production declined by 13.6 percent in 1959, by another 12.6 percent the following year, and by a further 2.4 percent in 1961 when the "leap" came to a crash landing.

After the disastrous "great leap forward" and the subsequent five years' efforts at economic readjustment between 1961 and 1966, the third FYDP began. But its implementation was again abruptly interrupted by the "great Cultural Revolution" that Mao instigated in 1966. Nationwide political chaos, social disturbances, and economic disruptions of unparalleled proportions ensued. From 1971 to 1980, the fourth and fifth FYDPs supposedly were drafted and implemented, but the government never made public either the plan outlines or the accomplishments of these two plans. Many Western experts doubted that these plans ever existed.[3] It was only by September 1976 that China was able to utter a muted sigh of relief. Mao's physical presence, if not his ghost, finally passed away from China's tortured history for good.

Economic Readjustment: 1961–1966

The disastrous aftermath of "the great leap forward" drastically reduced the already meager ration of staples such as rice and wheat. With the exception of higher ranking officials, preoccupation for personal survival drained the energy of the entire nation. Millions of families lost loved ones, and hundreds of millions had personal experience with starvation and widespread loss of lives in rural regions.

Famine-induced deaths and mass starvation weakened Mao's position as the nation's "great helmsman." Mao discreetly ceded his public leadership position and retreated from the forefront of publicity. Liu Shaoqi replaced him at the helm. A "readjustment" policy, formulated by Premier Zhou Enlai and Politburo members Chen Yun and Deng Xiaoping, was hurriedly promulgated. Implementation of the policy promptly began throughout the country.

By the winter of 1960, the Central Planning Committee of the CCP acknowledged, at least among CCP leaders, the error of the Mao-instigated "great leap forward." At the Ninth Plenary Session of the Eighth Central Planning Committee, a communiqué was issued, introducing a "readjustment, consolidation, filling out and raising standards" program. "Readjustment" meant realigning sectoral priorities, deemphasizing existing fixation with industrial growth while accentuating the imperative of agricultural development and production. "Consolidation" entailed the suspension or termination of unwarranted industrial projects on the one hand while consolidating or downsizing nonproductive enterprises on the other. And, "filling out" meant the strengthening of weak economic linkages by emphasizing more consumers needs and wants.

The centerpiece of the readjustment policy was based upon agricultural production and development. Measured administrative decentralization took place, granting wider parameters for enhanced lower-level decision-making authority. On another front, limited material incentives were also permitted both on farm and in industrial enterprises. In rural regions, small plots of land were allotted to members of the collectives and communes for private cultivation. The pace of industrial growth was henceforth to be commensurate with agricultural growth, from which much of the industrial raw materials originated. Increased investment in agriculture was to come from corresponding planned decreases in industry, particularly in the subsectors of heavy industry. Economic normalcy began returning and productive incentives also swiftly reemerged. Impressive gains, particularly in agricultural production, enabled Premier Zhou Enlai to declare in late 1964 that "the plan for national economic development should be arranged in the order of priority of agriculture, light industry, and heavy industry."[4] With Mao still being behind the scene, normalcy, however, did not endure. The infamous "great Cultural Revolution" began in 1966.

"THE GREAT PROLETARIAT CULTURAL REVOLUTION": 1966–1976

Sustained economic growth consequent upon readjustment policies strengthened leadership positions of the reformers, correspondingly weakening Mao's relevance in China's affairs. More liberal expressions in arts and literature accompanying economic readjustment emerged. Though compelled to play the second fiddle during the relatively brief period of readjustment, Mao managed to periodically make enough noises criticizing the policies of reform-minded "revisionists." From time to time, he demanded political vigilance and waging class struggle against the real or concocted enemies of socialism.

To Mao, the nation was deviating from the path of socialism he had envisioned. Whether genuinely an ideological purist or not, Mao warned against the reemergence of "capitalist tendencies." He repeatedly called for a return to his favorite term: "politics in command."

In September 1962, Mao demanded that the Tenth Plenary Session of the Party's Eighth Central Committee revive the "class struggle." Mao "asserted (at the session) that throughout the historical period of socialism, the bourgeoisie would continue to exist and would attempt a comeback and become the source of revisionism inside the Party."[5]

To Mao, the reform-minded revisionists had infiltrated the leadership rank of the Party and of the government while positioning themselves to turn back the tide of his vision of the socialist revolution. The reformists were seen by Mao as usurpers of legitimate authority of the CCP and therefore must be purged from all levels of the Party and administrative positions. However, lacking support both from within the Party's own Central Committee and from outside of the Party, and failing to derail the reformists' sustained effort at economic reform, Mao increasingly "relied more and more on an army, politicized under Defense Minister Lin Biao, to restore the spirit of socialism…"[6] By 1966, Mao was ready. With the support of Defense Minister Lin Biao, he called upon students from universities and high schools as well as leftist ideologues to close ranks with the army to form a "revolutionary committee." Their responsibility was to purge revisionists from the Party and the government administration at all levels. Return to economic normalcy and political rehabilitation of Party leaders previously disgraced by Mao were not to continue.

Students wearing red arm bands, with the words "Red Guards" on them, began invading and ransacking public offices, homes, and factories throughout the country. Any Party functionary, government official, teacher, or factory worker suspected of not being in line with Mao and his version of socialism was dragged out of his or her workplace or home and either publicly humiliated or severely beaten. Many were imprisoned and given harsh sentences in labor camps. Scholars both in and outside of China have estimated the number of victims of the "Cultural Revolution" to be in the tens of millions. Among the victims were former Party Secretary General and CCP Chairman Liu Shaoqi, former defense minister Peng Dehuai, and Deng Xiaoping, who later became China's paramount leader after Mao's death. A number of high Party and government leaders, including Liu Shaoqi, lost their lives while in prison. Mao regained his leadership position at the expense of countless lives lost and families shattered. The CCP's own official record acknowledged that:

> The "Cultural Revolution," which lasted from May 1966 to October 1976, was responsible for the heaviest losses suffered by the party, the state and the people since the founding of the People's Republic. It was initiated and led by Comrade Mao Zedong.[7]

Political Economy under Mao

Political parties other than the Communist Party existed in China prior to 1949. When they were first formed, they were political in orientation, either espousing patriotism during the Japanese occupation or opposing Chiang Kai-shek's Nationalist Party. Leaders of these parties were mostly intellectuals who had earned advanced degrees from prestigious universities in the West. Some of these parties continued existing alongside the CCP after 1949. Their continued presence on the scene presented the new China to the world as a country with a political system comprising of multiple political parties. Noncommunist parties were accorded due recognition and room for accommodation, at least from early on. However, there was never the slightest uncertainty as to who was in total control of the decision-making processes.

Since 1949, the power of making ultimate decisions in China rested with the top CCP leadership, comprising of members of the Politburo. In theory, the vote of each of the Politburo members carried the same weight, ostentatiously referred to as "democratic centralism." In practice, especially during the Mao years, predilection of the "Great Helmsman" more often than not predisposed the other members of the Politburo to cast their lots his way. China's economic development policies during the Mao era thereby invariably bore the imprint of his personal penchant. The Politburo's decisions were then pro forma approved by members of the CCP's Central Committee.

These same decisions were then "proposed" to the Congress of the Peoples' Representatives, which then routinely approved such "proposals." It was then the responsibility of the branches of the government to implement the decisions handed down from above.

As previously mentioned, "politics in command" was one of Mao's favorite dicta. And he perfected that dictum to an art form, including liquidating with impunity a significant number of his close comrades of long-standing since the civil war years.[8] With the progression of time since the founding of the PRC in 1949, Mao correspondingly became an authoritarian and whimsical leader of China. His pronounced objective was to transform the hundreds of millions of Chinese into a single-purposed society in pursuit of Marxist and Leninist ideals according to his own preference and interpretation of ideologies at a given time. Subjecting economic objectives and policies to political dictation was a logical deduction. If economic rationality diverged from the larger mosaic of his political agenda, then the former more often than not was either simply cast aside or ingeniously "reinterpreted" by Mao "according to the objective conditions existing in China."

The disproportionately skewed emphasis on capital formation in heavy industry, the accelerated farm collectivization and communization, the "great leap forward" and the "great Cultural Revolution" were all a part of Mao's legacy on China's recent economic history. Each of these political movements yielded disastrous consequences for the hundreds of millions of Chinese people, which still did not deter Mao from weighing in forcefully on the decision-making processes thereafter whenever it was expedient for him. Mao's legacy on China's economy is given a brief review in the remainder of this chapter.

The Economy under Mao: Performance

The command system, through central planning, centralized budgetary processes, and state monopoly over the production and distribution systems, rendered all economic activities being stage-managed. Producers depended on the state to dictate to them as to what, when, where, and how much to invest, produce, and deliver, while consumers were limited to how much of what each person was permitted to purchase per specified time period. Microactivities must all conform to macrodesign. Overproduction of unwanted industrial outputs and severe shortages of basic consumer goods became a perennial phenomenon in an economy that was structurally rigid and functionally inefficient.

A macro overview of China's economic performance in select domains, alternately reflecting the years when Mao was at the helm and those few years when he was sidelined, is discussed below. A few broad-spectrum observations suffice to highlight the more deep-seated anomalies that existed prior to the inception of reform that finally began in 1979.

Population grew from 541.7 million in 1952 to 975.4 million in 1979, an 80 percent increase, whereas indexed gross national product (GNP) increased from 100 to 594.7 for the corresponding period. However, a closer examination of the data reveals numerous anomalies in the growth patterns, of which only a few need highlighting.[9]

First, the long-term growth path not only lacked relative smoothness, it was erratic at best. In 1953, the economy grew by 15.6 percent. The following year the growth rate was a modest 4.2 percent. It then rose by 6.8 and 15.0 percent, respectively, in 1955 and 1956. By 1958, however, the reported growth rate was an inexplicable 21.3 percent. Shortly thereafter, the economy experienced year-to-year negative growth rates of 16.0 and 5.8 percent, respectively, for 1961 and 1962. Similar negative growth rates of 5.1 and 2.8 percent, respectively, recurred in 1967 and 1969.

Second, population increased by 13 million people between 1958 and 1962. Nevertheless, agricultural production decreased by 13.9 percent in 1959. It decreased further by 11.2 percent in 1960 from the previous year and did not regain its 1958 production total until 1962.

Third, while the agricultural sector was experiencing only modest or even negative growth over the decades, the industrial production was growing by leaps and bounds in select years while declining sharply in others. For instance, industrial output grew by 35.8 percent in 1952, 34.5 percent in 1956, and 52.9 percent in 1958. In 1961 and 1962, however, the secondary sector witnessed a 39.7 and 7.7 percent decrease, respectively. Similar decreases occurred in 1967 and 1968, with a decline of 14.1 percent in 1967 and a cumulative decrease of 10.5 percent the following year.

Fourth, despite significant budgetary deficit for numerous years, there was remarkable relative price stability between 1952 and 1979. For instance, budgetary deficit in 1959 was 11.5 percent of revenue while the composite price index rose by a meager 0.9 percent. Similarly, there was a 12.5 percent deficit in 1960. But the year's price index rose by only a modest 3.1 percent, strongly suggesting the absence of objective pricing for basic consumer goods that were perennially in short supply and for the cumulative buildup of repressed inflationary pressure.

Finally, between 1952 and 1979, the GNP grew by slightly less than six times. During the same time period, however, in a country where more than three-fourths of the population still resided in rural regions by 1979, production from the primary sector increased by less than 3.7 times. During the same period, growth in the secondary sector exceeded 13.6 times. The magnitude of structural imbalances and deformities is self-evident. The disproportionate growth in the industrial sector relative to agriculture during the 27-year interval is only the external manifestation of inherent structural deformities and their resulting functional inefficiencies.

Mao's Legacy

Economic efficiency requires efficient resource allocation in order to fully actualize the potentials of comparative advantages. China's economy was backward when the Communist regime came to power. It lacked capital and technologies. What it did possess was an overabundance of human resources, though an overwhelming majority at that time was still engaged in agricultural production. Dismantling the century-old landlord–tenant relationship via the land-to-the-tiller program in itself would have unleashed extensive productive incentives, initiatives, and potentials. Not only could there have been adequate food supply for a rapidly growing population at competitive prices, the savings from the farm sector could have been expeditiously accumulated and propitiously channeled to the nascent industrial sector.

However, Mao's penchant for control via the absolute centralization of not only productive, distributive, and consumptive activities but also all the means of production rendered all ownership and factors of production in the hands of the state. Private ownership was abolished, including farm land that the farmers had only recently acquired through land reform. Every decision, including how much consumer goods each citizen could consume each month, was made by the state. Individuality and freedom ceased existing. Entrepreneurial initiatives disappeared, discretion on the microlevel over investment and production was usurped, and competitiveness rendered obsolete. Individuals, in whom productive and entrepreneurial potentials inhere, were forcibly mutated into factors of production comparable to material inputs. Survival mentality took precedence over initiatives, passivity supplanted creativity. Under Mao's more than a quarter century's authoritarian rule, anomalies permeated throughout China's economy. Only a select few are briefly outlined below.

Aberrant Investment Patterns

As the state quickly consolidated all means of production into its hand after 1949, all profits accrued to the state rather than to the microresource owners. Instead of the private sector making rational reinvestment decisions, the state determined all allocations of investment resources in capital construction (ICC). The annual increase in ICC for 1954 was 9.4 percent. The following year, it declined to 1.3 percent. By 1956, the ICC increased by 54.7 percent, only to fall back to a negative 7.7 percent the succeeding year. The year 1958 marked the inception of the second FYDP. ICC increase in

1958 soared to 87.7 percent, coinciding with Mao's single-minded push for the "great leap forward" movement. After the dismal failure of that movement, whereby millions upon millions died of starvation and malnutrition, the ICC decreased by 67.2 percent in 1961 and then another 44.1 percent in 1962 when Liu Shaoqi replaced Mao as the chairman of the PRC.[10] The period of relative economic rationality ended when Mao began reasserting his power prior to the "Cultural Revolution" in 1966. As a result, not only was there no consistency in China's investment patterns during Mao's reign, the investment policy by the state resulted in deep-seated sectoral distortions and imbalances.

Sectoral Imbalances

China's population grew by 63.0 percent between 1952 and 1976. The GNP increase during that period was 333.5 percent. However, total value product from the agricultural sector rose by only 182.1 percent whereas the increase in the secondary sector was 843.0 percent. As the overwhelming majority of China's population was still engaged in primary sector production, the general public's purchasing power was low. Mao's insistence on accelerated industrialization meant deepening accumulation of unwanted industrial products, of which mostly originated from the heavy rather than from the consumer-oriented light industries. Furthermore, not only the consumers did not possess the purchasing power to buy household appliances, the general public was unable to purchase even sufficient quantities of basic consumer goods such as rice and flour. Although agricultural production on the surface increased notably faster than the population increases, all basic consumer goods that included rice, wheat, sugar, cooking oil, and textile products were severely rationed. Alternately stated, much of the increase in production from the primary sector went to trading for investment goods in heavy industries from the then other socialist countries. By the time of Mao's demise, aside from other anomalies in the economy, China was excessively top-heavy in industrial capabilities.

Absence of Market Forces

Central planning, centralized decision-making, state-determined prices, production quotas, and a directive distribution system meant the unmitigated absence of competitive forces. Risk avoidance and passive adherence to commands from above transformed the productive and consumptive entities into robots. There was no occasion for risk-taking initiatives and no opportunities existed. Personal thinking was neither required nor safe. On the production front, meeting assigned quotas reigned supreme. Once produced, neither marketing skill nor the needs to market were needed. What was produced was distributed to designated buyers at state-determined prices. The channel for commodity circulation was reduced to one: the state. Planned losses by state-owned enterprises (SOEs) mounted. At the same time, underinvestment in the potentially high-yielding productive activities translated into exorbitant opportunity costs. When the systemic transformation process did finally begin after Mao's permanent departure, China remained an agriculturally underdeveloped but industrially overinvested and overproduced country.

Nonexistence of an Objective Valuation System

Economic efficiency requires efficient allocation of scarce resources, including labor. The convergence of supply and demand in a market-driven system yields objective pricing for goods as well as inputs, accurately reflecting unbiased relative scarcity or abundance in both factor and product domains. Price functions as a rationing device, allocating scarce resources to markets promising the highest return to producers or value to consumers. The planned command system, on the other hand, surreptitiously assigns subjective values to both factors and products, hazardously distorting objective values present in either inputs or outputs.

Irrespective of a political or economic system, an individual is motivated by self-interest. Unless due to ideological values the self-interest is voluntarily subsumed under the umbrella of collective well-being. Short of ideological convictions, it is personal gains that motivate an individual to economize, minimizing inputs while maximizing returns. Administrative determination of prices during the Mao's era thus resulted in severe and extensive waste in scarce capital as well as human resources.

Passivity of Financial Resources

Financial flow in a rational system allocates material and human resources to accompany the real flow. A primary function of financial resources is facilitating the flow of productive factors that is natural, smooth, speedy, and balanced. Prior to reform, however, all financial resources were centralized in the hands of the state. Capital markets did not exist. Nor were profit-oriented private banks or other financial institutions permitted. The People's Bank of China (PBC) and special-purpose banks served as mere conduits for the collection and distribution of financial resources on behalf of the state. Extension of credits free of interest to SOEs adhered strictly to the plan, irrespective of whether a given SOE was a viable or a perennially loss-incurring entity. Administered flow of financial resources would not permit what Joseph Schumpeter termed as "creative destruction" of nonviable enterprises for substantive macrogrowth. Furthermore, passivity of financial institutions in a command system also effectively suppressed the possibility of realizing the potentially productivity-enhancing initiatives via competitive activities. Suppression of free mobility of financial resources consequently led to contrived growth that appeared strong in muscles but critically lacking in wholesome fitness.

Economic Isolationism

Development experience suggests that capital and technology are two of the primary engines for economic growth. From early on during his reign, Mao relied heavily on the former USSR for the much-needed capital and technology. Trade was limited mostly to exchanges with members of the Council for Mutual Economic Assistance (CMEA) countries in general and with USSR in particular. After Mao's open quarrel with Khrushchev in 1961, China's economic relations with USSR came to a screeching halt. Mao thereby stressed the imperative for self-sufficiency. Self-reliance, however, also meant opportunities foregone for speedier actualization of development potentials through capital and technology imports. Self-sufficiency also meant increased isolation from the world community, reducing China to nearly an island in the world community. Planning and mandating increased productivity and production from the mentally, emotionally, and physically fatigued general public,[11] in combination with ever tighter political grip on the masses, became a standard policy of the regime. Appearance of faithfulness to socialism aside, what the administration received from the work force in return was deepening passivity and growing disinclination for conscientious efforts.

Workplace Aberrations

SOE directors were appointed by the state, often on the basis of Party affiliation and ideological purity rather than their administrative expertise or managerial abilities. Without having to compete for acquiring input at competitive prices, nor needing marketing skills for product distribution, the enterprise director's primary tasks included meeting assigned production quotas, securing as much factor supply and low production quotas from above, and currying favor with higher authorities. The practice of underreporting the productive capacity while overestimating factor needs was commonplace among enterprise directors. Corollary to the above was to ensure that all plan-assigned inputs were used up. This was to insure that future factor allocation by higher authorities would not be trimmed. Compromising productive efficiency was not much of a concern for the management.

Another relatively commonplace practice on the part of the management responsible for preparing reports—and this was particularly true in rural regions—was filing inaccurate information when needed.[12] As long as the management's efforts at cultivating a close relationship with higher authorities were successful, then anomalies within the productive unit could be conveniently overlooked, including perennial enterprise losses. Since the FYDPs were formulated on the basis of past and current data, inaccurate reports led to false assumptions and unrealistic projections for the next planning period.

On the part of the workers, there was little pride or incentive to over perform. Objective reward system linking wages to productivity was absent. Wages were a function of allocated budget from the state. Even with low wages and low purchasing power, what was essential for daily sustenance was further curtailed by the parsimonious rationing system. Striving for higher productivity through personal effort was not high on one's priority list. Meeting mandated production quota did not entail qualitative performance. Product quality took a backseat to fulfilling production quotas, taking little interest in pride or satisfaction over what one's hand produced. The net losers were, then, household consumers or industrial users of the products from these hands.

CHAPTER 2

THE POLITICAL ECONOMY OF REFORM AFTER MAO

CHANGING POLITICAL LANDSCAPE

Deng Xiaoping was tagged as a "right opportunist" by Mao's fanatic "Red Guards" during the 1966 "Cultural Revolution." The "Red Guards" placed a dunce cap on Deng's head and paraded him along the streets for public humiliation. Deng was sidelined on the national scene thereafter until Mao finally permitted him to resurface as an architect for returning China's economy to a more normal path of development. By 1976, however, Mao initiated yet another nationwide "movement" to criticize Deng Xiaoping, though it would be the final act of his dictatorial irrationality. The cause for Deng's downfall the second time was because he criticized the mistakes of the "Cultural Revolution," implicitly holding Mao responsible for being the initiator of the "movement." Deng was shunted to the sidelines once again. That same year, at the recommendation of Mao, Hua Guofeng was elevated to the post of First Vice-Chairman of the Central Committee of the Chinese Communist Party while serving concurrently as China's premier.

Upon Mao's demise in 1976, Hua succeeded him as the CCP's general secretary. Hua was a second generation Party leader, lacking both in political statue and finesse. He needed support. Shortly after Mao's death, with perhaps more than encouragement from many of the old-time Party leaders, Hua promptly ordered the arrest of the "Gang of Four" that included Mao's ambitious and ruthless widow Jiang Qing.[1] However, since Hua's ascendancy to the pinnacle of power in China depended solely on Mao's benevolence, he still believed that he could hold onto power by relying on Mao's statue. In a public speech, he announced that "we firmly uphold whatever policy-decisions

Chairman Mao made, and we unswervingly adhere to whatever instructions Chairman Mao gave."[2] It was a miscalculation on Hua's part.

Vivid memories of the incalculable disasters from Mao's failed "great leap forward" and the "Cultural Revolution" movements hardly died with the first generation party leaders. While Hua was still learning the ropes of being the leader of the party and the nation, Premier Hu Yaobang courageously moved forward to rehabilitate the previously disgraced party leaders and countless average citizens wronged by Mao. Deng Xiaoping and his previously disgraced colleagues were rehabilitated and brought back to center stage. In time, Deng replaced Hua as Mao's successor. A new chapter in China's development began. The groundwork for systemic transformation began in 1978, with steps for initial reform steps taken in 1979.

Deng recognized that continuing a rigidly planned system would leave China's economy increasingly farther behind Japan, the "Four Asian Tigers," and the rest of the developed economies.[3] After the third Plenary Session of the 11th Central Committee of the Communist Party in December 1978, the seventh and current reform and modernization phase officially began.[4]

By 1980, Deng had consolidated his power as China's de facto supreme leader. However, reluctant of being perceived as sitting on the throne vacated by Mao, Deng only assumed the official title as a vice military commissioner. He nevertheless sat on the throne behind the scene, allowing the posts of Communist Party secretary general and the premiership to go to Hu Yaobang and Zhao Ziyang, respectively, both being communist leaders with genuine concerns for the well-being of the masses.

Imperative for Reform

Toward the end of the 1970s, Deng and his more liberal elements within the party began the push for reform. Both the Party and the People's Congress officially sanctioned the reform movement in late 1978. The rationale was self-evident. China was being left farther and farther behind on the world stage economically and technologically. After nearly 30 years of Mao's "socialist construction," China remained an underdeveloped country. Overcentralization, distorted production relations, perennial commodity shortages, low productivity, inflexible circulation channels, and administrative inefficiencies on both macro and micro levels were merely a few of the anomalies plaguing China's landscape. Mao's "self-sufficiency" isolationism had deprived China of the opportunities of actualizing its vast productive potentials for decades. The cumulative opportunity cost for maintaining negligible foreign economic and political relations was prohibitive. Status quo was no longer an option.

On December 22, 1978, the Party's Third Plenary Session of the 11th Congress adopted a resolution, outlining the imperative for reform. It admitted the flaws of undue centralization in the past and mandated bold decentralization measures under the government's guidance. Some of the perceived needs by the Party delegates included but were not limited to the following: establishing appropriate relationship between planning and market, self-determination for enterprise management, recognizing the merits of the market's value system, discontinuing the existing practice of commingling state affairs with that of the Party, and introducing a workplace responsibility system. Concurrent with these reform initiatives were also the need for reform in the broad spheres of planning, statistics, finance, taxation, pricing, banking, foreign economic relations, and legal and wage systems. The needs for reform were fundamental and the task arduous. The resolve for reform was nevertheless firm.

THE "FOUR PRINCIPLES" FOR REFORM

A torrent of official pronouncements came in quick succession after that Third Plenary Session of the 11th Central Committee meeting. The meeting resolution declared the imperative of refocusing China's energy from Mao's favorite "class struggle" to resolving the serious problems deeply entrenched in China's economy.

Comparable to Khrushchev's denunciation of Stalin, China needed first to downsize Mao statue somehow in the public. An official communiqué from the Sixth Plenary Session of the 11th Central Committee of the CCP stated that:

> During this period [the "Cultural Revolution"], his [Mao's] theoretical and practical mistakes concerning class struggle in a Socialist society became increasingly serious, his personal arbitrariness gradually undermined the democratic centralism in Party life and the (problem of) personality cult grew more and more serious.[5]

Although Deng's drive for reform began shortly after his rehabilitation following Mao's demise, it was the 11th Central Committee sessions that became the turning point in China's economic history. It was during these days that the foundation for structural reform and systemic transformation was laid and officially sanctioned.

Deng was an unwavering adherent to communism. Addressing delegates to the Party's Conference on Theoretical Works on March 30, 1979, Deng articulated the "four principles" for pursuing the "four modernization" objectives in China.[6] Modernizing China's economy was to be uncompromisingly premised on the four principles or preconditions. The four principles are: strict adherence to socialistic ideology, categorical insistence on proletariat dictatorship, unconditional supremacy of the Communist Party in leadership, and unwavering faithfulness to Marxism and the "thoughts of Mao." Broadly interpreted, Deng sought economic growth without compromising the communist regime's control and leadership. Party control, though with a notably lengthened leash, was the rule of the game.[7] The cost for failing to comprehend or abide by the rules of the game, as history would later prove, would be prohibitive.

Deng had foresight. He was well aware that democratization would be a logical trend consequent upon economic growth. Since his objective was developing China's economy and not relinquishing the party's position of absolute control, the public enunciation of the "four principles" in advance was to send a clear signal that democratization was not in the cards. In a later deliberation with Party leaders on December 30, 1986, when the students already began to manifest a trend of more liberal thinking, Deng cautioned those present in these words:

> The task of opposing Capitalistic democratization should endure for at least 20 years. Democratization needs being a process of gradual progression. The Western modus operandi is unacceptable. Emulating what takes place in the West unavoidably results in chaos. Our Socialistic construction must proceed on the basis of unified stability in an orderly manner.[8]

This theme of stability and order was emphasized time and again in both his public addresses as well as private conversations, and was repeatedly echoed by other top leaders of the Party and the government for years. Deng had the foresight because China was the first communist regime among the then socialist countries at that time to initiate wide-ranging systemic transformation. The disintegration of the Soviet bloc and the liberalization of Eastern Europe was still a decade away. Deng wanted economic restructuring without causing the downfall of the CCP, an approach which former leaders of the Warsaw Pact nations[9] did not assume, even though it would have been as easy ex post.

MODIFIED INTERPRETATION OF "SOCIALISTIC TRANSFORMATION"

For Deng, economic growth via systemic restructuring and reorientation was imperative. A frequently reiterated theme in his conversations with foreign dignitaries was that there would be no future for China without economic reform. He admitted that the past approach to economic growth proved unsuccessful after decades of implementation.

To ensure achieving his vision for a rapidly growing economy, Deng also became increasingly more creative in interpreting Marxism "in accordance with the objective situation prevailing in China." To him, opening up to international markets and making use of foreign capital and technology was a means to complement socialistic construction. It in no way implied a departure from socialist ideology. The central themes of Deng's speeches were then faithfully reiterated by Party and government officials at diverse levels during public functions. In time, Deng's interpretation of pragmatic socialism was codified into a theory propelling China's reform momentum.

To assure the smooth transition from Mao's model for growth to a structurally more balanced and functionally more efficient one, Deng insisted on the absence of social discord. To him, there could be no reform progress without social calm and public order. Attempts to deviate from proletariat dictatorship could not and would not be tolerated. Loosely translated, any call for democracy or freedom would face dire consequences.

Former Party Secretary General Hu Yaobang was too progressive and too broadminded for Deng's taste. Despite his ability to navigate between the so-called proletariat dictatorship and the progress he was achieving by liberalizing the economy, Hu fell into disfavor with Deng.[10] He tendered his resignation on January 16, 1987 and passed away shortly thereafter. Zhao Ziyang succeeded his former mentor Hu and continued pursuing economic reform. An effective leader, Zhao tirelessly moved economic reform programs forward. But his unwillingness to use force against the students and the workers protesting at Tiananmen Square in late May and early June of 1989 cost him dearly. After Deng sent tanks into Tiananmen Square and crushed the protesters on June 4, 1989, Zhao was summarily dismissed from his public office. Though not imprisoned, he was under virtual house arrest for the remainder of his life till his death in 2005. There was no room for free thinkers advocating capitalist-style democracy under communist rule. To Deng, CCP leadership was the sole guarantee for uninterrupted progress along the reform path and no challenge to it would be tolerated.

SECOND GENERATION PARTY LEADERSHIP: HU AND ZHAO

The immediate post-Mao era may be characterized by a drastic decline in the influence of the radical dogmatists and the corresponding ascendancy of the more liberal elements in the Party. The surviving first generation Party leaders had all witnessed firsthand the undesirable consequences of Mao's countless political moves.[11] Many of them were also victimized by Mao's "class struggles," especially during the years of the "Cultural Revolution." The harsh memories helped facilitate acceptance of the reform agenda put forward by the more moderate party leaders in the late 1970s.

Deng has traditionally been accredited as the prime mover of the current reform. Deng was indeed the main political force behind economic reform. However, he was no China's Gorbachev. Separation of party control from day-to-day management of state enterprises was permissible. Political reform that could compromise the Party's absolute authority was not.

Real architects and movers of reform—both economically and politically—were Hu Yaobang and Zhao Ziyang, the two successive Party Secretary Generals brought to power and subsequently rejected by Deng. After the downfall of Hua Guofeng, Hu became the party's secretary general, with Zhao the premier. This team of two open-minded reformers took on the arduous task of reforming an economy, the structure of which had been fossilized for nearly three decades by Mao. Both Hu and Zhao were humanistic pragmatists. Communists they were, yet both were practitioners of their belief. Namely, the well-being of the general public should take precedence over ideology.

Hu Yaobang: Party Leader and Charismatic Humanist

One of the first landmarks for Hu was his bold initiative to rehabilitate the millions of innocent citizens wronged by Mao's perennial "class struggles." A vast number of individuals imprisoned or exiled as "rightists" under Mao were restored to their rightful place in society. Under the close scrutiny of Deng, however, neither Hu nor Zhao strayed far from the direction Deng had articulated. The focus of their successive administrations was economic reform.

Zhao, while still secretary general of the Sichuan province, had already pioneered an experimental reform measure in the farm sector. Instead of working as commune members, farmers were permitted to enter into an agreement with the government. As long as the farmers could deliver the assigned production quota, they could operate independently from the commune system. It was a revolutionary novelty in China at that time. It was the exceptional successes from this reform measure on farm that agricultural reform during the subsequent years received its initial momentum. After Zhao became the nation's premier, with the support and cooperation from Hu, farm reform deepened with land-leasing agreements and the initiation of free market for cash crops.

On May 8, 1980, the Office of Structural Reform was created to draft the reform agenda. Mining foreign investment capital and exploring foreign markets became a major focal emphasis for enhancing domestic productivity. Economic zones were created one after the other and foreign investment and foreign trade initially aimed at the Four Asian Tigers became prominent in China's reform effort. For Deng, who also believed in "feeling the pebbles while crossing the river," the phenomenal successes on farm and from foreign investments vindicated his call for reform. By 1984, reform began widening into industrial and service sectors, with the general public fully trusting in Deng's frequently repeated motto that China's reform policy would remain unchanged for a hundred years. The pace of reform accelerated and China's economic growth rate during the first decade of reform gained the recognition and notice of the international community.

Economic growth invariably evolved into craving and calling for political reform, individual freedom, and democracy. By late 1986, germination for democracy and political reform matured into fermentation, especially on university campuses. More of a democratic and humanistic socialist than a communist ideologue, Hu was more than understanding toward the students. His hands-off approach toward the students was more than tacit sanction of the students' sentiment, which went contrary to Deng's political philosophy. On January 16, 1987, Hu "tendered his resignation" as the party's secretary general under pressure.

ZHAO ZIYANG: THE REFORMER

Upon Hu's de facto dismissal from his post, Zhao was named as his successor. Though deprived of Hu's dynamic support and close cooperation, and plagued by the party politics between the ultraconservative and the more moderate elements within the party, Zhao resolutely forged forward with his reform agenda. Simplifying macroplanning mechanism, decentralizing central authority, defining managerial authority in state-owned enterprises (SOEs), broadening horizontal circulation channels, reforming financial systems, and developing financial markets while initiating capital markets were a few of the more strategic domains that Zhao focused upon. Zhao's aim was achieving clear separation between the state and the enterprises. Instead of central planning, the role of the state would henceforth be macro coordination, relegating market coordination to micro entities. Concurrent with reform measures directed at developing market forces within, Zhao toiled tirelessly for integrating China's growing economy into the world community. The model would resemble more of a market socialistic economy for China than a centralized socialistic one.

More notable among Zhao's efforts was the initial steps he took toward democratizing China's political system. For him, unless economic reform was also accompanied by political reform, deepening of the former could not be sustained. Economic reform by then had yielded bountiful dividends. Since Deng had also advocated the eradication of bureaucracy in the Party and state apparatuses, Zhao began experimenting with free elections in basic political units of rural regions. It was his firm belief that, given free elections, unworthy officials could be rooted out of public offices. During Gorbachev's visit to China on May 16, 1989, Zhao even solicited the former's view on the merits of a multiparty political system.

Zhao's idealistic vision for China and his accomplishments during his years as China's premier, aided by his unassuming public image, earned him domestic admiration and international respect. However, the idyllic prospect did not endure. Zhao's predecessor Hu, another widely admired humanistic communist leader passed away less than three years after being pressured to relinquish his position and the party Secretary General. The deep grief felt by the masses precipitated the students' open call for democracy.

Tiananmen, the counterpart of the former USSR's Red Square, became the theater of student demonstrations. The throng grew larger and larger, drawing participants from all walks of life and from distant parts of China. Protests evolved into hunger strikes by some of the university students. Caught between the Party hardliners and the growing social unrest in major urban centers, Zhao visited the students who were on hunger strikes in the hospital. Political pressure mounted from both sides of the camp within the Party leadership, for and against deploying the military to quell rising unrest. On June 3, 1989, Zhao waded into the demonstrating masses at Tiananmen, apologizing that he had not visited with them sooner. A day later, Deng ordered the tanks to roll into Tiananmen Square. The rest is history. Despite his proven record on expeditiously moving reform forward, Zhao was swiftly dismissed from his office. A chapter of China's reform history came to an end.

In his written statement to an assembly censuring his conduct during the student protest movement, Zhao maintained his unwavering belief as articulated below:

> From my work experience, I became acutely aware that the time had changed. Changes have taken place in Society and in the way people think. Worldwide, democracy has become the tide of our time. Democratic ideals have gained strength pervasively. Therefore, we must adapt to new demands of the time and to new situations, learning new democratic ways for problem resolution. I feel that sooner or later we shall have to walk that path. Instead of doing so passively, it would be more desirable that the steps be taken proactively.[12]

Instead of self-criticism, as prescribed for anyone accused of straying from the Party line, Zhao maintained his integrity. For refusing to acknowledge his error in being sympathetic to the protesters, Zhao was placed under virtual house arrest for sixteen years till his death in early 2005.

THE THIRD GENERATION PARTY LEADERSHIP: JIANG ZEMIN

Deng did make clear from the outset his "four principles." No one was to challenge the absolute leadership role of the Communist Party. Zhao's public expression of sympathy toward the protesters defied Deng's declaration.

Deng summoned Jiang Zemin, the Party chief of Shanghai to Beijing and "recommended" to the Politburo that Jiang replace Zhao as the Party's Secretary General. Jiang, not a household name at that time, became the "third generation leadership" in China.[13]

Within weeks of being the Party's Secretary General, Jiang followed the script and publicly reaffirmed the policy of continued economic reform and foreign economic relations. Jiang, however, was neither Hu nor Zhao in action. With the hardliner Li Peng as the premier,[14] the two left-leaning members of the leadership team set about to slow down the reform momentum. Instead of continuing the trend for decentralizing and liberalization, Jiang worked covertly to recentralize administrative authority, emphasizing the merits of the public sector in the economy and concurrently promoting collective farming. Partly owing to the "Tiananmen Square incident" and partly to Jiang-Li's policies, the rapid growth rates of the past decade came to an end.

Deng, who was still intent on economic reform, recognized the need of continuing the reform momentum generated by Hu and Zhao. At the advanced age of 88, employing inspection as an excuse, Deng traveled south to Guangdong, Shenzhen, Zhuhai, Shanghai, and a few other key economic sites in China in late January, 1991. In his major policy speeches while en route, Deng reemphasized the imperative of sustained economic reform. Indirectly rebuking Jiang's course of action, he reiterated the merits of the responsibility system by individual farmers, the need for deepening and broadening market forces, and the importance of liberalizing foreign economic relations. He went so far as issuing a direct warning, stating that "the person who does not reform goes down." The message was not lost on Jiang and Li.

By 1991, Deng recognized the need for someone knowledgeable in economic affairs that was also proreform to guide the reform program forward. Zhu Rongji, a well-known professor at China's most prestigious university, was brought into the power structure and was named as a Vice-Premier and Minister of Finance.[15] Zhu had no political ambition. His focus was on managing the nation's economy while continuing the path of systemic reform and structural readjustments. A respected person of integrity and honor, Zhu was a straightforward and candid individual who often made public statements that ushered in a breath of fresh air to a society that longed for a leader whom they could trust. One of the statements he made regarding the widespread corruption among the elite was: "Prepare 100 caskets. Ninety nine are for the corrupt bureaucrats and one for me." Deng apparently appreciated Zhu's competency as an administrator, recognizing him as a person that China needed. When Li's term as the Premier ended in 1998, Zhu was appointed to succeed him. China's reform program during much of the 1990s and the early years of the 2000s bore the imprint of Zhu's administration.

THE "THIRD GENERATION" PREMIER: ZHU RONGJI

Zhu entertained laudable intentions. The legacies from the Jiang-Li administration, however, posed acute predicaments for Zhu. By the late 1980s, the momentum generated by reform successes on farm had dwindled. Average income disparity between workers in major urban centers and the rural masses kept widening. With tax obligations and local officials imposing dreamt up "fees," innumerable farmers simply abandoned their farms and joined the rank of the rising unemployed in urban centers. The halting progress on the privatization of SOEs, in contrast, became a gold mine for the power elite who secured titles to the more lucrative SOEs by financing cheap purchases with credits from state banks. "Connections" meant easy access to credits, and the facility to effectuate the undervaluation of the more competitive SOEs. A rich minority emerged amid the vast majority of the poor who were getting poorer. Bad credits both to nonperforming SOEs and to the power elite kept mounting, with a good number of the moneyed class migrated abroad with their ill-gotten wealth.

Zhu was a brave soul. One of his purposeful statements was that, irrespective of whether it is a minefield or a bottomless chasm ahead, keep advancing. Nevertheless, his good intentions were to a large measure thwarted by impediments inherent in the system. He vowed to restructure the large SOEs. A number of the largest SOEs, though broken up into smaller SOEs, still were able to exercise monopoly power within their respective markets. He wanted to reform the financial system, but had no effective means of bringing to a halt the bleeding of state banks by the SOEs and the more corrupt elements within the power elite. He did succeed in transferring housing units from the state to the private sector, but ended with much of the prime pieces of real estate properties in the hands of the moneyed elite with political connections. He intended to provide a stronger safety net for the growing unemployed as well as those who needed assistance the most, but there were not financial resources to do so. Zhu was able to maintain China's growth rate at a respectable pace. But that was due mainly to the transient boom of the housing market following the transfer of housing units from the state to the private sector, to the growth of the stock market, and to significant foreign injections in the form of foreign investment and foreign trade.

There were some major achievements that could be attributed to Zhu. He managed to crack a few cases of organized smuggling involving some second-level Party leaders and their associates. He succeeded in stripping the military of its earlier privileges to engage in all forms of commercial activities. And he managed to isolate China from the Asian financial crises and was a vigorous proponent of China's entry into the World Trade Organization (WTO). Zhu is a much respected former leader, mainly due to his integrity and to the circumscribed successes he was able to accomplish as a Premier. His vision and ambitions for China when first assuming the premiership, however, were to a large measure unfulfilled because, as he himself acknowledged, he was an idealist and not a versatile politician.

THE INTERREGNUM POSITIONING

By late February, 2003, the CCP leadership finalized the list for successors to the Jiang–Zhu administration. The list was to be "proposed" to the forthcoming People's Congress (PC) for approval. Hu Jintao, whom Deng had designated as Jiang's successor, topped the list. Hu was to be not only the Secretary General of the CCP, he was also "proposed" to the PC as the Chairman of the PRC. The Premier, as "recommended" by the CCP to the PC, was to be Wen Jiabao. As expected, the PC obliged and the Hu–Wen team became the fourth generation communist leaders. That Hu was to succeed Jiang was beyond the latter's control. Though Deng had passed onto the nether world in 1997, Jiang dared not go against Deng's edict. However, Jiang retained the post as the military commissar. Deng was confident of his leadership. Once he reestablished himself as China's leader in the late 1970s, the only position Deng accepted was being the Vice Commissar of the Military. Having command over the military in China meant power. After consolidating his position, Deng later became Chairman of the Central Military Commission. Jiang's charisma paled dismally when compared with that of Deng's. By retaining the position as the chief of the military, Jiang managed to salvage some political deference due him, thereby compromising the new administration's ability to effectuate its own reform agenda.

Covert dissent between the Hu–Wen administration and the Jiang clan over major reform policies quickly emerged. In reality, covert struggle between leaders of the two generations was apparent even during the interregnum period. Before handing over power, Jiang began chanting the "three representations" hymnal. The ideological essence of the "three representations" was: perpetual "democratic dictatorship" under the communist rule. The "three representations" would have the people believe that the CCP represents the vast population of China, that it embodies China's advanced civilization, and that it epitomizes China's advanced productive capacity. Logical conclusion to acceptance of the novel theory was that power would permanently be vested in the power elite. Using state-controlled media, the chant grew to such a pitch that the circle with vested interest called for its incorporation into China's Constitution. Understood was that the ones with vested interest would be guaranteed with continued ability to translate their positions and influence into economic gains. However, opposition to such a move was equally strident, even amidst the rank of the first generation revolutionaries and more progressive members of the Party leadership.

What Hu inherited, therefore, was a system of "democratic dictatorship" created by Mao, maintained by Deng and used by Jiang for the Party's absolute control over the nation. What Mao said carried more weight than either the law or the constitution. After Mao, what Deng and senior Politburo member Chen Yun agreed to and decided on, constitutionally acceptable or not, was acted upon.[16] During Jiang's administration, difference in the application of laws and regulations remained alive between the powered elite and the commoner, especially in the domains of economic laws and regulations.

In his first public statement after assuming the reign, Hu emphasized the importance of rule by law in accordance with the constitution. The constitution, at least on paper, guarantees the rights of individual citizens as well as circumscribes limitation of the state. People in and outside of China held high expectation of the Hu–Wen administration, especially in terms of political democratization. It was hoped that there would be rule by law instead of rule by political and economic connectedness. However, there has been little indication that political liberalization and democracy are to gain any grounds during this current administration. Press censorship has increased instead of decreased. The more vocal dissidents have been more closely monitored than before, and the much-expected proposal to amend the constitution has been sidelined. Instead, the administration's focus seems to be centered on sustained economic growth and structural/functional reform while enforcing the rule of the Party's "democratic dictatorship."

THE "FOURTH GENERATION" LEADERSHIP: HU AND WEN

Power sharing between Hu and Jiang translated into covert skirmishes between the Hu and Jiang camps from early on. When reform began in 1979, emphasis was placed on permitting a segment of China's economy to reap reform benefits first, yielding indirect benefits to the rest of China through the "trickle-down" effect. Internally, reform began in rural areas. Toward the outside, the special economic zones and open cities were established along select coastal provinces and regions, relegating the China's vast interior to playing the second fiddle. Economies in the coastal provinces of Guangdong and Fujian, and China's traditional commercial center Shanghai began to boom by leaps and bounds while provinces in the interior continue languishing in poverty and underdevelopment. It was particularly so in the northern provinces of China. In time, Shanghai—where Jiang was the party secretary general before his elevation to his crowning position in Beijing—became the center of prosperity in China, benefiting many of the power elite associated with the Shanghai circle, As reform progressed, provinces closer to the Pearl River and the Yangtze River Deltas also began reaping largesse from enhanced economic activities.

The Hu–Wen's intended strategic move differed from that of Jiang's. The new administration proposed developing northern provinces instead of the already more developed provinces as a priority for the much-needed macro realignment. The rationale was clear-cut. Much of China's industries are located in the northern provinces. The region had sustained high unemployment rates following industrial reform. Equalizing economic opportunities throughout the country could be instrumental in mitigating social unrest in the region and for maintaining social calm throughout the nation. Hu's proposal did not suit those with vested interest in the more developed provinces. The Party Secretary General of Shanghai, who was also a member of the party's Politburo, warned the premier in July of 2003 that his proposed macro realignment scheme had already caused harm to Shanghai's development, the negative consequences could ripple throughout the country, and that Premier Wen would be personally held responsible for the proposal. A month later, the *People's Daily* carried a front-page article that indirectly aimed at those with vested interest in the direction of China's reform policies. The central theme of the article was that reform would need courage. The article pointed out that obstacles to reform and restructuring was no longer ideological. Instead, they were coming from groups comprised of those with vested interest. Perhaps by coincidence, reports of corruption involving family members of the new leadership also began circulating in some area publications. With the current and the previous administrations poised on opposite sides of the aisle, there has been little movement from the current administration to implement its original reform schemes.

The fourth generation administration's economic policy is fundamentally a continuation of the policies enunciated by former Premier Zhu, maintaining an annual growth rate of between 7 and 8 percent while deepening foreign economic relations. Aside from tending to the basic needs of the unemployed and the needy and continuing the previous administration's reform focuses, the sole new emphasis of the Hu–Wen administration has been to tend more to the glaring needs of the agricultural producers. Other than this new emphasis, the new administration's reform philosophy remains nearly identical with that of the previous administrations.

As for the new initiative tending more to the agricultural producers, there is discussion of a permanent transfer of land ownership to the farmers in place of the current land-leasing program. If adopted, the tillers would be granted the right to purchase the land from the state. On another frontier, which has driven countless younger farmers into the already overcrowded urban centers, the administration intends to reduce the financial burdens placed on them by reducing farm taxes while concurrently prohibiting corrupt local officials to impose arbitrary "service charges" and surreptitious fees. Since reform on farm would neither be a serious drain on budgetary resources nor siphoning off economic opportunities away from the power elite, it is a new initiative that both sides of the aisles could live with.

After eight years in office, it has been more of a status quo than a progressive administration on economic issues for the Hu–Wen years. The issue of social malaise in the form of persistent corruption has not been publicly addressed. The earlier talk of rule by law in accordance with the Constitution has faded into the background. Regional parochialism is commonplace while genuine concern for those falling through the cracks of the meager social safety net has been less inspiring. There also does not seem to be effective and viable means for stemming the tide of some serious threats posed at the doorsteps of the fourth generation administration. Among such threats are: rising nonrecoverable bad credits extended by state banks, sustained budgetary deficit, mounting public debts, questionable ability of the state banks to meet obligations to depositors in the private sector, massive capital flight consequent upon emigration by family members from a good number of the power elite, rising unemployment, unequal regional development, growing disparity between the rich minority and the poor majority, alarming increases in the demand for energy imports, environmental deterioration, deep-seated risks in the stock and real estate markets and rising incidents of social unrest. The Hu–Wen administration's successes on the economic front have been built largely upon the past administrations' reform policies. In terms of introducing momentous structural and functional reforms, the Hu–Wen administration pales notably relative to their predecessors' administrations.

A Cursory Observation

A casual assessment of macro data may lead to the conclusion that China's economic growth and bulging trade surpluses should be the envy of the world community. Its apparent successes have also been of intense interest to reform architects in former socialistic countries elsewhere. However, a fundamental difference exists between reforms in the former socialist countries in Eastern Europe and China. Economic reform in Eastern Europe has been concurrently accompanied by political reform. It has not been so in China. New power structures arise in the former, even though the old guard communists may still remain an enduring force on the political stage. In China, "democratic dictatorship" under the leadership of the Communist

Party remains. Democratic elections, even if they be flawed, have taken place in the former. Western style democracy neither exists nor is it tolerated in China. Corruption exists in Eastern Europe, but not as pervasive as in China during the early years of reform. The power elite in all reforming economies benefit from the privatization process whereby state-owned assets are transferred to the private sector. But only in few countries, such profiteering ventures are as palpable as in China. Gaping income disparity exists in the former, but the Gini ratio is notably higher in China than in Eastern Europe. Unemployment has been a commonplace phenomenon in reforming economies. But, given the sheer population size in China, the number of unemployed, underemployed, and disguised unemployed are more of a serious threat to social calm than in other transitional economies. The poor remain abundant in Eastern Europe, but not to the extent as in China. Social unrest also takes place in some of the Eastern European nations, but not in a scale as frequent or as large as in China. Unsatisfactory officials on all administrative levels could be voted out of office in reforming economies in Eastern Europe. No election by popular votes has occurred since 1949 in China. Corrupt officials remain a primary cause of many of the social ills. China's economic growth has indeed been impressive. But moving economic reform forward without parallel political reform can create deep-seated anomalies that would incur high social cost and high opportunity cost in the longer run. Sustained successes along the economic frontiers require more than systemic and structural reforms by decrees. Tall structures require in-depth foundations. China has achieved heights, but is lacking in depth.

No system is perfect. Systems are relatively static whereas the general public is adaptive. In democratic societies, functional institutions are preserved while flawed ones are either discarded or modified over time. Given the institutions, implementation of game rules therein is entrusted to designated representatives. Responsible trustees are retained and unworthy ones are relieved of their trust within a predetermined time period. Functional institutions thereby generate progress and improvements in the domains identified with these respective institutions. Such improvements, growth, and progress take place because they evolve from dependable and securely rooted adaptive institutions that were designed for the well-being of those affected.

In societies of systems that differ from the democratic format, rule is more by decree than by laws. Such laws may well institutionalize practices in favor of the ruling minority. Objectively acceptable laws do exist in such societies but are either selectively enforced or at times arbitrarily interpreted. If it is rule by decree more than by objective laws and regulations based on reason, then there is little recourse that the adversely affected party may resort to. Unequal distribution of institutionalized benefits creates unequal classes of constituents. The state is not static since it involves self-motivated components. Disparity between or among classes of constituents amplifies. Such an evolutionary process may endure for an extended period of time, or it may swiftly germinate tension among conflicting interests. Other issues aside, social and economic anomalies may either persist or evolve over time. To remove or reduce such anomalies requires institutional modifications aimed at equalizing opportunities for accessing potential benefits.

China has achieved the economic recovery comparable to that experienced by the Japanese in the 1960s and the 1970s. Its accomplishment along the economic frontier has surpassed that of the "miracle decade" under De Gaulle in France and its economic growth rate has outshined the successes of the Four Asian Tigers.

China's economy under the current administration will continue growing at a relatively fast pace. However, it is questionable whether the current growth trend can endure without parallel and substantive institutional modifications. Sustained improvement in performance presupposes structural and functional modifications. Constructive structural and functional modifications in turn require adjustments in institutional frame and practices. The phenomenon of macro successes in China can readily be attributed to actualization of productive and entrepreneurial potentials of the masses. Given economic freedom and a rationalized pricing system, unwanted inventory dwindle while commodities high in demand receive corresponding increases in capital investment and resulting growth in production. Long-term success of China's economical miracle, however, hinges on whether the correspondingly needed institutional modifications take place alongside economic reform measures. The future remains to be seen.

CHAPTER 3

REFORM APPROACH AND FRAMEWORK

POLITICAL CHANGE: 1976–1979

Mao's demise in 1976 marked the most significant turning point in China's economic history. The tumultuous decade of the "Cultural Revolution" (1966–1976) also formally came to an end. The transitional period between 1976 and the inception of reform in 1979 was headed by Mao's designated successor Hua Guofeng. A politically unknown figure till his nomination by Mao to succeed him, Hua attempted to win popular support by pledging to follow in the footsteps of Mao while concurrently promising rapid economic recovery and growth. In 1977, he criticized the Central Planning Commission's (CPC) conservative estimates for the economy's growth rates. Later that same year, the CPC submitted its revised draft of the 10-year Development Plan, 1975–1985, to the CCP's Politburo. Echoing Mao and the late Premier Zhou Enlai's repeated call for creative resourcefulness in macroeconomic designs, the draft Plan's objective was that by the end of the twentieth century, there would be comprehensive modernization of China's agriculture, industry, national defense, and science and technology, propelling China's economy to the forefront of world economies. It was within the framework of such an ambitious target that the draft plan was presented to the CCP's Politburo. Among others, the proposal called for a 40.6 percent increase in food production between 1975 and 1985, a 151.0 percent increase in steel production and a 224.6 percent rise in crude oil production during the same period. The plan for inflated growth rates necessitated massive capital investment that led to a soaring budgetary deficit and mounting foreign debt. The crucial mistake of Hua's ambitious push for rapid economic growth, however, laid not so much in foreign borrowing or budgetary deficit as in exacerbating China's already severe problem of sectoral imbalances and glaring macro dislocations.¹ As a result, many of the scheduled investment projects had to be halted, abandoned, or scaled back. A valuable lesson was learned.

By the end of the Third Plenary Session of the Party's 11th Congress in late December, 1978, although nominally Hua was still the head of the Party and of the state, the leadership role was rapidly being shifted away from him and onto Deng. By the end of 1979, Deng effectively succeeded Mao as China's supreme leader and political strategist.

Reform Objective

When Deng reached the pinnacle of political power in China, China's per capita income was a mere fraction of that of Hong Kong, Singapore, South Korea, or Taiwan. The command system of Mao's era had left China farther and farther behind its Asian neighbors. Staying the course, therefore, was no longer an option. In preparation for the Party's Third Planetary Session of the 11th Congress, a four-week-long preparatory meeting was held. During that meeting the pivotal issue that was discussed at length was how to shift the Party's focus away from obsession with political issues and onto economic modernization. Hope began dawning on China's long-languishing economy.

A saying popularized by the administration at the time was "truth is to be found in evidence." For Deng, it "mattered little what color the cat might be. If it was good at catching mice, then it was a good cat." Loosely translated, pragmatic achievements were more important than political verbiages. Economic progress was what China needed more than either "class struggle" or rhetorical gobbledygook. Intended or not, it was a covert disparagement of Mao's ideological modus operandi and modus vivendi.

The reform objective was to raise the general standard of living for the population as a whole. The short-term objective was to double the population's per capita income between 1979 and 1990, and then redouble that during the decade thereafter. Deng termed the objective as "reaching a modestly comfortable level" by the end of the twentieth century. The longer term objective for Deng was for China's growing population to approach a per capita income level comparable with that of the developed economies somewhere between 2030 and 2050. Realistic and pragmatic that he was, Deng repeatedly emphasized that China was not aiming at catching up with or surpassing the developed economies' standard of living by the mid-twentieth-first century. Through reform, he only indulged in envisioning China's economy orderly shedding its past structure and practices while concurrently going through the process of continual reform, adjustment, growth, and integration into the world economy at a gradual but steady pace.² In brief,

Deng's vision for reform was to raise per capita income at a sustainable rate over an extended period of time on the one hand and to accumulate valuable reform experience by the end of the twentieth century so that China's development phase for the first half of the twenty-first century would be able to stand on a secure and firm footing on the other.

Ground Rules for Reform

Unlike the tumultuous decades of the Mao era, the political atmosphere among top Party leaders by the late 1970s and onward was tranquil, conciliatory, and relatively unified. All focus was upon reviving and developing the nation's economy. The two leading statesmen were Deng and his colleague of the civil war era, Chen Yun. Deng was the paramount leader in political spheres while Chen was the chief strategist and spokesperson in economic domains, especially during the earlier years of systemic restructuring. Both Deng and Chen publicly acknowledged mistakes of the past—thereby indirectly censuring Mao's flawed economic policies that unduly emphasized the accelerated development of heavy industries at the expense of agriculture, light industries, and consumer goods industries. It was Mao's irrational predilection for increasing production in heavy industries that led to severe structural rigidities, sectoral imbalances, and widespread macro dislocations. Two of the key words for reform were "realism" and "adjustment."

On January 6, 1979, Deng stated that China as a whole was in need of a comprehensive adjustment. Adjustment meant shifting development emphasis away from undue focus on developing heavy industries at the expense of the rest of the economy. Deng said: "Give priority to those (investments) which are easier, faster-growing and more profitable ones... The emphasis on imports should be on those that can produce quick results and can make more money."[3]

With variation on the same theme of needing adjustment, Chen Yun reminded his colleagues of the following during the Politburo's meeting of March 21–23, 1979:

> We must be clear as to under what circumstances that we are undertaking this task of the four-modernization program. Speaking of being realistic, we must be clear as to what "reality" is. Reality is that (we have) a population of more than 900 million (in 1990), 80% of them being still in the countryside. Thirty years after (our) revolutionary victory, there are still beggars. (We) must improve living conditions. Balanced growth promises the fastest growth rates. We made the mistake of overemphasizing steel production in the past. (Such growth path) cannot be continued.
>
> ...Some of our comrades only see the (development) situations abroad. Our industrial foundation is shallower than theirs; our techniques are

inferior than theirs... We need two to three years' period of adjustment first, preferably three years. The objective of adjustment is to arrive at the right proportions (for diverse sectors of the economy), and then move forward from there.

...The objective for adjustment is to achieve proportionate progress... Talk about food alone is not sufficient. Forestry, animal husbandry and fishery all need being considered.[4]

Echoing Deng and Chen's call for sectoral adjustment, Vice Chair of the People's Republic of China (PRC), Li Xiannian, addressed leaders of China's provinces, urban centers, autonomous regions, and the military saying: "Our direction for adjustment this time is: adjust, reform, consolidate, improve. Move forward while adjusting, reform while adjusting, consolidate while adjusting, improve while adjusting."[5]

Being the most senior and respected political leaders at that time, whatever reform policy approach Deng and Chen should agree on, their position then invariably became official reform policy for China.

Unlike Mao, both Deng and Chen were pragmatists. Nevertheless, both were also old revolutionaries who savored Mao's maxim of "politics in command," meaning absolute leadership of and control by the CCP in China. Corollary to that was the understanding that state intervention, whenever needed, remained a prerogative of the state, irrespective of how liberalized the nation's economic system might be.

A crucial difference between the approach to systemic transformation in China and that of many newly liberalized countries of Eastern Europe was that while loosening its grip on economic affairs, the CCP maintained tight political control throughout the process. Tight state control over the approach to economic liberalization, over the pace of reform and over the sequencing of reform policies was a key variable in the mechanics of China's economic restructuring. Unlike the majority of reforming economies of the early 1990s, China's approach to reform since the late 1970s has been deliberate, tentative, flexible, and steady. If an experimental reform policy produced desired results, then it was promulgated on a wider scale either regionally or throughout the country. On the other hand, if unforeseen flaws in either reform design or in implementation method were noted, then timely remedial measures were promptly taken. No large-scale macro disturbance was permitted and no prolonged macro dislocation went unchecked.

After nearly three decades of Mao's penchant for continual political "class struggle" and unsound economic development policies, the general public was more than ready for political calm and speedy economic development. The leaders of the CCP, however, though fully focused on economic restructuring, were neither complacent with evident successes of early years of reform nor were they impulsive in dreaming of unwarranted speedier growth rates. Even during the first months of the reform process, Chen Yun already began cautioning the leading cadres in the Finance Ministry that forward strides must be steady. As it was customary, Chen's position was then promptly echoed by other leaders of the CCP. In early April 1979, Vice Chairman Li Xiannian acknowledged that economic recovery, especially in 1978, was rapid. However, in the same breath he prudently cautioned that in the face of this initial success:

> ...we tend to look at our success too much while neglecting to pay due attention to problem and difficult areas. (We have been) too desirous for faster development, (as a result the development) steps have not been as steady...We want reform. But the steps must be steady. Because the problems are complex in our reform process. We cannot be overly impatient. Reform must depend on given theoretical studies, on economic facts and forecasting. More important is that we must proceed from experimental points and then draw timely conclusions.[6]

Therefore, the basic guiding principles for China's systemic restructuring include the following: (1) realistic assessment of existing conditions prevailing within the country; (2) significant investment retrenchment from heavy industries in order to restore sectoral balances; (3) liberalizing economic policies under tight political control; and (4) calculated and steady pace for introducing reform measures. Once the ground rules and guiding principles had been made clear, the stage for economic restructuring was set.

Inception of Reform

Reform began with a series of public pronouncements and official decrees. Accompanying different stages of reform progress were resolutions, decrees, laws, regulations, and guidelines from the Party committees, from the People's Congress, from the State Council, and ministries were formulated, adopted, and enunciated over time. When and where needed, laws, regulations, and guidelines were amended, while at diverse time intervals reform scope widened and speed modified. Officially, major reform initiatives and measures were promulgated either by the Party Secretary General or the premier. More often than not the major reform initiatives often originated either from Deng or from his Party elder and colleague Chen Yun. Both the party hierarchy and the People's Congress would then routinely endorse and sanction whatever reform proposal Deng and Chen formally recommended. In terms of actual implementation of reform resolutions, progress was the speediest and most orderly during the administrations of reform-minded Hu and Zhao than during their successor administrations.

The first definitive salvo for economic liberalization was fired by Deng. On December 13, 1978, at the conclusion of a work symposium of the central administration, Deng stated:

> Our system for administering the (nation's) economy at the present is overly centralized. It needs to be boldly decentralized in an orderly fashion. Otherwise, it would be difficult for the nation, for the regions, for the enterprises and for the workers to set in motion their productive dynamism. It would also be problematic for implementing advanced management techniques or for enhancing productivity. There should be greater administrative autonomy granted to the regions, enterprises and producing entities... Before a cohesive (reform) scheme can be prepared, we can begin with partial measures, beginning with one line of profession in one region, gradually widening its scope.[7]

Nine days later, a communiqué from the central government elaborated the theme as enunciated by Deng. After repeating nearly verbatim Deng's earlier remarks at the beginning, the communiqué declared:

> (We) should resolutely simplify economic administrative offices at all levels, transferring an abundant share of their administrative responsibilities to enterprise-level entities. We should purposefully implement management and organization reform according to economic laws, stressing the function of objective value. Under the single leadership of the Party, we should put an end to the (existing) practice of having no line of demarcation among the Party, the administration and the enterprise, ending the practice of Party supplanting the government, and of the administration commandeering the enterprise.[8]

The resolve for reform was evident. As if China in the late 1970s had already learned the painful lessons of extensive macro dislocations and social disturbances yet to unfold in the Eastern European countries in the 1990s, its reform approach was ever watchful. Although China's attempts at systemic transformation were a dozen years ahead of those of the Eastern European countries, the Chinese government exercised every measure of caution forestalling possible macro disturbances. China needed economic reform but permitted no changes in its political system or structure. Deng insisted on creating a socially stable reform environment and an orderly restructuring process. For Deng, there was reason for that insistence. The difficulties China was faced with were already sufficiently complex. The vast population that was comprised of complex ethnic diversities historically laden with parochial tendencies further compounded the complexity. Therefore, under the single leadership of the party and operating within the framework of "democratic dictatorship" was what Deng insisted upon.

Direction and Approach to Reform

The indirect objective was eventual market coordination of production, distribution, and consumption. But smooth functioning of the market system presupposes time-tested and well-developed institutional infrastructures, which were nonexistent in China. At the inception of reform, there was no market pricing in China. Timely and accurate flow of market information was neither present nor feasible. Furthermore, till that time, since surplus value accrued to the state, all social savings was accumulated by the state. Therefore, there were neither functional financial institutions nor financial intermediaries for market-based coordination of financial flows. On the legal front, even the most basic legal frame for regulating market activities was absent. On the issue of social security, since China was still a socialist country at that time, there was neither a labor market nor open unemployment. Therefore, a social safety net neither existed nor was it considered needed.

In short, no parts for the smooth functioning of a market existed in China. Instead of relying mainly on the market system's "self correcting mechanism" for adaptive modifications to changing conditions, the responsibility for mapping flexible adaptations to evolving conditions in China was readily assumed by the state. A gradualism approach to systemic transformation was deemed crucial. For instance, farm reform began with only eighteen members of one production team in a commune in Anhui province in China's southeast. On December 16, 1978, the eighteen former commune members entered and signed an agreement with the commune administration, promising the delivery of production quota assigned to them. The eighteen members worked collectively as a team but away from the commune's structure itself. That experiment was indicative of the administration's initial approach to reform: cautious and secretive. In other words, the commune could not and would not have ever granted such permission unless it had first been cleared and authorized by the highest of authorities. The experiment became public knowledge only after its phenomenal success had become the formalized model for agricultural reform later on. Pilot experimental projects thereafter became the pattern of reform in other domains of systemic transformation.

In the beginning, China was to allow one segment of society and, if desirable, one geographic region to sow the seed for generating market forces. The process was gradual, but reform was to begin.

The operational motto for reform was "enlivenment within and opening up to the outside." Enliven within necessitated administrative decentralization, not only granting increasingly more decision-making power to lower levels of government and enterprises but also to reduce the number of commodity items still being centrally purchased and distributed. Reform was to begin with the agricultural sector, broadening later on to include other sectors of the economy. Opening up to the outside meant absorbing advanced technologies, managerial expertise, and capital inflow. Other than improving the quality and increasing the quantity of domestic products from such inflows, there would be active searches for foreign markets in order to accumulate the much-needed convertible currencies. "Ceding benefits by the state" to entrepreneurial entities became an incentive for the potentially more productive enterprises in experimental regions.

Domains

The stated intent of systemic and structural reform was, through increased productivity and income, to achieve "modest economic affluence" for households at large. The key sectors wherein the productive potentials could be actualized included foreign investment and foreign trade, agriculture, industry, and financial markets. Each of these sectors will be discussed separately in the ensuing chapters. Some of the concurrent or sequential measures that would help unfreeze the productive potentials of these sectors included reforming the central planning mechanism, the legal system, administrative organizations, the budgetary and financial systems, and pricing and wage systems. The pace and scope of introducing reform measures in these spheres was to be a function of sectoral performances. If policy adjustments were in order along the way, then timely implementation of such fine-tuning measures was to be introduced. Once the proof of reform feasibility and merits was confirmed, either from experimental sites or from policy domains, then reform scope would be allowed to widen and the speed to accelerate. Once the mandate for reform had been issued by the resolution of the 3rd Plenary Session of the 11th Central Committee of the CCP in December 1978, the reform-minded Party Secretary General Hu and Premier Zhao promptly set the reform process in motion.

Decentralizing the Planning System

During Mao's era, central planning was the centerpiece of the orthodox command system. The Five-Year Development Plan, once approved by members of the Politburo and subsequently rubber-stamped by the People's Congress, became the blue print for the Central Planning Commission (CPC) to plan prime control mechanism for all facets of economic activities in the country for the duration of the Plan. Through the Plan, the entire nation's economy was to function as a giant conglomerate under the direction of a single board of directors. Which state-owned enterprise (SOE) in which part of a given province was to receive how much of what inputs and producing how much of what output(s) within a given period had all to be mapped and spelled out. The aggregated sums of investment, production, distribution, consumption, and savings, together with overall growth rates for the nation, all had to synchronize with the planned target numbers.

Within the Plan, the centralized purchasing system ensured that whatever was produced was also "purchased" by the state at the state-determined price. And centralized distribution system correspondingly ensured that what the state had "purchased" would also be allocated to SOEs or households and other economic entities according to the Plan. Financial resources were reduced to plain numbers, playing the simple and passive role as units of accounting only. The required skills for an administrator consisted in securing a larger share of state-allocated resources while being assigned a lower production quota. Production over and above the assigned quota would thereby earn merit points for the administrator as well as the producing unit.

A natural by-product of the centralized planning system was pervasive passivity on the part of enterprise management and producing units. Innate entrepreneurial potentials had no room for actualization. For the systemic transformation to yield the desired outcomes, therefore, it became imperative that the role of the central planning system had to be redefined.

To justify the dismantling of a primary mechanism of the command system, the ever-pragmatic Deng articulated the rationale behind it thus:

> Why equate market with capitalism and planning with socialism? Plan and market are only means. As long as (they are) constructive in actualizing productive potentials, then (they) can be used. If it serves the interest of socialism, then it is socialistic; if it serves the purpose of capitalism then it is capitalistic.[9]

At the inception of reform, at least on paper, the official line was that China's economy would remain as a plan-coordinated economy. That is, the plan would continue to play the leading role in coordinating overall economic activities. Market forces and market coordinating mechanism could exist alongside central planning, playing the role of the second fiddle. However, it was also made clear that the scope of plan-mandated targets would be reduced while the range of plan-directed activities and targets would increase.[10] The coordination of economic activities outside of either the compass of the mandated or directed sphere was then to be relegated to the market mechanism.

Plan-mandated spheres included economic activities that were the most vital and critical to the overall well-being and stability of the nation's overall economy. They included industries such as staple food items, steel, select industrial chemicals, energy, and transport. Plan-directed domains of economic activities on the other hand comprised of those products or services whose equilibrium conditions could be more readily brought about through macro policies or market incentives. Economic leverages were used to induce economic entities to pursue their respective interests by conforming to Plan-directed guidelines. In light of the Plan-directed targets, it would then be the decision of local governments and micro entities to evaluate the potential markets for appropriate investment and production/distribution decisions. The idea behind resorting more heavily to indicated targets was reminiscent of the indicative planning employed by the French government after World War II. There is ample room for market incentives to bring about a desired objective under the plan-directed approach whereas under the Plan-mandated approach, there was not even breathing room for market forces to make an appearance. Finally, the third category of economic activities were those whose supply and demand conditions were such that existing market forces at that time could already bring about the desired equilibrium levels. Therefore, activities such as in the service industries as well as those whose aggregate output could readily meet the prevailing level of aggregate demand at a stable price would all fall under this third category of market-coordinated economic activities. Over time, the scope of state-determined items kept declining, replaced by either state-directed or market-based coordination mechanisms. Function of the market's pricing mechanism thereby orderly and systematically began replacing Plan-determined pricing.

The longer-term strategy for reducing the role of the planning mechanism was to continually reduce the number of Plan-mandated items while progressively widen the range of Plan-directed and market-coordinated spheres of economic activities. Though not publicly enunciated, the ultimate goal in dismantling the command system is the eventual replacement of central planning in all spheres of economic activities by forces of the market's coordinating mechanisms.[11]

LEGAL REFORM

Prior to the inception of reform, China's Constitution and laws were drafted and adopted to ensure the Party's absolute authority over all spheres of people's lives. There was guarantee for the rights and privileges of individuals and legal entities, at least on paper. In practice, however, it was how the Party leadership interpreted the laws or the Constitution at a given time that mattered. In extreme instances, such as during the "Cultural Revolution" of the mid-1960s, it was neither the constitution nor the laws that ruled the land. Rather, it was Mao's wishes and pronouncements that reigned supreme. As a result, the Party Secretary General Liu Shaoqi, the former Defense Minister Peng Dehuai and numerous other old revolutionaries ended up in jail and died there because at one time or another they had offended Mao. In other words, laws and articles of the Constitution could at times be more words than substance.

Addressing the cadres of the central government's working team on December 13, 1978, Deng said:

> To ensure the people's democracy, (we) must strengthen the legal system. Democracy must be systemized and legalized so that the system and the laws do not change just because the leadership has changed, do not change just because either the view or the focus of the leader has changed. The problem right now is that the legal system is quite deficient. Many laws have yet to be enacted. (People) often take the leader's words as "law." Disagreement with the leader's words was taken to be "against the law." When the leader's words changed, so did the "law" changed.[12]

The remark was in clear reference to Mao, whose numerous actions, especially during the "Cultural Revolution," were in clear violation of laws and basic human rights, and of which Deng himself became a twice publicly humiliated victim. Nevertheless, under the communist system, it was not and still is not uncommon that political muscle carried more weight than laws and regulations.

For economic reform, however, the imperative of timely legal reform held far greater significance than merely ensuring that no one was above the law. Under the command model, all means of production were publicly owned. There was no room for entrepreneurial endeavors. Introducing market mechanisms into a planned system now meant that economic agents must be assured of legal protection against arbitrary measures or unfair practices. The rights and responsibilities of economic entities—whether they be domestic or foreign—required clear enunciations of a set of laws so that all concerned would understand the newly introduced rules of the game and abide by them. Confidence in and credibility of the regime, at least in economic relationships, was indispensable for the success of reform.

With the progression of reform successes, new laws and current regulations either had to be introduced or existing ones fine-tuned. As repeatedly emphasized by the party and government leaders from early on, new economic activities need to be fostered and strengthened and evolving new economic relationships need to be solidified and institutionalized within the frame of legal provisions. As a result, within the first ten years of reform, more than a thousand laws, decrees and directives were adopted, issued, and promulgated either by the People's Congress or by the Ministry of State Affairs, of which nearly 70 percent were either directly related to or were relevant to sustained economic restructuring and growth. Accompanying reform progress, there has been timely replacement of administrative control of economic activities and relationships by market coordination and legal mediation. Confidence in legal protection in economic relations thereby added a much needed layer of foundation for sustained economic restructuring process.

Administrative Decentralization

At least at the inception of reform, it was repeatedly stated that the prime mechanism for coordinating economic activities was to be state planning—with the market fulfilling only a supplementary role. The intent and direction of reform, however, were for the eventual replacement of the former with the latter. Though not articulated, it was understood from the outset that the command system would eventually be dismantled. Anticipating the declining role of central planning and therefore a more active role for diverse government agencies and levels of administrators in the years to come, administrative reform was in order.

Until reform began, government ministries, departments, bureaus, and agencies were administrative units. But they were administrative units only. That is, they only implemented policies and executed orders and directives as handed to them from "on high." The more immediate "on high" at each and every level of the leadership structure was not a higher-level agency or office. Rather, it was the office of the Party secretary for that same level of the administration, because for every administrative office—from top ministries of the central government to a local factory or school administration down below—there was, and still is, a corresponding office of the Party Secretary. Thus, for instance, while the nominal chief executive of a major city was the mayor, real power in the city resided (and still resides) with the Party Secretary of that same city. Similarly, a school principal is the administrator of a school. However, it is the Party Secretary of that school that has the ultimate voice in any major decision. Even though administrative positions, especially the higher ones, were invariably held by Communist Party members as well, having parallel Party Secretary offices would ensure that the ultimate authority at any administrative unit belongs to the Party representative rather than a political appointment. Such an organizational system was structurally wasteful and functionally inefficient. It became the breeding ground for nurturing a bureaucratic mind-set, for entrenched aversion toward decision making and/or responsibility bearing. Therefore, one facet of the administrative reform was the call for an effective separation of Party from the State while concurrently refining the mechanisms within the Party itself so that it would be more effective in exercising its leadership role.

The first order of measures for structural modification was reducing the administrative role of the central administration by decentralizing authorities and responsibilities to regional and local entities. The function of central planning was thereby effectively circumvented because an increasing number of decisions were to be made on the regional and local levels instead of being made by the center.

On the level of the central administration, the process of streamlining administrative procedures and practices also began from early on. With the mandate for decentralization being in place, a significant number of functionaries in the central administration were no longer required. In time, more than a dozen ministries and departments were either consolidated into other government institutions or abolished. As more authority and responsibility were decentralized to lower level administrations, the domains for fiscal authority and responsibility for central, provincial, regional, and local governments, respectively, also began to be continually more clearly defined and refined.

Fiscal Reform

Instead of the previous practice of the central administration collecting and disbursing all productive surpluses, domains of revenue sources and expenditures for both the central and lower-level administrations were now to be circumscribed, defined, and refined over time. Fiscal prerogatives and responsibilities of all levels of government were to become increasingly more detailed and transparent.

The central administration was still responsible for collecting revenues from and tending to limited operating needs for some enterprises of national interest. Similar fiscal schemes also came into existence on the provincial and municipal levels for enterprises owned by them. Demarcation of disbursement obligations for the central and provincial or local governments, respectively, was also made more transparent during the 1980s, enabling the central government to focus its concerns more on macro coordination rather than micro management.

The reformed system initially permitted the SOEs to retain a portion of the profit. During earlier years of fiscal reform, the government would collect a fixed 55 percent of the profit from the SOE. The government and the

SOE would then share the remainder 45 percent of the profit, with relative percentage shares by each of the two being dependent on the nature of the productive activity. After 1984, the tax structure was modified. Depending on the nature of productive activities, an SOE began paying taxes according to the "tax bracket" it might fall into in a given year. The tax rates varied from one industry to another even if two SOEs in different industries might achieve the same rate of returns. The after-tax income would then belong exclusively to the SOE.

On the expenditure side, the central government would no longer allocate investment or operating needs of the SOEs "gratis." Instead of the state collecting all depreciation charges prior to 1983, the rate of annual depreciation was raised from 5 to 7 percent and the SOEs could henceforth retain the charges for reinvestment purposes. There was to be a clear separation between the state and the SOEs in management as well as in fiscal responsibility. For needed financial resources, the SOEs should turn to state banks or other financial institutions rather than to the state. All such credits secured, at least in theory, should be repayable on time, obliging the management to administer investment, production, and distribution activities as business entities. In principle and at least in theory, the SOEs were to either reap the fruit of their own successes or bear the consequences of failures.

Fiscal reform on other fronts also began in the early 1980s. Since the state ceased collecting all surplus values from economic activities, which ranged from the largest to the smallest economic units, the state's financial needs had to be met from alternative sources of revenues. In time, value-added tax, sales tax, resource depletion tax, business and personal income taxes and property tax, among others, all came into existence.

Financial Reform

China's banking system prior to 1979's reform served as a clearing house for the state's budget and the Central Plan, not as an efficient conduit for financial flow. Unlike financial resources in market economies, money played no active role in China's plan-dictated economy. The traditional role of the central bank regulating money supply as an effective tool for implementing the nation's economic policy was also absent. Reforming the financial system, therefore, was essential not only so that a potent macro coordinating and controlling mechanism could be set in motion but also so that the financial flow can constructively and productively accompany the real flow in a growing economy.

Structurally, the People's Bank was officially transformed to become the state's central bank in September 1983. The purpose of converting the People's Bank to become the nation's central bank was so that it would focus on exercising the traditional functions of a central bank, setting reserve requirements, regulating money supply, charting its lending policy to member banks, and discharging its supervisory responsibilities.[13] Instead of previous practices, at least on paper, the central bank was to make its own decisions without interference from the state.

A branch bank, The Bank of China, was created from the former People's Bank, tending exclusively to foreign currency banking activities. A number of special purpose banks, such as the Agricultural Bank of China, the Chinese Investment Bank, and the Bank of Industry and Commerce of China were also either resurrected from the bygone years or newly created. All special-purpose banks owned by the state were to become independent commercial banks, supposedly operating independently from the state. Operating on the principles of commercial banks, the state-owned special purpose banks would reap the benefit of their own operational successes and/or suffer the consequence of their own mismanagement.

In time, private banks capitalized by domestic or external sources would also be permitted, helping to create a more competitive environment in the financial sphere. In addition to state-owned and private commercial banks, other forms of financial institutions such as insurance companies, investment banks, trust companies and the like were all envisioned to emerge in due time. The stock market was also to be institutionalized for facilitating the transfer of state shares in SOEs to the private sector and to mobilize financial resources for improved allocative efficiency. Through growing competitive forces in the financial market, not only mobilization and utilization of financial resources would become more efficient and vibrant, effective implementation of monetary policy by the central bank would also thereby become more realizable. However, as will be seen in a later chapter, functionally the state sector of the financial system is replete with ambiguities and anomalies, severely compromising the potential effectiveness of financial intermediaries.

PRICE REFORM

System-induced structural rigidity fossilized the plan-determined price structure. Plan-determined prices ranged from the most costly investment items to the cheapest consumer goods such as matchbooks and toothpicks. Timely or even just periodic price adjustment for tens of thousands of producer and consumer goods according to supply and demand conditions was neither feasible nor ever contemplated. Arbitrariness and rigidity in price determination resulted in extensive misallocation of resources. Perennial shortage of needed goods and services amidst accumulation of unwanted intermediate and finished products became a permanent feature of the planned command system. "Enliven within and opening up to the outside" necessitated price reform, because the success of reform impinged upon free-market-based pricing system.

Administrative decentralization, land-leasing program, individualized farming away from the commune system, and phased price liberalization program, among others, came one upon the heels of another in quick succession. Phased price reform began in 1979. A three-tiered pricing system came into existence. Controlled prices included essential factors of production and consumer necessities that were still short in supply relative to demand. Free pricing began for nonessentials that were either adequate or ample in supply relative to demand. The middle tier pricing comprised of either inputs or consumer goods and services that experienced neither severe shortages nor abundant surpluses. Within the state-determined parameter, the price of a given commodity within that category could fluctuate upward or downward to yield market signals to both the producer and the consumer.

The first phase of price reform began in 1979 and was concluded toward the middle of the 1980s. Although the prices of numerous nonessential commodities and services became free during that period, the focus of price adjustment was upon the gradual objectification of prices for the previously plan-determined essentials. The pace of price liberalization was the fastest for factors and commodities with the highest supply elasticities that could cause least hardship for consumers at large. For instance, the centralized purchasing prices for eighteen agricultural products were raised by nearly 25 percent in early 1979, while the prices on meats, aquatic and dairy products were adjusted upward by 30 percent later in that year. Increases in centralized purchasing price were then passed onto the consumers because producer elasticities for these commodities were high. The prices on other agricultural and industrial factors or products also saw periodic adjustment during a six-year span. However, prices on items that were neither abundant in supply nor price sensitive were the last ones to see adjustment. It was a two-pronged pricing system, administrative-determined prices for some and market-determined prices for others. With the progression of time, the number of regulated prices kept declining while the scope of free or partially freed prices continued rising. For goods and services produced or provided by private initiatives during that period, the prices were to a large measure outside of the state's intervention.

The second phase of price reform began in 1985. As the general public's earnings rose during the early half of the 1980s, aggregate demand correspondingly increased. Costs for factors and essential social services thereby underwent a series of upward adjustment. During the second phase of price reform, prices on factors and products that were still short on supply remained administered rather than market-adjusted. The goal was that, in due time, such supplies would augment and that the market would eventually be the flexible and readily adjustable coordinating mechanism for all factors, products, and services. To date, prices on nearly all factors and goods and services are already market-based rather than administered.

Wage Reform

Anticipating enhanced productive incentives, wage system reform also began to take shape. Wage system reform was deemed an integral part of systemic transformation because of the wastefulness of labor resources in the planned system. Before reform began, neither an individual nor an enterprise had the freedom of choice. For an individual, once reaching the age or stage of entering into the "job market," he or she was assigned which enterprise or productive unit in which location to go to and which job position to fill. Whether the assigned job suited an individual's educational background/training or not was immaterial. Conversely, whether an individual assigned to a job in a given enterprise or office was what the latter needed or was looking for was likewise inconsequential. Mismatching of labor with a producing unit was only one facet of the planned system's wastefulness. The equally important facet causing wastefulness in labor force was the planned system's wage structure. As an example, the beginning salary of a college graduate in the majority of academic disciplines was exactly the same for everyone. It mattered little whether the graduate was from one of the nation's most prestigious universities or from an unheard-of college. Likewise, whether one graduated from the college with the equivalent of a summa cum laude or one barely made the grades made no difference in starting salaries. Furthermore, since China was an avowed socialistic country, there could be no unemployment for able-bodied working age citizens. Quality performance or not on the job, the workers could not be readily fired, cultivating the so-termed iron rice bowl mentality. It is easy to logically deduce the consequence of this plan-determined wage system on human resource efficiency and on work incentives.

Supplanting the planned system's state-determined wage levels, management of SOEs that were granted increased discretionary power could henceforth adjust a given worker's wages in accordance with the company's performance as well as an individual worker's marginal productivity. Limited profit-sharing scheme also came into existence, injecting productive incentives into workplaces. For state employees, there were basic wages applicable to respective professional services at different levels of expertise. In addition, either merit raises or bonuses could be awarded for quality and/or length of service. Wage reform did not concern itself with the wages of private enterprise employees, since the state had no role in the operation of private economic endeavors. However, steady rise of the private sector within the economy over time has had a profound influence on wage system reform in the public sector. Financial remuneration in the private sector is a function of marginal value productivity of an individual. Since reform began permitting free mobility of labor resources, the more productive employees in the SOEs began moving into the private sector. For the SOEs to retain quality workers, therefore, appropriate upward wage adjustment was in order, effectively aligning wage with one's value product and correspondingly raised the productive incentives and overall productivity of China's vast labor force.

Gradualism Approach to Reform

The Politburo gave official endorsement to Deng's reform initiative. With the mandate from above, the Fifth People's Congress approved the government's proposal to coordinate central planning with market forces. The initial reform steps taken were experimental in nature and modest in scale. As senior Politburo member, Chen Yun affirmed at a working conference of the central government on December 18, 1980:

> We should reform. But the steps should be steady. Due to the fact that the issue of reform is complex, we must not hasten. Reform must rely on the necessary theoretical investigations, on economic calculations and economic projections. More important is to begin with experimentations, drawing timely conclusions on the experience. That is, "crossing the river by probing the pebbles underfoot." The beginning steps need to be small, proceeding with caution. This should in no way be construed as not reforming. It is to expedite measures for remedial adjustments. It also helps promote overall reform successes.[14]

The proposed approach to remedying past mistakes was to permit market forces playing a "subsidiary" role alongside central planning in order to mitigate the structural deformities among sectors as well as the perennial imbalances between aggregate supply and demand. For theoretical justification and ideological "clarification," reform leaders asserted that planning did not equate with a socialist system because market economies also resorted to planning. Conversely, relying on market forces did not mean capitalism since markets also existed in socialist economies. Despite rhetorical jargons and official apologetics, the role of the market began its official ascent in economic decisions in China and promptly replaced central planning as the mainstay of economic coordinating mechanism.

During the first five years of reform, planning remained as the principal means for coordinating commodity circulation, with the market mechanism playing a "supplementary" role. The overall approach was experimental in nature. After the Third Plenum of the Twelfth CCP Congress in 1984, the pace of reform accelerated and scope widened. On the basis of reform successes, the merits of the market as a coordinating mechanism were more than proven, they were confirmed. Central planning slowly but steadily faded in importance while the function of the market correspondingly increased over macro coordination. Lest the more liberal-minded segment of society should entertain any hopes for political liberalization, Party and government officials at varied levels kept emphasizing and reemphasizing the leading role of the Communist Party and the state's overall control of reform agenda. By the 1990s, market forces had effectually supplanted central planning in macro coordination. Rather than micromanaging each and every enterprise in the nation as it was prior to reform, the state's main function in the economy now devolved into macrocoordination. Market instead of the state now began coordinating information and input product flows. On their part, the state and the central bank became the mediating institutions functioning mainly in the domains of macro coordination and regulation.

CHAPTER 4

FOREIGN INVESTMENT

A BACKGROUND NOTE

The People's Republic of China (PRC) was founded in 1949. The West immediately imposed an embargo in an effort to isolate it from the outside world. Since China had no experience with establishing a communist state, it faithfully modeled its efforts after that of the former USSR. Its foreign economic relations revolved nearly exclusively around the USSR and other former members of the Council for Mutual Economic Assistance (COMECON) nations.[1] Since none of these countries permitted private economic initiatives, there was no free flow of investment resources into China. The main source of foreign investment came by way of intergovernmental treaties.

China relied primarily on the former USSR for credits and technical assistance. After Mao's open quarrel with Khrushchev in 1961 the USSR recalled all its technical experts. It also invalidated treaties on economic cooperation with China and demanded repayment of the credits advanced to China. China's major development projects that had been financed by Soviet credits and supervised by the Soviet experts came to a screeching halt. As a result, China became further isolated from the rest of the world. In response, Mao called for self-reliance. Foreign economic relations were perceived as a symptom of ideological impurity. A closed-door policy quickly ensued.

After a quarter century of centralized command system and severely curtailed foreign economic relations, China remained a poor country. Relative isolationism helped freeze China into a state of stagnant backwardness. In contrast, the economies of the Four Asian Tigers[2] continued reaping the bountiful benefit of sustained external economic relations. Ever pragmatic, as early as 1975, Deng proposed:

> ...Bringing in new technologies and advanced machineries broaden merchandise trade. Strive to increase exports so as to be able to increase imports

of crucial, key, high tech equipments...Enter into long term agreements with foreign economies. Bring in their technical equipments for coal mining, compensate them with coal exports.[3]

RATIONALE FOR NEEDING FOREIGN CAPITAL INFLOWS

Growth in developed economies decelerated in the second half of the 1970s. In Southeast Asia, in addition to Japan, the economies in Taiwan, Singapore, Hong Kong, and South Korea had all been bustling with impressive gains. China stood out as the sleeping giant in the Pacific Rim region. Reform-minded leaders in Beijing recognized the lost opportunities of the past decades. They also understood the vast potentials that still lied ahead if China was to redesign its development strategy. Other than introducing systemic reform measures, it recognized the merits and the imperative of opening up its economy to the outside world.

After nearly three decades of Mao's reign, China was sorely in need of advanced technologies, investment capital, and entrepreneurial skills. Foreign capital inflow can help mitigate investment capital shortage and induce the much-needed modern technologies and techniques. In addition, foreign investment can also help create jobs, improve labor quality, contribute to tax revenues, and be instrumental in systemic restructuring. That is, China's nearly fossilized economic structure could be most expeditiously thawed through foreign injections both in terms of capital and in ideas. Furthermore, China needed to modernize its infrastructure. Foreign direct investment (FDI), especially those from the transnational corporations, have both the financial and human resources to upgrade domestic infrastructure as a form of investment for their own benefit. Opening up FDI became a logical conclusion.

Politically, however, China was not ready to acknowledge its need for the capitalistic West. The more advanced economies in the Pacific Rim could be ready and willing candidates to provide what China needed. Opening up to the more developed economies in the region was both politically acceptable and strategically judicious.

China was also well aware that economies in the West were battling with severe recessions in the late 1970s. China held the promise of a vast outlet for the West's market-hungry investors and entrepreneurs. It would be easy for capital, advanced technology, and entrepreneurship from the West to channel their resources through Hong Kong into China. It was decided then that it was an opportune time for China to open its door to the outside world, not entirely but circumscribed opening. Comparable to its reform approach in agriculture, opening up a window to the Asian economies first was to serve as an experiment in amplified foreign economic relations.

Process of Inducing Foreign Capital Inflows

Capitalizing on a more relaxed political atmosphere after Mao, the leadership in Guangdong province petitioned the central administration in April of 1979 for greater autonomy in its economic relations with neighboring countries. More specifically, it requested that Shenzhen, Zhuhai, and Shantou be designated as export-destined centers for value-added activities. The targets for such exports would include neighboring Hong Kong and nearby Asian markets. Hong Kong would also serve as a ready conduit for channeling such exports to distant shores. The petition received Deng's unequivocal endorsement.

The central administration deliberated the petition. The outcome of the deliberation was a document titled "Select Provisions Governing Stepped-up Foreign Trade Endeavors for Enhanced Foreign Earnings."[4] The provisions first identified select provinces and coastal cities possessing geographical and infrastructural advantages for expanded foreign economic relations. Second, within such designated provinces and cities, only select districts were chosen as special economic zones (SEZs) for expanded relations with external economies. Alternately stated, these designated districts were granted special privileges for targeting foreign capital inflows from overseas, which included Hong Kong, Macao, and other neighboring countries. The primary focus was to channel foreign capital, advanced technologies, and foreign expertise into export-destined production and processing centers. Prior to reform, Mao's call for self-sufficiency relied on import substitution. With reform, the focus shifted to export promotion. The primary interest in inducing foreign capital inflow then was upon investments that would promote exports. Intended or otherwise, China transformed itself into the world's factory for manufactured goods destined for external markets.

In July 1979, the coastal provinces of Guangdong and Fujian were designated as the platform to launch China's new open door policy. Special legal provisions were more liberal and the two provinces granted greater flexibility in application. A year later, the central government designated the cities of Shenzhen, Zhuhai, Shantou, and Xiamen as SEZs.

Till then, SEZs were unique to China. It was an experiment to introduce pivotal free-market elements into what was, basically, still a socialist system. SEZs enjoyed the privileges of more liberal policies than the rest of the country. Administrations of SEZs were also granted greater autonomy from the center in decision making. The zones were not simply export-destined processing centers; they also served as special links and windows to external economies, inducing foreign capital and technical inflows.

Between 1979 and 1982, 949 agreements with foreign investors were reached within the designated SEZs. Out of the agreements, 922 foreign direct investments were made, totaling $6.01 billion. FDI in 1983 alone reached $1.73 billion, accounting for 470 additional investments. For hard-currency-starved China, the beginning of the open door policy promised bountiful dividends.[5] Whether foreseen or not by reform advocates, resistance to opening up to external economies dissipated. Hard core ideologues still existed, however, "money talks." Though overtly they still adhered to Mao's ideology, few failed to capitalize on the new economic opportunities. It became futile to call for a return to the old belief of building a socialistic society.

In early 1984, Deng toured the SEZs in southern China. Duly convinced of the merits of an open door policy in the SEZs, he took the next step to opening up China. In April 1984, fourteen coastal cities stretching from Dalian in the northeast to Beihai, a port city in the province of Guangxi in southwest China, were declared open to FDI.[6] Some of the open cities such as Shanghai and Tianjin had been under colonial occupation of foreign governments. In varying degrees, all of these open cities possess port facilities. All are better endowed with infrastructural foundations, which were not available to most of China's interior municipalities. Furthermore, many of them had been trade centers in the past. The intent was that by opening up these coastal cities to foreign capital and technological inflows, the foreign injections would be able to revive the long dormant commercial spirit of the past. Policies governing external economic relations within the open cities were not as liberal as those in the SEZs. Neither were the local administrations granted as much autonomy as in the SEZs. The primary focus of opening these coastal cities was to attract foreign capital and technologies and to stimulate and promote foreign trade.

The following year, instead of opening up individual cities to FDI, the State Council opened up three delta regions.[7] Major SEZs or cities like Shanghai, Guangdong, Shenzhen, and Xiamen were also included in the three delta regions.[8] As a result, the following year alone recorded 3,073 agreements for FDI, totaling $5.93 billion. When compared with China's foreign reserve of $2.18 trillion in late November 2009, it was a minuscule sum. In 1985, this figure, however, was significant and substantive. It must also be recalled that it was only a few years prior that China was still advocating self-sufficiency.

The quickened pace of opening up to FDI spoke silently but eloquently of the leaders' intent. On April 20, 1988, Hainan Dao, an island under the administrative jurisdiction of Guangdong province, became an independent province and was designated as open to external economic relations. Hainan Dao became the largest SEZ in China. To hasten export growth, the government resorted to export subsidies and tax refunds. Furthermore, in order for China's exports to remain competitive, the government purposefully kept the exchange rate favorable to convertible currencies. China's open door policy was gradual, cautious, and deliberate. However, once solid evidence presents itself to the merits of a given policy, the government was neither hesitant nor slow to confidently broaden and deepen a reform measure. In brief, China's opening up to external economies comprised primarily of three categories: SEZs, open cities, and open economic development zones (open regions).

By the end of 1990, the total number of agreements reached for using foreign capital was 29,693, totaling $68.1 billion. Appreciating the value of productively utilizing foreign capital, China also began borrowing as early as 1979. By the end of 1990, China had borrowed a total of $45.9 billion from external sources that included international financial institutions, foreign governments, foreign commercial banks, and financial institutions.[9] After a decade of reform, China had accumulated enough experience in fine-tuning, intensifying, and expanding its foreign economic relations. Shanghai, on its part, was well on its way to reclaim its past glory as China's financial and commercial center. Shanghai's economy was bustling with life. Shanghai itself, however, had no suitable land for expansion. Pudong, a rural district under the jurisdiction of Shanghai municipality, was situated across from Shanghai, separated only by the Huangpu River. Developing Pudong could add both depth and breadth to Shanghai being a world-class financial and commercial center. In June 1990, the central government declared Pudong a "new area." As a result, the former rural district of 467 square miles was transformed into an open region. In less than two decades, Pudong became a metropolis of more than 3 million people with a gross domestic product of $54 billion. Pudong, a former rural district, generated a GDP greater than many smaller economies in the world.

In addition to SEZs and open economic zones, technology development zones, industrial development zones, and free trade zones were also established. Because of geographic reasons or regional needs, each of the designated zones or districts enjoyed uniquely defined or circumscribed privileges in foreign economic relations. Furthermore, as the central government continues its policy of decentralization, provincial, and local administrations were allowed to also begin designating zones for promoting FDI.

LEGAL FRAMEWORK FOR ENCOURAGING FOREIGN CAPITAL INFLOWS

Laws and the Constitution had little relevancy in practice while Mao was alive. This was particularly apparent during the tumultuous years of the "great Cultural Revolution" in the late 1960s. What the leaders said or how they felt at a given time carried more weight than legal or constitutional provisions. Economic laws were essentially unnecessary since all means of production belonged to the state. Furthermore, it was the central plan that dictated and directed all aspects of economic activities, ranging from the largest state-owned enterprises (SOEs) to the lowest of microproducing entities.

The history of cooperating with foreign capital and technology was brief and the scope of cooperative efforts was limited during the 1950s and 1960s. Other than a few joint ventures with Poland and Tanzania in the early 1960s, there were less than a dozen Chinese overseas endeavors. By the mid-1960s, the atmosphere for cooperating with foreign economies worsened. In fact, cooperation with capital and technologies was scoffed at during the "Cultural Revolution." The need of foreign assistance was an insult to national pride and, therefore, unpatriotic. Foreign economic cooperation came to an abrupt halt.

Because Deng himself was a victim of the lawless years of the "great Cultural Revolution," he insisted on the imperative of legal reform. Law and order were perceived as a prerequisite for sustained economic reform and development. The People's Congress authorized the State Council to issue provisional regulations, decrees, and guidelines pertaining to foreign economic relations. Between 1979 and the end of 1986, more than half of the laws enacted by the People's Congress and more than half of the directives and decrees issued by the State Council pertained to economic relations. Among them were laws and regulations pertaining to the encouragement and protection of foreign investments.[10] The legal environment regulating foreign economic relations was founded on three legislations promulgated during the first ten years of reform: The PRC's Joint Venture Enterprise Law of 1979, the PRC's Foreign Capital Enterprise Law of 1986, and the PRC's Chinese-Foreign Cooperative Enterprise Law of 1988. The more distinct characteristics of each of the three are briefly highlighted in the following discussion.

THE PRC'S JOINT VENTURE ENTERPRISE LAW

Joint Venture Enterprise Law was adopted on July 1, 1979 by the Second Session of the Fifth People's Congress and promulgated on July 8 that same year.[11] A joint venture capital enterprise is a joint capital equity company. For broadening the PRC's international economic cooperation and technical exchanges, the law permits foreign corporations, enterprises, institutions, or individuals to establish joint capital ventures (JCV) with their counterparts in China. Establishment of such ventures must be premised on the principle of fairness for mutual benefit. The government will neither nationalize nor seize foreign capital ventures. Under exceptional circumstances, if so needed for public good, the government, in accordance with laws, may acquire such enterprises with due compensation. The law stipulated that registered foreign capital in a joint venture should be no less than 25 percent. Partners share benefits or losses according to the share of respective registered capitalizations. The share of investments by partners may take the form of cash, materials, or patented rights. If a foreign partner should make the investment in the form of techniques, technology, or equipment, then they must be advanced in nature and must suit the needs of the host country. If losses should occur due to a foreign partner's deception in terms of technology or equipment claimed to be advanced but in reality are not, then compensation must be made for financial losses incurred there from.[12] According to tax laws and administrative regulations, JCVs may be granted the privileges of tax reduction or exemption. If the foreign partner should reinvest financial gains from the ventures in the host country, then it may request reimbursement of a part of the taxes already paid. Materials, energy, parts, and other factors should be secured from the host country first, though it is also permissible for JCVs to procure the same from abroad with convertible currencies supplied by themselves. Upon expiration or cessation of the enterprise, according to foreign exchange regulations, the foreign partner may repatriate financial resources duly allotted to it.

On September 20, 1983, the State Council issued detailed directives governing the implementation of the Joint Venture Enterprise Law.[13] Of the 105 directives, a select few merit highlighting. Directive 41 required that technology transferred for use by JCVs should be advanced in nature. The products resulting from employing the induced technology should be either socially or economically beneficial (to the host country) or competitive on international markets. Directive 43 states that unless otherwise stipulated, the party transferring the technology may not restrict the recipient partner in terms of geographic regions, quantity, or pricing of products being exported by the JCV. In addition, upon the expiration of the technology transference agreement, the technology recipient partner may continue availing itself of the technique or technology. In accordance with another directive, the equipments and machineries and their parts that are not available from domestic sources may be imported. Such imports may receive tax reduction or exemption privileges. Similarly, raw materials, machinery parts, and packaging supplies that are needed for producing export-destined goods may be accorded similar privileges. When needed, JCVs may apply for convertible or domestic currency credits from either domestic financial institutions or from banks in Hong Kong and Macao.

Viewed as a whole, the JCV law and its corresponding operational directives accentuate two major points: China welcomes foreign capital in the form of JCVs and it actively and demonstrably seeks advanced technologies and modern techniques.

The earnestness in seeking advanced technology imports is made patently clear in the favorable provisions made for diverse forms of capitalization. The favorable conditions provided are manifestly evident especially under Article 4 of the law and in Directives 22 through 25, both inclusive. China wanted advanced technologies. Instead of all cash investment, foreign capital partners could apply advanced technologies or patented techniques as a part of its total contribution to a JCV. It is made even more transparent by the language of subsection four of Directive 43, which obliges any foreign capital partner to grant the domestic partner continual rights to utilize the imported technology even after the technology transfer agreement has ended.

THE PRC'S FOREIGN CAPITAL ENTERPRISE LAW

By the mid-1980s, China's leaders were duly convinced of the valuable contributions in which foreign capital and technology could make in the country's effort at systemic restructuring. China had by then accumulated sufficient experience in and knowledge of administering foreign capital and technology inflows. However, the bulk of capital and technology inflow came through neighboring Asian economies. China was ready to broaden its scope. On April 12, 1986, the Fourth Session of the Sixth People's Congress adopted the Foreign Capital Enterprise Law. The intent of the law was to encourage the expansion of foreign capital and technology inflows. The law was amended on October 31, 2000 by the 18th session of the Ninth People's Congress. In order to broaden the scope of foreign economic cooperation and technology exchanges, and to stimulate the country's economic development, the PRC permitted foreign enterprises and other economic organizations as well as individuals to establish foreign concerns in China.[14] "Foreign enterprise" meant that all capital investments are made by foreign investors. The term does not include subsidiaries owned by foreign corporations or economic institutions.[15] Foreign capital enterprises may be established, if and only if, they are beneficial for China's economic development, for promoting its export industry and if foreign capital embodies advanced technology.[16] Earnings and associated legal rights of foreign investors are protected by China's legal system. In accordance with China's tax code, foreign capital enterprises may receive tax reductions or exemptions. If the enterprises should reinvest their after-tax gains in China, then they may apply for a tax refund for the portion that is allotted for domestic reinvestment purposes. After fulfilling tax duties, both foreign employees and the foreign capital enterprises may repatriate their earnings to their respective host countries.

The nuance of Articles 1 and 3 of the law is unmistakable. Investments by exclusively foreign capital are welcome, especially if they can contribute to China's export sectors. More important, through this law, China begins a new chapter in encouraging foreign investments. It marked the dawning of an era for major international investors to compete more actively in China's booming investment markets. The law is deliberately intended to attract deep-pocketed foreign capital and high-tech investments made exclusively by foreign investors. Such investments are normally made by more developed economies of the West.

Supplementing the earlier JCV law, this foreign capital enterprise law opens up a new channel for enhanced benefits to China's efforts at systemic restructuring and economic development. Capital and advanced technologies invested in China thereby plays a pivotal role in modernizing China's economy without corresponding need of expending the much-needed convertible currencies that must be earned through increased exports. In addition, the presence of major foreign capital investments could provide China's treasury with an added revenue source.

PRC'S CHINESE-FOREIGN COOPERATIVE ENTERPRISE LAW

On April 13, 1988, the First Session of the Seventh People's Congress promulgated the third major law governing foreign capital inflows into China. It is titled "PRC's Chinese-Foreign Cooperative Enterprise Law."[17] The major distinguishing characteristic of this law from the 1979 JCV law is that a Chinese foreign cooperative enterprise operates on the premise of contractual agreements for the parties to cooperate in a business endeavor. Capitalization by the cooperative parties, unlike in a joint venture enterprise, does not need to be translated into equity shares. Furthermore, profits or losses are shared by cooperative parties on the basis of contractual agreements rather than on proportionate equity shares. Other than the usual provisions for rights and privileges of foreign investments, the more relevant features of this law are briefly discussed below.

In accordance with provisions of this law, partners of cooperatives need to enter into contractual agreements pertaining to the following: capitalization and/or cooperation provisions, distribution of earnings and/or products, respective responsibilities and shares in loss and/or risks, administrative and/or managerial methods/techniques, and asset distribution upon termination of the cooperative endeavor. The host country encourages cooperative enterprises that espouse exports and advanced technologies. Provisions for capitalization and/or cooperation may take the form of cash contribution, materials, use of real estate properties, patent rights, nonpatented techniques, and varied property rights. Needed credits may be applied for from either domestic or foreign financial institutions. Liabilities and responsibilities for secured credits being used for investment or for cooperative endeavors are to be determined by the partners themselves. Insurance for cooperative enterprises should be purchased from domestic insurance institutions. According to China's tax code, cooperative enterprises pay taxes and may be accorded tax reduction or exemption privileges.

SOME PRELIMINARY OBSERVATIONS

A few preliminary observations may be made concerning China's foreign investment reform. Legal protections, option for credits, and tax privileges conjure up an attractive scenario for prospective foreign capital. Tax privileges were not uniformly applied to foreign capital. The pivotal consideration is—within a given designated zone, city, district, or region—what is the potential contribution of the prospective foreign investment to these respective administrative domains. The SEZs rank first in privileges because of their multiple potential contributions to systemic restructuring. Their proximity to Hong Kong and Taiwan rendered them as natural sites for inducing foreign capital, technology, and advanced managerial techniques. Their geographic closeness to other Asian economies also provided them with ready access to, as well as access by, foreign economies. Anticipating the British government's returning Hong Kong to China by 1997, the SEZ administrations could experiment with the "one nation, two systems" doctrine advocated and approved by Deng.

The primary intent for designating the fourteen open cities was to revive the economic vitalities of those cities that existed prior to 1949. The most direct approach to achieving that objective was by way of absorbing advanced technologies through induced foreign investment. Varying economic incentives were granted to foreign capital in the open cities, depending on distinctive characteristics and individual needs of the cities and their surrounding regions.

To further accelerate the pace as well as widening the scope of attracting and absorbing advanced technology and techniques, the central government designated thirteen specific economic and technology districts within these open cities. Foreign capital establishing manufacturing activities within these designated districts were accorded additional privileges. These designated districts then became gateways for the open cities to economies abroad.[18]

Growth in foreign capital inflow has been rapid and enduring. Early foreign capital inflows, though relatively modest, all had to be coursed through legal provisions and regulations delineated by the central government. Over time, increasingly greater autonomy was granted to provincial and regional administrations to articulate and define the provisions for attracting foreign investments. With increased capital inflows and resulting increases in foreign earnings, the government has been enabled to improve both the infrastructural support systems and overall investment environment.

Sources of foreign capital keep augmenting, widening, and deepening. In the beginning, the majority of foreign investment originated from relatively smaller investors in economies of the Pacific Rim. With the passage of time, investors with more advanced technologies and deeper pockets from more remote parts of the world began to invest in China, which is evident by a rising number of the Fortune 500 firms' bilateral governmental agreements, export-credit lending as well as issuance of government securities.

Initial foreign investments tended to concentrate in manufacturing and construction industries. With improved investment environment for foreign capital, investments from abroad have systematically branched into service industries that include financial services, communication, and transportation. The foreign injections also helped alleviate the two-pronged obstacle of foreign capital shortages and China's feeble export capacity. Modern equipments, state-of-the-art production techniques, and ready marketing channels enabled and empowered China to throw its doors wide open to its own export industries, actualizing and mining the rich potentials of earning convertible currencies.

Foreign investments have benefited China's production and exports. As policy makers continuously attempt to improve the quality of foreign investments in terms of payoffs, they also recognized that FDIs have not benefited China as much in terms of developing new technology on its own. That awareness led to China's increased expenditures on research and development (R&D) on its own.

Concurrently China has also begun improving its investment environment for foreign capital that focuses on R&D activities. According to a survey by United Nations Conference on Trade and Development (UNCTAD), "China has become the third most important offshore R&D location for multinational enterprises (MNEs)." The expected outcome for it would be a new generation of quality researchers increasingly more comparable with the best scientists in the world.[19]

It is through foreign injections that the entrepreneurial spirit in China has been awakened, fortified, and energized. Foreign capital inflows have also helped create jobs, increase government revenues, fuel the growth of the export sector, raise the general living standards, and empowered the general public to dream of sustained economic well-being. It is China's reformed foreign investment and foreign trade policies that have propelled China onto the world stage as a rising economic giant commanding international attention and continual assessment.

Development [Trend] in Foreign Investment

Political considerations aside, the primary objective for any investment abroad is profit. Capital flows into ventures and geographic regions when and where opportunities arise. Economic rationality is the guiding principle for capital flows.

When China began its open door policy, ideological resistance to foreign cooperation still lingered. Though Deng replaced Mao at the helm of the government, politically it would be safer for him to adopt a gradualist approach to major changes in policy direction. China, therefore, targeted only investment capital from neighboring economies where there would be greater cultural compatibility and historical parallelism. JCVs became the primary form of external capital flowing into China.

Historically, China has been a country with either imperial rules or authoritative regimes. For six decades, the communist regime has ruled China with a commanding presence. China was a planned economy. It is now an economy in transition. Instead of planning by rigidly managing micro entities, the government still resorts to planning. It is now planning by macro coordination, factoring in market forces, and international interactions. Before reform began, there were production targets. Now, targets are still very much a part of the five-year development plans (FYDPs). But the targets to be secured are by relying on the market's coordinating mechanisms and market forces that include entrepreneurship and capitalist greed.

When China first designated the five SEZs in 1979, JCV establishments began emerging and clustering in those designated zones. Relatively smaller in scale, the attention of the JCVs was on manufacturing and value-added industries destined for exports. Unlike transnational corporations intent on profits as well as market share, the foremost objective of JCVs was for profit and speedy returns on investment.

When reform first began, articles of the JCV law purposely circumscribed foreign capital's ability to dominate an enterprise's processes. Legal constraints on foreign capital's influence stemmed in part from the regime's predilection for its own ability to control. On the other hand, China's experiment with economic coordination via market forces was still in its embryonic stage. Deng opted for caution. Over time, larger foreign investors progressively sought to increase their shares in the enterprises. It was not until 1986 that the Foreign Capital Enterprise Law was promulgated, permitting enterprises in China to be wholly owned by foreign capital.

The principal form of single capital ownership was enterprise establishments by multinational corporations (MNCs). They enter with substantive capital, benefiting from economies of scale, and technical and organizational superiority.

Large capital investment by single firms from abroad also implied more advanced technologies. A central consideration for China to permit sole foreign capital ownership, therefore, was reaping the benefits of technical and technological externalities from MNCs. Of the 500 multinationals, nearly 450 have made sizable investments in China. Furthermore, foreign investment in China has progressed from primarily value-added activities at the inception of reform to quality and high-end products. For instance, the MNCs such as GM and Microsoft are their respective sole proprietors in China. A commonplace approach for becoming sole proprietors in China by large foreign capital is by way of mergers and acquisitions. The size as well as the number of foreign firms has increased in China. Activities also correspondingly branched and widened into the service sector and R&D domains. However, an estimated 90 percent of foreign capital in China is still invested along the coastal provinces and regions, causing unequal distribution of benefits from foreign capital infusion.[20] Policy aimed at inducing quality foreign capital into China's interior provinces has been on the drawing board. When will FDI flow into the less well-endowed regions and provinces in a more meaningful way depends on how far the central government is willing to grant regional governments greater autonomy in setting parameters for attracting foreign capital.

INJECTION OF FOREIGN CAPITAL

Consequences from China's planned command system between 1949 and 1978 and its open door policy thereafter provided a glaring contrast of the relative merits of the two systems. China was poor before its reform policy began. The country as a whole has since witnessed phenomenal growth. It is to a large measure due to its open door policy that China has today become an economic force and a major player on the stage of world economies.

Table 4.1 presents data illustrating growth in foreign capital inflows since reform began in 1979. Data in the upper portion of the table present the number of projects and their respective contracted values for select years. Foreign investments include projects financed by both investment firms as well as credits extended by private institutions and international organizations. The lower portion of the table, on the other hand, presents data on the total amount of foreign investments realized, or actually utilized, for the corresponding years.

Table 4.1 Foreign Capital Inflow, 1979–2008 (in $100 million)

Year	Total		Foreign Loans		Direct Foreign Investments		Other Foreign Investments
	Number of Projects	Value	Number of Projects	Value	Number of Projects	Value	
Amount of Contracted Foreign Investment							
1979–1984	3,841	281.26	117	169.78	3724	97.50	13.98
1985	3,145	102.69	72	35.34	3073	63.33	4.02
1986	1,551	122.33	53	84.07	1498	33.30	4.96
1987	2,289	121.36	56	78.17	2233	37.09	6.10
1988	6,063	160.04	118	98.13	5945	52.97	8.94
1989	5,909	114.79	130	51.85	5779	56.00	6.94
1990	7,371	120.86	98	50.99	7273	65.96	3.91
1991	13,086	195.83	108	71.61	12978	119.77	4.45
1992	48,858	694.39	94	107.03	48764	581.24	6.12
1993	83,595	1232.73	158	113.06	83437	1114.36	5.31
1994	47,646	937.56	97	106.68	47549	826.80	4.08
1995	37,184	1032.05	173	112.88	37011	912.82	6.35
1996	24,673	816.10	117	79.62	24556	732.76	3.71
1997	21,138	610.58	137	58.72	21001	510.03	41.82
1998	19,850	632.01	51	83.85	19799	521.02	27.14
1999	17022	520.09	104	83.60	16918	412.23	24.26
2000	22347	711.30			22347	623.80	87.50
2001	26,140	719.76			26140	691.95	27.81
2002	34,171	847.51			34171	827.68	19.82
2003	41,081	1169.01			41081	1150.69	18.32
2004	43,664	1565.88			43664	1534.79	31.09
2005	44,001	1925.93			44001	1890.65	35.28
2006	41,473	1982.16			41473	1937.27	44.89
2007	37,871				37871		
2008	27,514				27514		

Continued

Table 4.1   Continued

Year	Total		Foreign Loans		Direct Foreign Investments		Other Foreign Investments
	Number of Projects	Value	Number of Projects	Value	Number of Projects	Value	
Amount of Realized Foreign Investment							
1979–1984		181.87		130.41		41.04	10.42
1985		47.60		25.06		19.56	2.98
1986		76.28		50.14		22.44	3.70
1987		84.52		58.05		23.14	3.33
1988		102.26		64.87		31.94	5.45
1989		100.60		62.86		33.92	3.81
1990		102.89		65.34		34.87	2.68
1991		115.54		68.88		43.66	3.00
1992		192.03		79.11		110.08	2.84
1993		389.60		111.89		275.15	2.56
1994		432.13		92.67		337.67	1.79
1995		481.33		103.27		375.21	2.85
1996		548.05		126.69		417.26	4.10
1997		644.08		120.21		452.57	71.30
1998		585.57		110.00		454.63	20.94
1999		526.59		102.12		403.19	21.28
2000		593.56		100.00		407.15	86.41
2001		496.72				468.78	27.94
2002		550.11				527.43	22.68
2003		561.40				535.05	26.35
2004		640.72				606.30	34.42
2005		638.05				603.25	34.80
2006		670.76				630.21	40.55
2007		783.39	1471.57			747.68	35.72
2008		952.53				923.95	28.58

Although China's reform measures in foreign investment were tentative and experimental in the beginning, China has steadily and progressively removed covert restrictions or barriers lifting institutional impediments to foreign investors and adjusting to evolving conditions. Consequent upon the promulgation of successive reform measures, the total amount of contracted and utilized foreign capital also steadily mounted.

The primary forces attracting inflows were cost efficiency in the form of relatively inexpensive labor and complementary factors, tax and duty privileges, and abundant market opportunities, that is, low-cost manufacturing and assembly operations promising rapid returns.[21]

A few observations pertaining to Table 4.1 are briefly outlined below:

- For the first five-year period between 1979 and 1984, there were 3,841 projects totaling $28.1 billion. The main source of the contracted foreign capital originated from the "foreign loan" sector. That is, total contracted foreign investment was less than $11.5 billion. Viewed from a different perspective, slightly less than 41 percent of foreign capital inflow during that period originated from FDI. The balance came from international borrowings.
- Contracted foreign investment in 1988 was $16.0 billion, which was a 31.8 percent increase over $12.1 billion in 1987. However, the same category of contracted foreign investment suffered a 21.3 percent decrease during the following year. The cause of the abrupt decline in contracted foreign investment in 1989, together with the 1988 decline in realized foreign capital utilization, cannot be as readily ascertained. However, it may be recalled that the years 1988 and 1989 were also the years of mounting social tension, culminating in the "Tiananmen Square incident" on June 4, 1989. Uneasy social calm returned by the second half of 1989.
- There was a modest increase of 5.4 percent in contracted foreign investment by 1990. However, the 1990 contracted foreign investment was still 24.5 percent below that of 1988.
- With restored social calm and enhanced economic incentives, growth in FDI resumed in 1991. Amendments in 1990 to the JCV law extended a guarantee of nonexpropriation of JCV assets by the state (Article 1), permitted a foreign investor to chair the board of a JCV (Article 3), granted to the foreign partner the privilege of opening a foreign currency account with a bank other than the Bank of China (Article 5), and allowed an extension of the time limit on cooperative ventures (Article 6).
- A year later, the government granted additional tax privileges to foreign capital enterprises and contractual ventures if the investments

were made in priority domains suggested by the state. As seen in Table 4.1, the contracted foreign direct investment increased by 77.8 percent from 1990 to 1991, and realized inflow grew by 24.3 percent.

- With the passage of time, foreign investors were sufficiently reassured that the Chinese government was determined to maintain social calm, whatever the cost. For foreign investors, it meant predictability and security of their investments. Contracted foreign investment surged from $19.6 billion in 1991 to $69.4 billion the following year, a 254.6 percent increase.
- The fastest growth category in inducing foreign capital was in FDI. When comparing the 2006 contracted FDI of $193.7 billion with that of $6.3 billion in 1985, it shows a phenomenal 2,959 percent increase in a 21-year period. The increase in the corresponding number of projects for the same two years under comparison is also an impressive 1,250 percent. The conclusion that may be deduced is that larger FDIs were making their way into China's vast investment markets.
- During the five-year period of 1979–1984, foreign capital realized was $18.2 billion. It was a humble beginning when compared with the single-year realized foreign investment totaling $95.3 billion in 2008.
- The combined amount of contracted foreign investment for the three decades of open door policy was $1.66 trillion. Combining the 2005 contracted foreign investment of $192.6 billion with that of $198.2 billion in 2006, the two-year period's contracted foreign investment was $390.8 billion. That is, the sum of the two years' contracted foreign investment data accounts for nearly 24 percent of the total contracted foreign investment for the 30-year period of 1979 through 2008. The data speak eloquently of China's impressive accomplishments in the domain of attracting foreign capital through its reform policies that began three decades ago.
- Over time, investment domain by foreign capital has broadened from primarily the more labor intensive manufacturing activities to more capital intensive endeavors. Products from foreign investment during earlier years were mostly destined for exports. With capital deepening by larger foreign investments, the target market has been increasingly shifting toward domestic consumers.
- Variety of products from foreign investment has also been broadening over the years. When reform began, emphasis on productive activities by foreign investment was on value-added, processing, and low-cost manufacturing. Three decades after reform began, foreign capital has been carving out niches in electronics, communication, transport, banking, and a host of service-driven industries.

- Being the largest country in the world with a population in excess of 1.3 billion, China holds immense potential for both domestic and foreign entrepreneurs. One of the more pronounced trends of foreign capital flowing into China has been a notable increase in R&D activities in recent years. The concern is whether China has the appropriate number and quality of personnel to absorb the prospective investments in the near future desired by foreign investors.
- Potentials for both high-tech and capital-intensive research industries abound. However, a major weakness in China's ability to absorb greater volume and superior quality service-oriented foreign capital is its lack of appropriate infrastructural support and services needed by R&D-centered foreign capital.

MERITS AND CHALLENGES OVER FOREIGN CAPITAL INFUSION

The benefits of opening China to foreign investments are nearly immeasurable. Foreign capital has helped upgrade China's technical competence and elevated it to technological heights. Some of the larger foreign investments enter first with appropriate technologies for smaller scale production. Success leads to increased productive capacity and higher level technologies being introduced into China. An estimated 50 percent of new technologies introduced into the market since reform began are attributed to the infusion of foreign capital.[22] As a result of foreign capital and accompanying technology inflows, the open door policy has helped improve labor productivity and reawakened entrepreneurial spirit. Though MNCs are reluctant to share or sell its technologies to the host country, their entry into the host country invariably yields technological externalities. It thereby provides impetus to domestic enterprises to improve their own ability in research and development endeavors.

Accelerated introduction of market forces via foreign injections has also helped unclog commodity circulation channels that perennially plagued the command system. Foreign capital, therefore, has helped thaw China's structural rigidity, while reducing structural imbalances and improved functional efficiency.

Fueled by export-destined foreign investments, China's foreign reserve has surged and surpassed all other major economies in the world. Foreign capital increases competitive pressure for both the SOEs and private concerns, including establishments in the financial sector, to adapt and adjust to changes in the market for efficiency and productivity. Foreign injections have thereby obliged the less efficient SOEs in China to leave behind past practices and perform or expect an early demise.

Since China's accession to the World Trade Organization (WTO) in 1991 and its progressive dismantling of covert barriers to foreign insertions, foreign capital has introduced compelling new dynamics into China's hitherto closed financial markets. An increased competitive environment in the financial sector in China can help improve its functional efficiency in that pivotal sector of the economy. An improved financial system thereby can also lead to greater efficiency in the capital markets, effectively elevating the performance of both domestic and foreign resource flows.

That China's reform policy affecting foreign investment has yielded bountiful benefits is self-evident. Nevertheless, there have also been concerns associated with the introduction of an open door policy toward foreign capital inflows. Some of the less salient features consequent upon foreign investments are briefly highlighted below.

Since reform began, there has been gradual decentralization of decision-making authority granted to lower level governments by the central administration. Provincial and regional governments have been granted greater autonomy, including mapping out their respective foreign investment policies within the parameters circumscribed by the central administration. Reward for economic performance is political promotions. Self-interest, therefore, influences lower level administrations' evaluating and processing applications by foreign investors. Within given parameters, the lower level administrations resort to more generous policies in order to attract foreign investments. Stretching central administration's directives and parameters occur. Latent anomalies and irregularities in policies in order to attract foreign investment ensue.

SOEs became beneficiaries of Beijing's decentralization policy. If the SOEs were of vital importance to the overall well-being of the economy and if losses were incurred, they could still receive subsidies and unsecured credits during the early phase of reform. Over time, easy credits and subsidies began drying up. For survival and for possible personal gains, the SOEs of less strategic importance to the nation began looking for foreign capital. By way of mergers or undervalued buyouts, extensive state assets became lost in the process.[23] Corollary to such mergers or buyouts, cost cutting and personnel trimming measures resulted. The previously disguised and underemployed became openly unemployed helping to swell the rank of the already unemployed.

Consequent upon rapid economic growth, an adequate supply of energy and a deteriorating environment have surfaced as two of the major concerns for Beijing. A number of foreign ventures in China are energy-intensive users as well as high polluters. Even as China has been tightening up its processing procedures for new FDI, there is no effective means to curb existing foreign capital firms and cooperative ventures that are less than ideal on these two fronts.

On the other hand, foreign capital firms, often, provide social benefits and associated fringes that domestic enterprises cannot match. Consequently larger foreign investors are in a position to lure quality personnel into their employment. It in effect siphons off the more productive labor force from domestic enterprises. That translates into the weakening of domestic concerns' productive efficiency and competitiveness.[24] Another concern, though not a demerit, is that the rapid increases in foreign investment in China during early decades of reform were to a large measure due to privileges and competitive incentives. After being admitted into the WTO, however, the privileges had to be orderly phased out. The main strategy to sustain the momentum of foreign capital inflow now rests with an improved investment environment. The jury is out as to what extent China is able to timely improve its foreign investment milieu to remain competitive in this regard.

Foreign investment flows where expected returns are the highest. The eastern seacoast provinces and major ports benefit the most from foreign investment. Geographic concentration of foreign capital thus creates uneven distribution of benefits. Though local administrations in interior provinces strive to lure foreign investments, the share has been meager. Unequal distribution of benefits accentuates the predicament of China's rapidly rising Gini coefficient. Rising social tension in China may be attributable to unequal distribution of economic opportunities and income. It is a pressing concern requiring more attention from the central government.

If future-induced capital inflow emphasizes what China's growing economy needs, then foreign investment can be beneficial. China needs sustained efforts at structural readjustment. Constructive new FDI can also simultaneously assist in synchronizing China's productive activities, transiting from mass production to quality products and from secondary to tertiary activities. However, if future FDI keeps flowing mostly into activities that are highly polluting and are resource- and energy-intensive, then long-term harm may outweigh its short-term gains.

FDI increases competitive pressure for China's industries to adapt and adjust. In light of China's current development situation, this is particularly true for China's financial sector, which has thus far been one of the least affected sectors in its economy. The weakened dollar and the Euro's purchasing power in recent years compromise China's competitive position as a haven for foreign capital in search of investment opportunities. On the one hand, China must be able to anticipate frequent and rapidly changing conditions in the world economy. Yet to, increasingly integrated into the world economy, China needs alternative strategies to weather possible vicissitudes consequent upon the globalization process.

In brief, China's open door policy has yielded positive results far beyond the early decision makers' expectation. The glaring consequence of its reform policy based on the slogan of "enliven within and opening up without" is for the world to see and for other transitional economies to covet. Behind the veneer of successes, however, there are also hazards not as readily perceived. China's 10th FYDP has addressed some of the concerns.[25] Given the momentum of self-interest bred by systemic restructuring and the introduction of market forces, to what extent the 10th FYDP will succeed in these respective domains remains to be seen.

CHINA'S DIRECT INVESTMENT ABROAD

Consequent upon China's unparalleled success in its open door policy, its foreign reserve keeps mounting. Foreign infusion has helped China restructure its economy internally while continually expanding its export capabilities. Mounting trade surpluses led to rising antidumping sentiments against China. To achieve relative current account balance and to secure needed factors of production short in supply domestically, China looks outward for investment opportunities by increasing its capital account.

China opened its door for gains. Gains breed increased appetite for greater and wider gains. The initial aim for attracting foreign investment policy was to help restructure China's economy and to increase domestic productivity. Well-defined, gradual opening up to foreign capital began with the designation of SEZs. Success led to successive opening up of cities, regions, and deltas. From economics zones to coastal cities and then regions, sustained success yielded improved production, living standards, and optimism.

The principle of comparative advantage led China from "coming in" to "going out." The objective is to alleviate domestic shortages in crucial factors while concurrently benefiting from cost efficiency abroad. Cost efficiency dictates efficient resource allocation. The globalization process continues. Integration of world economies and allocation of scarce resources globally is in full force. "Early birds get the worms." China is in a position to capitalize on the trend by "going out." Ideal targets abroad for investing its immense foreign reserves were wherever comparative advantages existed. The "going out" policy became official.

The motto of 'going out' began resonating in the 1990s. China has since made the transition from foreign capital inducement as one-way traffic to a new phase in its open door policy by combining capital inflow with that of outflow. Rapid and sustained economic growth entails equally rapid increases in raw material and energy consumption. To be able to nurture continual growth, China needs secure and adequate supply of essential factors of production. China ranks among the highest energy consumers in the world. The trend will continue and more likely than not accelerate. Investing and producing abroad saves factory needs domestically while exporting pollution that accompanies productive activities to countries abroad. The "going out" policy therefore is economically rational. This is particularly true when investments are made in energy- and resource-rich developing economies.

"Going out" also makes sense politically. China has become the second largest economy in the world. Economic power yields political power and prowess. The by-product of spreading its economic resources, especially into the third world countries, leads to ascendancy on the political scale internationally. Investing abroad also serves to broaden China's markets abroad. "Going out" can reap the dual benefits of securing cheaper resources from abroad while making China's presence felt globally. It is politically expedient.

Even before China embarked upon reform, it began looking outward to Africa, though the objective was more for political support than economic gains. It projected itself as a nation standing with and standing by the former colonies of the West. Goodwill missions such as helping build infrastructure in select African nations began decades before China became an economic power itself. With mounting foreign reserve and recognizing the inevitable process of accelerating globalization, China began looking outward financially two decades ago. Faced with increasing needs for markets as well as investment opportunities, there was much to gain by investing abroad for efficient resource allocation globally. China's first quarter investment abroad in 2008 exceeded that of entire year of 2007. Its investment abroad in 2002 was $2.5 billion. By 2007, it soared to $18.8 billion. Though still minuscule when compared with many developed economies' FDI abroad, the rate of increase was what attracts the attention of developed as well as developing economies alike.[26]

The voiced concern among developed economies with respect to China's "going out" policy is China's rapidly increasing investment in Africa. In 2003, China's investment in Africa totaled less than half a billion dollars. By 2008, however, it had soared to $7.8 billion. Accusation mounts, fearing that China is intent on vigorously competing for energy and mineral resources with rich countries in Africa. While en route to a visit to Egypt on November 7, 2009, China's Premier Wen Jiabao said:

> "Energy cooperation is just one area... The aim for China in helping Africa is to reinforce its own role in development."[27]

> Two days later, the Premier "...pledged $10 billion in low-interest loans to African nations" over a three-year period. To strengthen his contention that China's investment in Africa was more than self-serving, Wen reported that "...despite the financial crisis (worldwide), Chinese investments in Africa were up 77% in the first three quarters of 2009."[28]

The criticism against China's FDI policy in Africa is not likely to fade anytime soon.

The reality is that China's investment abroad is broader than merely investing in less developed economies. It also means investing in developed countries. Declining value of convertible currencies against the Chinese renminbi translates into improved ability for China to invest in developed economies. Japan and numerous European economies invest in the United States. In practice, domestic establishments financed by foreign capital means products are domestically produced. When marketed in domestic markets, the products are strictly speaking, not imports. The strategy can avoid covert trade barriers on the one hand while helping stem the tide of antidumping sentiment against China on the other.

According to the State Administration of Foreign Exchange in Beijing, China's foreign reserve before reform began was $2.3 billion. Two decades after reform began, it grew to $146.2 billion. Ten years later, it soared to $2 trillion. By the end of April 2009, China's foreign reserve was $2.01 trillion. Eleven months later, the reserve increased by $444 billion to $2.45 trillion.[29] China is in an eminent position to go shopping globally. By year end in 2009, China still ranked only fourteenth in cumulative investments abroad. The glaring evidence is for all to witness. Its growth in direct foreign investment abroad, therefore, is likely to mirror that of its foreign reserve increases.

In the middle of 2005, China's third largest oil company, Oceanic Petroleum Corporation, Ltd., (OPC), offered $18.5 billion to buy the U.S.-based Unocal. An estimated 70 percent of Unocal's estimated energy deposit is located in Asia and the Caspian Sea. The concern was that, if the offer was to be accepted, OPC would have gained access to possessing the rights of petroleum and natural gas rights in the region. OPC's offer invited strong negative reactions in the United States. A Congressional hearing led to a resounding "no" to OPC's initiative. Prior to that, China's "Ideal Investment Group" made an offer of $17.5 billion to purchase IBM's computing division. And China's Haier Group offered $12.8 billion to take over U.S. company Maytag.[30] By year end in 2006, more than 5,000 investment firms in China had made an investment in 172 economies abroad, totaling $90 billion.[31] The "going out" call is now for investment funds from China to flow wherever the promised return is the highest or is the most pivotal in insuring China's sustained growth. Growth in China's investment abroad is likely to accelerate as speedily as its growth in foreign trade and foreign reserve.

China's 11th Five-Year Development Plan (2006–2010)

China passed its 11th FYDP on March 14, 2006. In Chapter 36, the Plan calls for actively capitalizing on foreign capital inflows and in the following chapter the Plan directs focus on increased international cooperation for mutual gains.

Addressing the government's policy for attracting and utilizing foreign capital inflows, the Plan explicitly states the following objectives: obtain advanced technologies, bringing in advanced managerial talents and experiences, and synchronizing the utilization of foreign capital with improved domestic productive and technical capabilities.

For effectuating sustained foreign capital inflows, the Plan called for fine-tuning legal and administrative tools for greater transparencies pertaining to prospective foreign investors. It also called for steering foreign capital toward high-tech productive activities, advanced service industries, infrastructural development, and environmentally friendly ventures. The plan also called for attracting foreign capital flowing into established industrial bases in midwestern and northeastern parts of China. It also attempted to encourage the MNCs to establish regional headquarters, and research and personnel training centers. Its other objective was to promote cooperation between domestic enterprises and MNCs so that the latter could help restructure and improve domestic firms' productive endeavors.

On the front of the "going out" policy, the Plan called for support to qualified domestic enterprises, empowering them to make FDI abroad while concurrently engaging in transnational exchanges. In Section one of Chapter 37 of the Plan, it is also clearly stated that: "According to the principles of mutual gains and comparative advantages, expand and broaden cooperative endeavors (with others) for developing natural resources." China does not deny its interest in developing mineral and energy resources abroad. But, as stated in the Plan, it is on the basis of equality and mutuality. Explicitly stated or not, China's burgeoning financial assets will keep flowing outward in search of its much-needed factors of production and product markets.

A Concluding Note

China's open door policy followed a gradual, orderly, and progressive trail. The glaring successes of its foreign investment policy are self-evident. Its development policy is a model for the less-developed economies in the world to analyze and study. Its approach to systemic and structural reform has effectually become a chapter in the book of development studies and comparative economic systems. However, there is still ample room for China to tweak and modify its foreign investment policy, both for capital inflows and outflows.

Having achieved its initial intent of capitalizing on foreign capital inflows, China's new direction in encouraging future foreign investment aims at, among others, high-tech externalities, at R&D, at environmentally friendly productive activities. It is a noteworthy change in direction. Initially, the emphasis had been on quantity. The new direction emphasizes quality. It is not a sweeping change away from manufacturing and value-added activities. It nevertheless is a clear call for upgrading the quality of FDI. New focus on foreign capital entering China is on modernizing, upgrading, and widening activities in the service sector. These desired foreign investments are high-stake ones requiring substantial capital outlays. To achieve the desired objective, a host of new measures are called for. A select few include special tax privileges may help entice capital intensive FDI into China. Tax privileges are not the sole or even the main concern for MNCs entering a host country. More important to such prospective high-end FDI is a tax system that is fair and transparent. Independent and reliable judicial system is (also) important to foreign investors.[32]

Similarly, quality personnel from MNCs' own headquarters does accompany their entry into a host country. They nevertheless also need highly educated and qualified personnel in the host country to collaborate in activities such as R&D. The quality of China's high-tech and well-educated personnel has been on the rise. However, China must compete with new developing nations like India and Eastern European economies. The question is how competitive is China in terms of having sufficient quality human capital to accompany such desired FDIs.

The service sector accounts for nearly two-thirds of MNCs' overall investment abroad. However, service-oriented investment in China from abroad is less than one-third.[33] It is an indication that China is still wanting in some essential services. There is the need, therefore, to identify these infrastructural and fundamental services required by quality FDI from abroad.

China has been opening up its capital market to foreign investors. However, a major front that China should pay due attention to is the inflow of capital from the less than legitimate sources. Hot money seeks investment opportunities abroad wherever it promises speedy returns. Speculative activities by such financial inflows are highly mobile. They can become a source of destabilization to China's nascent financial sector.

China has been encouraging large domestic enterprises to invest abroad. The growth rate in China's FDI abroad has been significant. On the part of the government, however, multiple fronts require measures appropriate for and supportive of China's growing direct investments abroad. For instance, there has been too much administrative bureaucracy. There are "too many hands in the pot" that are caused by different offices examining the same application repetitively using different standards. A related issue is that undue emphasis is being placed on application processes without accompanying administrative supervision.

In conclusion, China's phenomenal economic growth during the past three decades has been achieved to a large measure through its systemic transformation and its open door policy. Success in foreign trade has been instrumental in China's success. Success in China's foreign trade policy is in turn premised on its success in its foreign investment policy. Flexibility in drawing timely conclusions and implementing judicious corrective measures when needed have been some of the characteristics of the designers of China's reforms. Given the dynamic nature of the globalization process, sustained adjustments, modifications, and refinement remain imperative for China's continual success in its development policy.

CHAPTER 5

FOREIGN TRADE REFORM

A BACKGROUND NOTE

Faced with embargo imposed by the West after taking over the reign from the Nationalist government in 1949, China's communist leaders relied on the former members of the Warsaw Pact. Among the Warsaw Pact nations, the former USSR was the nation that China most relied on for military assistance and economic relationships.[1] Soviet advisers were quick to oblige China to model its economic system after that of their own. China's policy for foreign economic relations, therefore, patterned closely after that of its "big brother," the former USSR.

The command system adopted by China was based on centralization of resource allocation, output targets, and budgets that took into account needed imports and exports for a given year. Until reform began, China's foreign trade policy was premised on three decrees issued by three different state administrative and policy offices. The first decree, which appeared in September 1949, was titled "Implementing Trade Controls and Policy for Protecting Foreign Trade." It stipulated "centralized sovereignty" by the state in foreign trade. The second decree titled, "Provisional Administrative Regulations for Foreign Trade," was promulgated in December 1950. That same month, the Bureau of Foreign Trade issued the "Provisional Implementation Details Governing Foreign Trade."[2]

The regime wasted little time socializing all means of production. First of all, privately owned enterprises became "jointly owned" with the state. Fanned by propaganda and frightened by being labeled "capitalists," all former owners of productive assets "willingly and proudly" ceded their ownership rights to the state. Furthermore, the state's foreign trade agency exercised full control over all imports and exports. Trade volume soon after was determined by the state's Five-Year Development Plans (FYDPs). These FYDPs assigned production quotas of export-destined goods to state-owned productive entities. Most of the planned exports had to originate from the primary sector. Given food shortages and needs for minerals in the former Warsaw countries, primary products became exportable commodities from China. As a result, the state assigned export quotas to China's collectivized farms and state-owned mines. Ironically, the state itself did not produce. The state did, however, plan, mandate, and manage the entire process, from assigning production quotas to exchange and distribution of imports.

The Soviet advisors recommended planned import items. Emphasis was on heavy industrial and reproducer goods. Production quotas were assigned to primary good producers, while imports were allocated to industrial goods producers. As prices for goods and services were state-determined, there were no objective measures for gains or losses. Inflated prices for industrial goods with undervalued consumer goods rendered measurement of gains or losses meaningless. Furthermore, since trade was the state's monopoly, it was the state that supposedly reaped all the benefits or sustained whatever losses.

Political decisions dictated enterprise operations. The entire system was "command" by definition. Efficient resource allocation premised on the market's pricing system was absent. Measurement of success was on fulfillment of plan-dictated quotas, not on efficiency. Motivation on the enterprise level was therefore irrelevant.

China's foreign trade declined drastically in the late 1950s and early 1960s for two reasons. First, Mao's development strategy witnessed dismal failures, which were the most pronounced in the farm sector. Farm collectivization and communization led to a severe grain shortage between 1959 and 1961. Mass starvation followed, costing an estimated 30 million deaths. In addition, China did not have sufficient exportable commodities for imports. Second, with Mao's open quarrel with Khrushchev in 1961, economic cooperation agreements between the two countries were nullified. The episode deepened China's distrust of foreign powers. Mao called for self-reliance and self-sufficiency. Import substitution was the result of self-imposed isolation from external economies. Focus of central planning was shifted onto domestic supply and demand. Foreign trade suffered a further setback in the late 1960s during the "Cultural Revolution." Extreme leftist ideology supported by Mao called for a cessation to foreign economic relations. Foreign trade was frowned upon as acknowledging superiority of foreign producers. After the tumultuous years of the late 1960s, the administration of Premier Zhou Enlai began efforts at restoring some semblance of normalcy. Limited foreign trade began.

EARLY PHASE OF TRADE REFORM

Any unwavering loyalty to or faith in Maoist ideology was lost with the aftermaths of the "Cultural Revolution." Without freedom of expression, muted resentment helped translate suppressed frustration into questioning the merits of the command system. The public had no free access to outside information. The leaders were aware that the rapid growth of the "Asian Tigers" was due to their expanded external economic relations. The successes of the neighboring economies casted a long and dark shadow over China's underdeveloped economy. So long as Mao was alive, reform ideas could be secretly entertained but not voiced. After removing the extreme leftist ideologues from power, Deng began implementing the open door policy.

China's overall approach to reform adhered to gradualism. Therefore, "open door" did not suggest free trade. It meant stepwise decentralization of trade by state-owned enterprises (SOEs). The first phase of foreign trade reform began in early 1980. Prior to reform, the FYDPs dictated which authorized SOEs were to produce how much of which export goods and which SOEs receive how much of which plan-determined imports. All transactions with foreign trading entities were coursed through the state's Ministry of Foreign Trade (MFT). Political decisions prescribed enterprise-level activities. When reform began, the MFT still maintained its monopoly over imports and exports. However, the state no longer micromanaged enterprise-level activities of the authorized SOEs. In line with overall reform policy of decentralization and separation of ownership from management, SOEs were able to enjoy some latitude of autonomy.

China was sorely in need of modern technology and reproducer goods. Foreign trade had a direct bearing on China's ability to procure its needed imports. Contractual agreements were signed between the state and export-related SOEs, specifying production quotas. Aside from the contractual obligation of delivering the agreed upon export-destined commodities, the SOEs were at least in theory on their own. Factor procurement, investment decisions, and product distribution were henceforth the responsibilities of the SOEs. In theory, the trade-related SOEs were to be financially independent from the state budget. These enterprises were permitted to retain a share of the profit. Incurring losses, however, was a different issue. In light of needed imports, the state must also determine the necessary exports to finance these needed imports. Import and export prices, however, were determined by supply and demand on the international market. Incurring loss in some productive activities was unavoidable. State subsidy for such losses remained an item of the state budget.

In the early 1980s, the government needed all the foreign reserve it could garner. All foreign exchange earned was controlled by the central government. As foreign investors in China began exporting their products, China's foreign reserve began rising. Beginning in January 1984, the central government permitted the provinces where export-oriented SOEs concentrated to retain a share of the convertible currencies earned from exports. A year later, the state permitted the authorized export SOEs the freedom to use 50 percent of their retained foreign earnings.[3]

A more significant aspect of trade reform during the period was the institution of foreign trade agencies. The agencies became extension arms of the MFT. Instead of the MFT monopolizing all trade activities, these select agencies became the go-betweens for domestic and foreign trading partners. They represented authorized importers and exporters and determined respective prices. They also stipulated other desired trading terms with foreign exporters and importers. At least in theory, they are individually responsible for their own losses. The profits, after paying what was due to the state, henceforth belonged to the domestic exporters or importers. To the authorized agencies representing them, a service charge is paid. It is the responsibility of the agencies to represent the authorized domestic importers and exporters in signing trade agreements with foreign partners. The decentralized trade policy thereby granted domestic exporters and importers the rights of self-determination for the first time. With rights also came responsibilities. The new policy was significant in that there was a clear separation of rights and responsibilities between the state and domestic enterprises authorized to engage in trading activities. Beginning in 1988, the trade agencies became the universal vehicle for foreign trade by SOEs.

Institution of trade agencies and the overall decentralization policy combined empowered the establishments under the jurisdiction of regional governments to become the prime movers of foreign trade. The next phase of trade reform began in March of 1987.[4] This new phase of reform consisted of three focal elements. First, the government specified the objective or working toward overall financial independence. Budgetary coverage of losses incurred by enterprises engaged in trading activities was in the process of being discontinued. Secondly, the state began emphasizing the imperative of establishing the linkage between production and distribution. It was a notable departure from the past practice. In the past, the focus was on production not on marketing. It was the state alone that allocated outputs to designated recipients according to the plan. No market existed. The new direction was then to keep prospective demand in perspective prior to making investment and production decisions by the SOEs. Third, instead of micro managing trade activities, the central government relied on foreign exchange regulations and tax and tariffs for coordinating trade policy.

The government premised its overall trade policy on the initiatives of provincial and regional governments. The central government set targets for export and import growth. Export firms signed "responsibility system" agreements with local jurisdictions to which they respectively belonged. The central government then collated all export information from the local jurisdictions to ensure steady growth in China's exports. Central planning in production had by then to a large measure discontinued. However, the state still maintained its role in specific export activities by assigning production quotas to select SOEs. In addition, the government also provided overall direction to some other export activities. Market-coordinated export activities by other SOEs by then were already the leading exporters of goods produced by the state sector. Over time, the scopes of assigned export quotas and directed exports kept declining while that of market-based exports correspondingly kept growing.

Early Administrative Provisions

The 1998 Decree

Prior to reform, foreign trade was under the jurisdiction of the Ministry of Foreign Economic Relations and Trade (MOFERT). The name was later changed to Ministry of Foreign Trade and Economic Cooperation (MOFTEC). The ministry administering foreign economic relations was under the direction of the State Council. In line with decentralization policies, bureaus and administrative agencies corresponding to the ministry were established on provincial, regional, and municipal levels. Such administrative agencies issued import-export permits, supervised productive entities for compliance with legal provisions, and ensured that trade treaties with foreign countries were fulfilled.[5]

There was no official legislation regulating foreign trade prior to May 12, 1994. Until then, foreign trade was conducted by fiats issued by the State Council and implemented through the MOFERT. The primary vehicle for promoting foreign trade was through authorized trade agencies. On February 26, 1988 the State Council issued its initial decree on foreign trade in order to actualize more fully the rapidly growing economy's export capacity.[6] Effective immediately, the system of trading through authorized agencies became universal. It meant substantive decentralization of benefits from the central administration to provincial and regional authorities.

Prior to the decree, it was the central government's trade scheme that shaped the economy's total imports and exports. Planned imports and exports were then allocated to lower-level administrations for fulfillment of the master plan. It was then the responsibility of lower-level administrative units to accomplish the respectively assigned targets. Lower administrations in the decree also included state-owned enterprises authorized to engage in foreign trade.

Universalizing the trade agency system meant that instead of central allocation, lower-level administrations and authorized SOE exporter enterprises now submit their respective import and export plans to the appropriate authority. These plans would include expected foreign earnings, remittance of the same to the central administration, and subsidy requests. The decree pledged no change to this procedure for three years. With the abolishment of existing control over how retained foreign earnings could be utilized by lower level administrations, they could henceforth expend authorized portion of retained foreign earnings at their own discretion. The measures were designed to be a stimulus package to mine the potentials of lower level authorities for upgrading their export efforts.

Another indication of a gradualism approach to decentralizing foreign trade pertained to subsidies. The decree made it known that, beginning in 1988, subsidies to imports and exports of products in industrial, textile, and handicrafts would be discontinued. Implicit in the statement is that subsidies, when needed, would continue for other import and export activities.

The decree affirmed the merits of trade decentralization by way of institutionalizing the trade agency system. Decentralization helped resolve the anomaly of the state owning and directing enterprise-level operations at the same time. Profit motivation was absent on the part of the enterprises. With it, the sense of assuming responsibility for decision-making was lacking. By instituting the trade agency system, opportunity was given to all capable of profiting from trade activities, albeit through the conduit of the trade agencies.

However, as the decree pointed out, despite the reform measures, there were still incongruities and flaws inherent in the existing system. First of all, responsibility system was not thorough. The practice of export subsidies lingered. There were discriminatory trade policies being applied to different regional governments and state enterprises. This meant that both rates for foreign earnings and subsidies granted differed from one region to another. The result was unequal opportunities for trade development for diverse regions of the country. That in turn led to disproportionate growth in some regions while the others were being passed over with minimal progress. In addition, motivated by profits, enterprises converged on value-added industries that promised rapid returns on investment. Consequent upon this short-term gain strategy, China's exports were disproportionately of lower-level commodities. Yet, given China's measured approach to reform, the 1988 decree decided on a three-year period for the system to adjust before the next reform measure was to be implemented.

The 1991 Decree

On January 1, 1991, the State Council issued a decree entitled "Decisions Concerning Issues Involving Systemic Reform and Development of Foreign

Trade."[7] The communiqué first affirmed successes of China's foreign trade during the past years. Trade volume had been soaring, foreign reserve kept mounting, and the structure of imports and exports continued improving. It then acknowledged existing flaws and incongruities in trade practices. The communiqué aimed at actualizing more fully the potentials of the central and local governments as well as export-oriented enterprises with respect to foreign trade. At the same time, the provisions of the directive clearly indicated the state's pervasive role in foreign trade. Select highlights of the communiqué are briefly discussed below.

First, all regional and administrative entities must abide by the state's unified trade regulations and policy. Effective January 1, 1991, export subsidies would be discontinued.[8] Second, it restructures the retention rates of foreign earnings according to export categories. As an example, exporters of state-contracted crude and refined petroleum could retain 4 percent of earnings in convertible currency. Exports of the same beyond that, however, need to remit only 30 percent to the state while retaining 70 percent of the foreign earnings. In general, exporters of nonspecific commodities could retain 50 percent of foreign earnings whereas value-added exporters could retain up to 90 percent and remitting only 10 percent of export earnings to the state treasury.

The 8th FYDP (1991–1995) specified export growth targets for each of the five years. For each of the targets, provincial, regional and autonomous municipal administrations entered into agreements with the central government. Each of the agreements detailed categories of export goods, and the quantity and value and expected foreign earnings. The aggregated annual exports and their respective values and foreign earnings were to be in line with the central plan for each of the five years' growth. It would then be the responsibility of the lower-level administrations to ensure that the contracted commodities and their respective quantities and values would synchronize with the agreements.

The communiqué continues the existing policy of privileges to encourage export promotion. Current policy of export tax rebate and credit privileges for exports are to be maintained. In order to further develop and promote value added activities for exports, policies that have been effective to promote "One Subsidy-Three Inward Bound Sources" practice would continue.[9] It notes that it is the responsibility of MOFERT to administer the licensing of trade permits according to categories of commodities. Exports were grouped under three categories. The MOFERT must obtain the State Council's permission before adjusting the composition of export commodities belonging to category one. If needed, the MOFERT was authorized to adjust the composition of category two commodities which included 72 items. This category of exports included products such as live hogs, frozen beef, garlic, and the like. The third category of export commodities comprised of seventeen items over which MOFERT could exercise its discretionary power for needed adjustment.[10] The state's control over foreign trade during early phase of reform was both comprehensive and patent from this provision alone. Finally, the communiqué strengthens the central and local governments' administration, ensuring foreign exchange balance. All local and regional administrations must progressively improve the planning and coordination of imports and exports vis-à-vis their respective foreign exchange balances.

Measured Reform Progression

Social tension was high in the late 1980s. GDP growth in 1987 was 11.6 percent. The following year the growth rate decreased slightly to 11.3 percent. Student demonstrations led to the so-called Tiananmen Square incident in June 1988. The GDP growth rate for 1989 decreased to 4.1 percent and then declined further to 3.8 percent the following year.[11] After nearly a decade of reform, nonmarket elements in China's economy still persisted. Unless China's economy was to become more fully integrated into that of the world, the rapid growth rate experienced could come to an end. Toward the end of the 1980s, China began actively negotiating for membership in the World Trade Organization (WTO). The WTO was founded on the principle of free trade among nations. Free trade also presupposes minimal intervention by the government in micro entities' activities. During the years paralleling WTO membership negotiations, China gradually began removing obstacles to formal accession.

Beginning in 1991, nearly all subsidies and coverage of loss-incurring exports by SOEs came to an end. Furthermore, other than issuing permits for specific export commodities, there was to be a general relaxation of export licensing procedures. That is, unless for items otherwise stipulated, all SOEs would have the rights to produce and export marketable commodities via the trade agencies. By 1992, the state ceased assigning production quotas to those previously receiving such directives.

On the domestic front, another significant modification in trade policy was to unify the retention rates of foreign earnings by state-owned exporters. Prior to that, the retention rates varied from one geographic region to another. By unifying the rates, the state effectually gave the previously less-endowed regions greater incentives in export promotion for the SOEs located under their respective jurisdictions.

Foreign Trade Law of 1994

The law titled "Foreign Trade Law of the People's Republic of China" was adopted by the 17th Session of the Standing Committee of the Eighth

Congress on May 12, 1994. It came fifteen years after the reform began. The law stipulated that exchanges with external economies be on the bases of equality and mutual gains. Corollary to the stipulation is that China could retaliate if treated unfairly by a trading economy. Article 3 of the law affirmed the authority of the MOFERT in administering the entire nation's foreign trade activities. Legal entities engaged in foreign trade must first secure permits from MOFERT or its authorized representative offices. Enterprises with foreign capital, however, according to the law governing foreign investment are exempt from such permits. According to Article 8 of the trade law, firms with foreign capital may import the following without having an import-export permit: importation of articles by the firms both for productive or non productive uses, equipments, raw materials, and other factors of production. These firms may export their own products without a trading permit. Firms having no permits may entrust the authorized trading agencies to conduct trading activities on their behalf.

Article 16 of the law categorized articles whose imports or exports may be limited or restricted. Among those limited or restricted are those for national security and social well- being, resources that are either short in supply domestically, or are likely to face possible depletion, and articles that may oversaturate the market of a trading country's or region's capacity to absorb. Others include any type of agricultural, livestock, or fishery products that require limitations of imports, and any limitations of imports in order to maintain trade balance and financial stability.

Special provisions in Articles 24 and 25 of the law were also itemized for the limitation or prohibition of trade by foreign service industries in China. For national security reasons and for environmental protection, certain foreign service industries are restricted from entering China's market. Furthermore, if a service industry that the state has singled out either for establishment or accelerated growth domestically, then import restriction also applies. In addition, Article 29 of the law permits that if a surge in imports adversely and seriously affects domestic producers of the same, then restrictions of imports could materialize.

Protracted Accession Process to the WTO

The General Agreement on Tariffs and Trade (GATT) was formed in 1949. Member nations of GATT agreed on free trade of goods among themselves. The scope of GATT was augmented to include trading in service and intellectual properties. With new obligations placed upon members, it was transformed into the current WTO in 1955. The fundamental principle for both GATT and WTO is free trade among nations. China was a signatory to the GATT agreement while it was still under the Nationalist government.

When the communist regime was established later that year, it discontinued its relationship with the organization. With the thawing of political relationship between the United States and China under President Nixon starting in 1972, the PRC displaced Taiwan as the sole legitimate member in the UN. With the opening up of China's economy to external economies by the late 1970s, China secured its membership with the International Monetary Fund (IMF) and the World Bank. By the mid-1980s, it became evident that China's economic successes were to a large measure due to increased interactions with foreign economies. By then, there was also a concern over a possible future decline in the growth rate.[12] Since China's rapid growth was founded on foreign exports fueled by growing foreign investment, membership in the WTO was the logical step taken. It formally applied to the WTO for membership.

One challenging hurdle to gaining accession to WTO was that members having concerns over China's trade practices could negotiate separately with the Chinese government. Only when such respective negotiations resulted in terms of agreements would China's application for membership be forwarded to the General Assembly. According to WTO rules, any member country of the organization may challenge an applicant over its trade practices and policies. Thirty-seven countries, including the United States and the European Union (EU), expressed concerns over China's membership. In order for China to gain full membership, bilateral negotiations had to be conducted so that agreements could be secured or concessions granted. Most of the challenging nations questioned China's economic system because of its pervasive role in economic activities. That is, free trade is premised on a market-based system. China's economic system was progressing toward market coordination. It nevertheless was still not a free economy. In addition, individual challengers had their respective concerns more unique to their own situations. The most drawn out negotiation China had to endure was with the United States, which had multiple and serious concerns against it. In addition, the United States had numerous negotiation points with China. It was not until September 17, 2001 that China succeeded concluding agreements with all the challenging nations. After fifteen years, China's application to WTO membership was formally approved in November 2001.

A press release announcing the successful conclusion of agreements between WTO representatives and China stated:

> As a result of the negotiations, China has agreed to undertake a series of important commitments to open and liberalize its regime in order to better integrate into the world economy and to offer a more predictable environment for trade and foreign investments in according with WTO rules.[13]

There are a few salient reform measures that China agreed to adopt that should be highlighted. China agreed to the progressive elimination of trade barriers against foreign imports, the elimination the practice of dual pricing and special treatment of goods being marketed abroad, and the revision of relevant economic laws in compliance with WTO articles. It also agreed to granting import and export rights and privileges to all enterprises, eliminating restrictions on foreign enterprises in China after three years from the day of accession to WTO, and discontinue and cease initiating subsidies to agricultural exports. The exception was that the state could continue its exclusive rights in the trade of products such as cereals and select minerals.

On December 11, 2001, China was officially admitted as a member during the organization's meeting in Doha, Qatar. One of the conditions was that China had to admit that it was still a nonmarket-based economy. Consequent upon the admission was that there would be a transitional period for China to remove impediments to free trading. By the end of that period, China must abide by all of WTO's rules and regulations governing trade practices with member nations. Consequently, China had to make an umbrella concession that there would be a twelve-year transitional period.

> China agreed to allow WTO members to apply a special safeguard rule, the "transitional product-specific safeguard" (TPSS) that applies only to China and will remain in effect for the twelve year transitional period. The TPSS allows other WTO members to impose quotas and tariffs on Chinese goods upon a minimal showing of injury, and it restricts China's ability to retaliate.[14]

During this transitional period, if a trading partner perceives that China's exports to it would threaten or cause disruption to its domestic producers, then the country may take appropriate actions to restrict China's exports to it. As noted, this TPSS was never applied to other nations applying for WTO membership. The fact that China agreed to this discriminatory protective mechanism imposed upon it for twelve years evinces the intensity of its desire for membership in the WTO.

Concessions for WTO Membership

The one major contention that China insisted on throughout the negotiation process was that it was still a developing nation. Given that status, a developing nation applying for membership into the WTO could expect to receive more lenient considerations. China succeeded in being accorded the developing nation status, but it did not quite receive all the special privileges granted to members with that status.[15] In fact, no accession process had ever been as drawn out as the one experienced by China. China's low per capita income at the time did qualify it to be classified as a developing nation and the world economies did welcome China's progressive integration and participation in world affairs. Nevertheless, the developed economies, in particular the United States and the EU nations, entertained grave concerns over the prospect of China's rapid trade growth at their expense. As a member of the WTO, other member countries trading with China would have to permit China's exports at significantly lowered tariffs. China's ability to rapidly increase its low-cost exports to developed economies was likely to endure for some time to come. That promised to pose a considerable threat to domestic industries. For, once the transitional period is over at the end of 2013, grounds for protective measures by developed importing nations would to a large measure be no longer as effective. Negotiations with the developed economies, therefore, were protracted and strenuous. China had to make concessions, especially to the developed economies in the end. However, compromises by China at the negotiating table would be more than compensated for by prospective gains in the long term.

To illustrate the concessions that China had to make during the negotiations with challenging nations, the more significant concessions ceded to the United States are briefly highlighted below:[16]

- An overall reduction in tariffs from 22.1 to 17 percent, with the most significant reduction in industries such as computers and semiconductors from the existing 13.3 percent to zero percent by 2005.
- U.S. telecommunication concerns would be permitted to own up to 50 percent of China's communication enterprises.
- U.S. manufacturers would be permitted to enter, to market, and to service their products in China without the intermediation of the Chinese trade agencies.
- Foreign banks would be allowed to establish branch banks and to provide renminbi (RMB) services to individual clients in China.
- There would be an overall reduction of tariffs on agricultural imports from the existing 31.5 to 15 percent.
- U.S. investors would be able to compete for ownerships in enterprises with state assets and SOEs and China's SOEs must abide by WTO rules and regulations in their business practices.
- China would eliminate all export subsidies for agricultural products.
- Removal of restrictive barriers to foreign investment, including demands for domestic content and tech transfer.
- Within fifteen years of China's accession to the WTO, the United States would have the rights of adopting protective measures against China's surge in exports to the United States.

Given the concessions granted to the United States and to other nations during the negotiations, there would be ample challenges to China's domestic enterprises. Increased competitive forces from abroad will compel domestic producers to either perform or face elimination from the marketplace. Demands will be the greatest on the less efficient SOEs accustomed to subsidies from the central government. In the long run, however, membership in the WTO will yield substantive systemic and structural changes to China's economy. Given China's productive potentials and development policy, membership in the WTO will help integrate China's economy and society more fully into the world community. It is also the conditions and concessions attached to accession that would help lead to substantive reform measures. With the passage of time, vestiges of the command system of the past will progressively be erased from China's economy as well as society.

Foreign Trade Law of 2004

China's new Foreign Trade Law was promulgated in 2004, three and half years after accession into the WTO. It consisted of 70 articles in 11 chapters. The 2004 law basically amended the old 1994 Foreign Trade Law, which contained only 44 articles in 8 chapters. The 1994 law contained articles pertaining to general provisions, defining the term "foreign operators," trade in goods and technology, trade in services, orderliness in foreign trade, trade promotion, legal liabilities, and supplementary provisions. These eight themes remain in the 2004 version. The three new chapters in 2004 law dealt with the topics of trading in and protection of intellectual property, and investigation into irregularities in trade practices and trade promotion that includes covert subsidies.

Some articles in the 8 chapters of the 1994 law were deleted from the 2004 version of the law. Under the same eight themes of the two laws, there were also articles added to the 2004 law not present in the 1994 version. And some of the articles that were in the 1994 law continue to be in the 2004 version, but with some modifications.[17]

Observations over some aspects of the 2004 law are given a cursory review.[18] Article 2 under Chapter 1 titled "General Provisions" mentioned specifically the protection of trade-related intellectual property. Three articles in Chapter 5 of the law specifically dealt with intellectual property protection. Article 29 of the law states:

> Where the imported goods infringe intellectual property rights and impair foreign trade order, the authority responsible for foreign trade under the State Council may take such measures as prohibiting the import of the relevant goods from being produced or sold by the infringer within a certain period.

Incidents of producing pirated intellectual properties such as print materials, movies, and musical pieces for exports by illegal businesses in China were one of the concerns for many developed economies. Article 29 authorizes appropriate authority to interdict the production and marketing of unauthorized intellectual property "within a certain period." Since the words "certain period" are not defined, it raises the question of how strictly the intellectual property clause can or will be enforced.

Less transparent is the meaning behind Chapter 2, Article 11. The caption for Chapter 2 reads "Foreign Trade Business Operators." Article 11 states:

> The State may implement state trading on certain goods. The import and export of the goods subject to state trading shall be operated only by the authorized enterprises unless the state allows the import and export of certain quantities of the goods subject to state trading to be operated by the enterprises without authorization. The lists of the goods subject to state trading and the authorized enterprises shall be determined, adjusted and made public by the authority responsible for foreign trade under the State Council in conjunction with other relevant authorities under the State Council.

Perhaps Article 11 was intended to be purposefully indefinite. The words "may" and "on certain goods" in the first sentence of the article seem to provide ample latitude to the state for monopoly power over trading activities in chosen fields. And the words "lists of the goods subject to state trading and the authorized enterprises shall be determined, adjusted" imply that these authorized trading items may be modified when expedient.

According to the official translation of the law, Article 15 states that the responsible authority should approve application for "automatic import and export licensing (of) certain goods subject to free import and export and make public the list thereof." The original words in Chinese for the passage, however, used the words "a part of" the goods subject to free import and export. The law itself does indeed, but only in general terms, outline the kinds of goods or services that are either restricted or prohibited for imports or exports under Article 16. However, if trade is supposed to be free after the "transitional period," then no list of the nonrestricted or prohibited goods and services needs published. Furthermore, the words "a part of" in the article raises more questions than providing answers. If only "a part" of the goods are subject to free import and export, then the remainder "part" of the same goods are not subject to free import and export. Once again, intended or not, the language of the law is ambiguous.

Article 24 accords foreign trading partners the same standing as Chinese nationals. The article is noteworthy in that the provision was absent in

China's Foreign Trade Law of 1994. With the provision, some of the free trade barriers for foreign partners are removed.

One of the major contentious topics during the negotiation phase of China's accession to WTO concerned communication industry and Internet services. A concession made by China at the negotiating table was that foreign-owned communication enterprises would be permitted to own up to 50 percent of shares in China's telecommunication enterprises after 2003. It was a major concession on the part of China for the simple reason that communication had always been under strict supervision and tight control by the state. With up to 50 percent of ownership in telecommunication enterprises in China, representatives from such foreign investments would also be permitted to hold key positions in China's communication enterprises. In addition, foreign capital would also be permitted to invest in Internet industries, including enterprises whose Internet contents were at that time restricted or prohibited by the state.[19] However, Article 26 section 1 explicitly states that restrictions or prohibitions are needed "to safeguard the state security, public interests, or public morals." To what extent communication would be genuinely free and unrestricted, therefore, would be subject to wide interpretation of the law.

A new chapter titled "Foreign Trade Relief" was added to the amended 2004 law. Compliance with WTO statutes prohibits unjustifiable export subsidies. Articles of the chapter, therefore, provide a protective shield in case of need. This chapter of the law contains 11 articles, conferring ample coverage for the interest of domestic producers and exports. Select instances for protective measures by the government include the following:

Article 41 empowers the administration to take appropriate actions against imports that can cause substantial harm to domestic interests. Foreign dumping or threat of foreign dumping, therefore, calls for antidumping measures.

Articles 41 and 42 state that imports that impede the development of nascent domestic industries will be met by government measures.

Article 43 dictates that if imports directly or indirectly receive special subsidies from an exporting country or region, then appropriate steps will be taken by the Chinese authority.

Article 44 necessitates that if an unexpected surge in imports causes substantial injury to a domestic industry, financial assistance to the same would be in order.

Article 49 establishes a system by the appropriate authority for monitoring and disseminating information cautioning domestic concerns of possible deviant trend in trade activities.

Another new chapter added in the 2004 trade law was Chapter IX "Foreign Trade Promotion." The chapter consists of nine articles. Promotion of trade, especially for export industries, assumes varied approaches. One of the more noteworthy articles is Article 53, which states: "The state promotes foreign trade by applying such measures such as (providing) import and export credits, export-credit insurance and export tax refund." In developed economies, instruments such as import and export credits and credit insurance are the proper domain of the private sector. This provision in the law renders it evident the government's intent of preserving its central role in foreign trade, especially in export promotion.

The 2004 rendering of China's foreign trade law fulfilled two principal functions: complying with articles of agreement with the WTO and, in light of concessions made to the agreements, establishing parameters for protective measures. The "transitional period" comes to an end in 2013. Since gaining membership into the WTO, trade frictions between major developed economies and China have not been lacking. The jury is still out as to how China's future relationship with its major trading partners will be. China has tasted the success of its foreign investment and trade policies. It has accumulated valuable experiences in foreign economic relations. Anticipating the closing years of the "transitional period," it is actively in search of strategies for adapting to the rapidly changing process of globalization and international relationships. Three decades of reform has yielded a stark contrast between the rigidity of the command system of the past and the more flexible and adaptable process of market-based and market-driven global integration.

A Synoptic Overview of China's Foreign Trade Performance: 1978–2008

Japan's economic recovery after World War II was powered primarily by its rapid growth in the export sector. The lesson was not lost on China's leadership. When reform began, the greatest comparative advantage China possessed was its vast potential inherent in low labor costs. What China needed was to unleash the population's desire for freedom and personal gains. However, the regime recognized the potential peril of permitting unbridled freedom.[20] China's population had suffered from and endured nearly three decades of Mao's merciless rule. Abrupt release of social tension would lead to political chaos. Systemic transformation therefore, including trade reform, was to combine phased economic liberalization under tight political control. As a result, cautiously calibrated measures were applied to trade liberation.

Overview of China's foreign trade development may be appraised from three perspectives: (1) overall growth; (2) composition of imports and exports; and, (3) geographic distribution of trade relations.

Overall Growth

Table 5.1 presents a broad perspective of China's foreign trade growth since reform began in 1979. In 1978, the year prior to China officially began its open door policy, the total imports and exports were $ 20.6 billion, of which exports was $ 9.8 billion and imports $10.9 billion, with a negative balance of $1.1 billion. In 1980, a year after reform began, total trade increased by nearly 85 percent due to exports increasing by 86 percent while imports rose by 84 percent. For the decade 1980–1990, total value of imports and exports increased by 203 percent. The more pronounced increase was in the export sector where the growth for the decade was from $18.1 billion in 1980 to $62.1 billion in 1990, an increase of 243 percent. Imports also grew rapidly, from $20.0 billion in 1980 to $53.4 billion in 1990, a nearly 167 percent increase. The most significant import increase was in 1985. For that year alone, imports exceeded exports by nearly 55 percent, incurring a $14.9 billion trade deficit. It was also the year when China's negative balance was the highest ever. The surge in imports in 1985 was fueled by two factors: Deng's decision to open up fourteen additional coastal cities to direct foreign investment in addition to the five existing SEZs; and investors were convinced that China's reform policy in general and its open door policy in particular were irreversible. At the same time, foreign trade kept expanding rapidly with export increases surpassing that of imports in all the subsequent years, with the exception of 1993 when China's imports exceeded exports by $12.2 billion.

China's total trade volume in 1990 was $1.15 billion. Five years later, it increased to $28.1 billion, a 143.3 percent increase. Exports for the same duration increased 139.6 percent while imports increased 147.6 percent. The average annual growth rate was 28.6 percent. Two points merit mentioning. First, for the same five-year period, the amount of foreign investment realized and actually utilized experienced a 367.8 percent surge, from $10.3 billion in 1990 to $48.1 billion in 1995.[21] Second, despite the fact that trade surplus had increased by 91.1 percent during the five-year period, the rate of growth in imports still exceeded that of exports. That is, despite China's rapid export expansion, its imports during that period grew even more rapidly. It was the import of productivity-increasing factors that was powering China's rapid growth in exports.

For the next five years, total trade volume rose from $28.6 billion in 1995 to $47.4 billion in 2000, a 68.9 percent increase. Though the average annual growth rate was still an impressive 13.8 percent, it paled when compared with the previous five-year period. It was not by coincidence that the annual growth rate for utilized FDI for the same five-year period was slightly less than 4.7 percent. The year 2000 was also the year before China's application

Table 5.1 China's Foreign Trade 1978–2008 (Select Years) ($100 million)

Year	Total Imports and Exports	Total Exports	Total Imports	Balance	Exports		Imports	
					Primary Commodities	Manufactured Goods	Primary Commodities	Manufactured Goods
1978	206.4	97.5	108.9	−11.4	—	—	—	—
1980	381.4	181.2	200.2	−19.0	91.14	90.05	69.59	130.58
1985	696.0	273.5	422.5	−149.0	138.28	135.22	52.89	369.63
1990	1154.4	620.9	533.5	87.4	158.86	462.05	98.53	434.92
1991	1357.0	719.1	637.9	81.2	161.45	556.98	108.34	529.57
1992	1655.3	849.4	805.9	43.5	170.04	679.36	132.55	673.30
1993	1957.0	917.4	1039.6	−122.2	166.66	750.78	142.10	897.49
1994	2366.2	1210.1	1156.1	54.0	197.08	1012.98	164.86	991.28
1995	2808.6	1487.8	1320.8	167.0	214.85	1272.95	244.17	1076.67
1996	2898.8	1510.5	1388.3	122.2	219.25	1291.23	254.41	1133.92
1997	3251.6	1827.9	1423.7	404.2	239.53	1588.39	286.20	1137.50
1998	3239.5	1837.1	1402.4	434.7	204.89	1632.20	229.49	1172.88
1999	3606.3	1949.3	1657.0	292.3	199.41	1749.90	268.46	1388.53
2000	4742.9	2492.0	2250.9	241.1	254.60	2237.43	467.39	1783.55
2001	5096.5	2661.0	2435.5	225.5	263.38	2397.60	457.43	1978.10
2002	6207.7	3256.0	2951.7	304.3	285.40	2970.56	492.71	2458.99
2003	8509.9	4382.3	4127.6	254.7	348.12	4034.16	727.63	3399.96
2004	11545.5	5933.2	5612.3	320.9	405.49	5527.77	1172.67	4439.62
2005	14219.1	7619.5	6599.5	1020.0	490.37	7129.16	1477.14	5122.39
2006	17604.0	9689.4	7914.6	1774.8	529.19	9160.17	1871.29	6043.32
2007	21737.3	12177.8	9559.5	2618.3	615.09	11562.67	2430.85	7128.65
2008	25622.6	14306.9	11325.6	2981.3	779.57	13527.36	3623.95	7701.67
2009	22100.0	12000.0	10100.0	1900.0	—	—	—	—

Sources: www.chinaview.cn; http://www.gov.cn/english/2010-02/25/content_1541738.htm

for accession to the WTO was formally approved by the organization. The respective growth rates for both FDI and foreign trade would have been the envy of most nations. For China, however, the decrease in growth rates in both FDI and foreign trade was exhibiting the fatigue syndrome. Namely, the initial open door policy had reached the point of diminishing returns in terms of growth rates. Given the relative institutional constraints in 2000, opportunities for both foreign investments into China and China's own trade expansion began dwindling. China was in need of a revitalizing dose in order to revive the sustained rapid growth as during the past two decades. Accession to the WTO in 2001 was the timely injection from the judicious prescription.

The first decade of the twenty-first century witnessed a new cycle of rapid growth both in imports and exports as well as trade surplus. A year after accession into the WTO, China's total value of trade witnessed an unparalleled surge of 21.8 percent. Exports increased by 22.4 percent to $325.6 billion while that of imports rose by 21.2 percent to $295.2 billion. Only five years after accession to the WTO, the total trade volume swelled by 245.4 percent, from $509.7 billion in 2001 to $1.76 trillion in 2006. Growth in imports for that five-year period was 225.0 percent and exports 264.1 percent. The average annual growth rates for imports and exports for the period of 2001–2006 were 45.0 and 52.8 percent, respectively. Speedier growth in exports than that of imports for that five-year period resulted in historically unprecedented surge in positive trade balances. The trade surplus in 2001 was $22.6 billion. The trade surplus for 2006 alone was $177.5 billion. That the widening of China's open door policy yielded the desired consequence in trade expansion is self-evident.

China's total trade volume for 2008 was $2.56 billion. That is, its foreign trade rose by 45.6 percent between 2006 and 2008, averaging 22.8 percent a year for the two-year period. In 2009, however, China's foreign trade experienced a severe decline for the first time since reform began. Exports fell by 12.2 percent to $1.2 trillion and imports by 10.8 percent to $1.1 trillion. Two principal factors may have contributed to this episode. First, the world economy has been experiencing an acute downturn since 2008. Second, the "fatigue syndrome," or the principle of diminishing returns seems to have reappeared. An economy that aspires to sustained growth either in any of the sectors or for the economy as a whole, timely and appropriate adaptations must be made. Without such needed adaptations, the growth would taper off and eventually decline. For China, the primary commodities that have been driving its export growth have value-added or light industrial manufactured goods. Unless China reconfigures and upgrades the composition of its exports, then continual and sustained growth cannot be expected.

TRADE COMPOSITION

EXPORT

An overview of the composition of China's imports and exports may also be observed in Table 5.1. A close relationship exists between China's imports and exports. This is evidenced by the fact that a high percent of China's exports originates from value-added industries.

In 1980, a year after the inception of the open door policy, China's exports was comprised mainly of primary and manufactured goods with the former accounting for $9.1 billion and the latter $9.05 billion.[22] Five years later, primary good exports still accounted for 50.6 percent with the balance being derived from manufactured goods. Primary good exports rose by 51.7 percent during the five-year period 1980–1985. For manufactured goods, it was 50.2 percent. The first half of the 1980s was also the years when China's primary sector, together with the foreign sector, enjoyed most the benefits of reform while little reform was taking place in the rest of the economy. It helps explain the primary sector's ability to increase its exports during these five years alongside manufactured goods financed by foreign investment. However, the landscape was significantly changed by 1990. Reform measures were extended to the industrial sector by the mid-1980s while little progress was made by producers of primary goods in this regard. The average annual growth rate for primary exports between 1985 and 1990 was a modest 3.8 percent whereas for manufactured goods it was 48.3 percent. As alluded to earlier, it was in 1984 that fourteen coastal cities along China's waterfront were added to being open to direct foreign investment. Fast-paced growth in China's manufactured goods sector kept soaring past growth in primary goods exports. Between 1990 and 2008, the average annual growth rate for primary goods export was 21.7 percent. For manufactured goods exports, the annual growth rate for the corresponding period was 157.1 percent. Viewed from another perspective, exports of primary goods 1980 was $9.1 billion. By 2008, it rose to $78.0 billion. For manufactured goods, however, the increase was from $9.01 billion in 1980 to $1.35 trillion in 2008. It is thereby appropriate to deduce that China's export growth since 1980 has been fueled mainly by its growth in export-destined manufacturing sector. However, there was little component of technologically more advanced finished products.

IMPORTS

China's imports of manufactured goods have always surpassed that of primary goods, even during the years of great famines between 1959 and 1961. With China's reform in the farm sector beginning in 1979, food productivity kept rising, reducing the demand for imports of staple produce. Concurrently, as expected, there were rapid increases in demand for imports of manufactured goods.[23] Imports of primary commodities in 1980 were nearly $7.0 billion and that that of manufactured goods it was $13.1 billion. Import of primary goods between 1980 and 1995 was 250.8 percent, averaging 16.7 percent annually. The growth in manufactured goods import, on the other hand, was from $13.6 billion in 1980 to $107.7 billion in 1995, a nearly sevenfold increase.

By 2008 year-end, China's total imports of primary commodities were $362.4 billion. For that of manufactured goods, the imports were worth $770.2 billion. When compared with the corresponding data for 1980, imports of primary commodities rose by 36.7 times between 1980 and 2008. The increase for manufactured goods for that same period was 58 times. As China's economy keeps striding the greased wheels of growth, the most pronounced components of imports include machinery, electric equipments and accessories, minerals and, select chemicals. Alternately stated, the increase in the imports of advanced electronics and precision instruments has been scarce.

Examined from a different perspective, the category of imports as it relates to China's exports can help shed additional light on the development of the country's export structure. As presented in Table 5.2, the data presented by the National Statistical Bureau of China[24] are grouped the "Total Value of Imports and Exports by Customs Regime" under three categories: "Ordinary Trade," "Processing Trade," and "Others." China's total exports in 1981was $22 billion. Exports of "ordinary trade" for the year was $20.8 billion, accounting for more than 94.5 percent, with "processing trade" and "other" comprising of the balance. Imports for the same year was $21.9 billion, consisting of $20.4 billion in "ordinary trade" and only $1.5 billion from "processing trade" and "other" combined. That is, imports of "ordinary trade" in 1981 accounted for 91.5 percent. Imports of "processing trade" items for 1981 were $1.5 billion, a meager 6.8 percent.

A decade later, imports of "ordinary trade" commodities grew by 45.0 percent to $29.5 billion in 1991, an annual increase of 4.5 percent. Imports for "processing trade"–related commodities, on the other hand, climbed by 1,564.0 percent to $25.0 billion. The average annual growth rate for each of the ten years was 156.4 percent. Exports from "processing trade" in 1981 were $1.1 billion. Following the surge in imports of processing related commodities in 1991, exports of "processing trade" also skyrocketed. The total growth of China's exports of processed goods between 1981 and 1991 was 2,767.4 percent, averaging an annual growth rate of 276.7 percent. When compared with the swift growth of the processing industry, imports of "ordinary trade" commodities for the same duration increased from $20.4 billion in 1981 to $29.5 billion in 1991. It was a 45 percent increase for the entire decade. Exports of "ordinary trade" also rose, but by a paltry 83.3 percent for that ten-year period. When compared with the growth in the processing industry, it is evident that the fastest sector of export growth in China for the years between 1981 and 1991 was the processing industry.

With the progression of time and the rise in per capita income, imports of consumer goods also began gaining ground. As a result, imports of "ordinary trade" began rising swiftly beginning with the latter part of 1990. Imports of "ordinary trade" items grew from $29.5 billion in 1991 to $113.5 billion in 2001, a 284.8 percent increase in a ten-year duration. Exports of ordinary trade category goods for the decade also rose, but by 91.3 percent less to 193.5 percent. Imports of processing related commodities, on its part, rose from $25.0 billion in 1991 to $94.0 billion in 2001. The increase for the decade was 275.4 percent, which was slightly shy of that of "ordinary trade's" growth in imports. Yet, the growth rate for exports of processed goods between 1991 and 2001 was still an impressive 354.6 percent.

China was officially admitted as a member into the WTO in 2001. It was also the dawn of the period when exports of both "ordinary trade" and "processing trade" commodities witnessed unprecedented increases for the ensuing years. Imports of "processing trade" goods increased from $94.0 billion in 2001 to $378.4 billion in 2008, averaging 43.2 percent annually for that seven-year period.[25] Exports of processed goods for the same period, on the other hand, rose from $1.47 billion in 2001 to $6.8 billion in 2008, growing at an average of 65.4 percent a year for the duration.

As future growth of China's exports depends on its ability to improve the composition of exports, the need for productivity enhancing imports is imperative. The quandary is whether developed economies of the West can trust China sufficiently to permit the exports of their advanced technologies and equipment to it without compromising their own national security on the one hand and global competitiveness on the other. On the part of China itself, its future performance of the foreign trade sector also depends heavily on its ability to adapt to the world market's changing conditions and its ability to restructure export compositions for high-quality exports.

GEOGRAPHIC DISTRIBUTION OF CHINA'S TRADE RELATIONS

Geographically, China's primary trading partners have been the economies in Asia. Within the Asian market, Japan ranks first and Hong Kong second. Hong Kong was reverted to the Chinese jurisdiction in 1997 but maintains its status as an autonomous economy divorced from China's central government. The other more significant markets for China in the region are South Korea, Taiwan, and Singapore. Developed economies in Europe make up

Table 5.2 Major Trading Partners, 2005–2008 ($ billion)

Region/Country	2005			2006			2007			2008		
	Total	Exports	Imports	Total	Exports	Imports	Total	Exports	Imports	Total	Exports	Imports
Total	1,421.9	762.0	660.0	1,760.4	968.9	791.5	2,173.7	1,217.8	956.0	2,563.3	1,430.7	1,132.6
Asia	807.9	366.4	441.5	981.1	455.7	525.4	1,187.8	567.9	620.2	1,366.7	664.0	702.6
Hong Kong, China	136.7	124.5	12.9	166.1	155.3	10.8	197.2	184.4	12.8	203.6	190.7	12.9
Japan	184.4	84.0	100.4	207.3	91.6	115.7	235.9	102.0	134.0	266.7	116.1	150.6
Africa	39.7	18.7	21.1	55.5	26.7	28.8	73.7	37.3	36.4	107.2	51.2	56.0
Angola	7.0	0.4	6.6	11.8	0.9	10.9	14.1	1.2	12.9	25.3	2.9	22.4
South Africa	7.3	3.8	3.4	9.9	5.8	4.1	14.0	7.4	6.6	17.9	8.6	9.2
Europe	262.1	165.6	94.4	330.2	215.4	114.9	427.5	287.8	140.0	511.5	343.4	168.1
Germany	63.3	32.5	30.7	78.2	40.3	37.9	94.1	48.7	45.4	115.0	59.2	55.8
Netherlands	28.8	25.9	2.9	34.5	30.9	3.7	46.3	41.4	4.9	51.2	45.9	5.3
Latin America	50.5	23.7	26.8	70.2	36.2	34.2	102.7	51.5	51.1	143.4	71.8	11.6
Brazil	14.8	4.8	10.0	20.3	7.4	12.9	29.7	11.4	18.2	48.7	18.8	29.9
Mexico	7.8	5.5	2.2	11.4	8.8	2.6	15.0	11.7	3.3	17.6	13.9	3.7
North America	230.8	174.4	56.2	286.0	219.1	66.9	332.5	252.1	80.4	368.4	274.3	94.1
Canada	19.1	11.7	7.5	23.2	15.5	7.7	30.3	19.4	11.0	34.5	21.8	12.7
United States	211.5	162.9	48.6	262.7	203.4	59.2	302.0	232.7	69.4	333.7	252.4	81.4
Oceania and Pacific Islands	30.9	12.9	18.0	37.3	16.0	21.3	49.5	21.1	28.4	66.1	25.9	40.2
Australia	27.2	11.1	16.2	32.9	13.6	19.3	43.8	18.0	25.8	59.7	22.2	37.4
New Zealand	2.7	1.4	1.3	2.9	1.6	1.3	3.7	2.2	1.5	4.4	2.5	1.9
Others	0.02	0	0.02	0.04	0	0.04	0.06	0	0.06	0.06	0	0.06

Numbers may not add up due to rounding off.

the second largest trading bloc with China. Among economies in Western Europe, Germany and the Netherlands lead the way in trade volume with China. UK and French markets are the next largest trading partners with China in the European theater. For the North American continent, the United States leads the way as the most significant export market in North America for China, with Canada following in a distant second.

North America is followed by the continents of Latin America and Africa. The growth rates of imports from and exports to economies in Latin America and Africa have been accelerating at a phenomenal pace. As of 2008 year-end, however, the trade volume of the two continents combined still valued at nearly 50 percent less than that of the sum of the United States and Canadian markets.

The largest economies in the Oceanic and Pacific Islands are Australia and New Zealand. This is the continent whose economies' trade value with China is growing like those in other continents, but the total value of trade trails after that of China's trade with African nations.

The distribution of China's trade relations with economies of the six continents is presented in Table 5.2. Six separate brief analyses are briefly presented describing China's trade with each of the six continents and the two leading trading partners within each of the continents during the recent years.

Asia, Japan, and Hong Kong

China's total trade value in 2005 was $1.42 trillion. Asian economies' trade with China accounted for 56.8 percent, totaling $807.9 billion. China's open door policy began with the Asian economies. Asia also is the most populous continent in the world. In addition, it is the Asian markets that China's value-added products are more marketable than in developed economies. By 2008, China's total trade with Asian economies alone rose to $1.37 trillion, averaging 32 percent annually for the three-year duration. Ironically, the share of Asian economies' trade with China declined from 56.8 percent in 2005 to 53.3 percent in 2008. Despite Asian economies' declining percent of trade with China between 2005 and 2008, its total trade volume in three years grew to nearly that of China's total trade volume with all economies of the world only three years earlier. Unlike trading with most of the major import/export partners in the world, China's trade balance with the Asian economies as a whole was negative for the four years under consideration. No detailed categories of China's imports from the Asian economies have been available. One possible reason for China's negative balance against the Asian economies during these years is that much of the imports are factors used for value-added activities

China's largest trading partner in Asia is Japan. China's exports to Japan in 2005 were $84.0 billion while that of imports were $100.4 billion. By 2008, its exports to Japan grew by 44.6 percent and imports by 15.6 percent. Japan has poor resources and its exports are comprised mostly of quality or technologically more advanced products, which might explain the negative balance China carries with Japan. China's second largest trading partner in Asia is Hong Kong. For the period 2005 through 2008, China's exports to Hong Kong far exceeded that of imports. In 2008, China's exports to Hong Kong were $190.7 billion and imports only $12.9 billion. The reason for the imbalance may be that Hong Kong is a port city and has an ample supply of relatively cheap labor. Additionally, Hong Kong no longer has commodities that China cannot itself produce or need.

Europe, Germany, and the Netherlands

China's trade with European markets was $262.1 billion. Three years later, it nearly doubled to $511.5 billion, averaging 31.7 percent annually for the three-year duration. In 2005, China's exports to Europe were $165.6 billion whereas its imports were only $94.4 billion. European economies' trade balance with China for the year, therefore, was a negative $71.2 billion. By 2008, with China's exports to Europe being $343.4 billion and imports $168.1 billion, the negative balance for that year alone more than doubled to $175.3 billion. Within the European theater, China's largest trading partner has been Germany. There is relative trade balance between China and Germany for the four recent years under consideration. Germany's imports from China for 2005 were $32.5 billion and its exports to China were $30.7 billion. The scene continues into 2008 when its imports were $59.2 billion and exports $55.8 billion. The scenario is significantly different for the Netherlands' trade balance with China. China's second largest export market is in the Netherlands. In 2005, China's exports to the Netherlands were $25.9 billion while importing only $2.9 billion worth of goods and services. The result is Netherlands' negative trade balance with China was $23.0 billion. It surged to $40.6 billion by 2008. Without detailed trade statistics available between China and Germany and between China and the Netherlands, no attempt is made to explain the causes of relative trade balance and imbalance situation depicted above.

The North American Markets

The North American economies trail after the Asian and European markets in their trade with China. However, North American trade activities with

China are carried out almost exclusively with the United States.[26] China's imports from the United States in 2005 were $48.6 billion. The same year, China exported $162.9 billion worth of commodities to the United States, resulting in a $113.3 billion trade deficit for the latter. Three years later, The U.S. imports from China climbed to $252.4 billion. Its exports to China for that year, on the other hand, were $81.4 billion, netting a negative trade balance of $171.0 billion in a single year. For three consecutive years between 2006 through 2008, inclusive, the negative trade balance incurred by the United States exceeded that of the EU's combined trade deficit against China every single year. The consequence on the value of the U.S. dollar, therefore, is unmistakable.

The other major economy trading with China on the North American continent is Canada. Imports into Canada from China were $11.7 billion in 2005. Canada's exports to China that year were $7.5 billion, netting a negative trade balance of $4.2 billion. By 2008, Canada's imports from China were $21.8 billion while its exports to China were $12.7 billion. Canada's imports from China grew by 86.3 percent in three years. Its exports to China also rose, but slightly less by 69.3 percent. Canada's negative trade balance against China, however, increased by 116.7 percent within that three-year period. The predicament facing the developed economies of the West in its trade relationship with China is the continual and mounting trade imbalances. It has also as a result become a major source of trade disputes against China by the West. It is a quandary that promises no solution in the foreseeable future. It is a concern that both sides must adequately address for improved future trade relations.

LATIN AMERICAN ECONOMIES

Latin American economies make up the fourth largest trading bloc for China. The two largest export markets for China in Latin America are Brazil and Mexico. In 2005, China's exports to Latin America were $23.7 billion and imports $26.8 billion. Three years later, both China's exports to and imports from Latin America more than doubled. Latin American economies imported $71.8 billion worth of goods and services from China in 2008 while exporting $71.6 billion to China. The Latin American countries are rich in natural resources while at the same time their markets more receptive to value-added commodities from China. Brazil's imports from China were $4.8 billion in 2005. It soared by 291.7 percent in the three-year period between 2005 and 2008. For all of the four years under consideration, China's imports from Brazil exceeded that of exports to it by far. Its negative trade balance with Brazil was $5.5 billion out of the total trade value of $14.8 billion. By 2008, the negative balance slightly more than doubled to

$11.1 billion. China's trade with Mexico ranked the second on that continent. Unlike China's trade with Brazil, Mexico consistently incurs a negative trade balance with China between 2005 and 2008. China's imports from Mexico were $2.2 billion in 2005 while exports were $5.5 billion, scoring a trade surplus of $3.3 billion. Three years later, Mexico's negative trade balance rose to $10.2 billion. Though minuscule when compared with that of the U.S. negative trade balance with China, it is sufficiently considerable for a relatively small economy like Mexico. The concern is how long the trend might persist for a comparatively weak economy like Mexico.

Oceania and the Pacific Islands

China's principal trading partner in this region is Australia, followed by New Zealand in a distant second. China's exports to Australia in 2005 were $11.1 billion, with imports for the year being $16.2 billion. That same year, New Zealand imported $1.4 billion from and exported $1.3 billion of goods and services to China. While China imported more from Australia than its exports to it in 2005, there was minimal trade imbalance between China and New Zealand. By 2008, China's imports from Australia grew by 130.9 percent while its exports to it exactly doubled. Australia is geographically large and is well endowed with minerals and natural resources, which China sorely needs. On the other hand, it is not a densely populated country that is as much in need of value-added exports from China. It might be the possible explanation for Australia's positive trade balances against China for all of the four years under consideration. For New Zealand, its exports to China grew by 46.2 percent and imports by 100 percent between 2005 and 2008. The rates of growth are significant but the amount in terms of China's total trade volume is low. What is of significance is that China is trading with any and every country in the world that has what China needs and can absorb Chinese exports at the same time. It presents a stark contrast between China's dynamic productivity with a liberalized system and the lack of accomplishments during the Mao decades.

Trading with Africa

With the exception of Oceania and the Pacific Islands, the combined African economies carry on less trade with China than all the other continents. However, at least for China, Africa is the up and coming continent. With a population of 680 million and the economies relatively less than developed, the potential for China's exports to Africa is promising for decades to come. For the more immediate future, the potential of African exports to China, especially minerals and raw materials, is crucial for China's sustained growth.

In 2005, the total value of trade between China and Africa was $39.7 billion. China exported $18.7 billion worth of goods and services to Africa and imported $21.1 billion from that continent. In 2008, China's exports to Africa were $51.2 billion, a 173.8 percent increase. The average annual growth for the four-year duration was 57.9 percent. More important, China's imports from Africa in 2008 climbed to $56.0 billion, averaging 55.1 percent annually between 2005 and 2008. China's exports to Africa will continue to grow. Nevertheless, the growth rate of the continent's purchasing power will be relatively slow. Therefore, the growth rate of China's exports to Africa is unlikely to climb rapidly on a sustained base in the foreseeable future. For China, however, its need for primary productive factors which Africa is well endowed will not only surge but could swell in a nearly geometrical fashion. Cultivating goodwill and providing assistance to Africa has increasingly become more important in China's policy decisions. The formation of the Forum on China-Africa Cooperation (FOCAC) in 2000, Premier Wen Jiabao's visit to Uganda, Tanzania, Egypt, Ghana, the Republic of Congo, Angola, and South Africa in June 2006 and his visit to Egypt in November 2009 tellingly reveal China's interest in the African continent.

TRADE FRICTIONS

Since the inception of reform, focus of the central administration was upon enlivening domestic productivity by opening up China for increased external relationships. Foreign capital inflow was then to serve as a main catalyst for enlivening foreign trade. Value-added industries in SEZs, open cities, and open coastal regions spearheaded China's surge in exports. China's import needs correspondingly rose. Among China's desired imports are advanced high-tech exports from developed economies. However, led by the United States, severe restrictions have been in place for such exports to China. Such desired imports would have been high-end items that could help achieve a more balanced current account. Foreign earnings from exports keep mounting. Imports do not rise as quickly, amplifying China's foreign reserves. That in turn translates into trade disputes and frictions. There have been more trade disputes involving China than any other major trading economies.

One of the main disputes is over the exchange rate. As part of China's trade strategies, the exchange rate between the Chinese renminbi and major convertible currencies were purposefully kept low by the government. Foreign purchasers of Chinese exports reap the additional consumer surplus. China's exports kept rising, resulting in swelling negative trade balances incurred by the importing economies.

Another dispute concerns the products being exported. Most of China's exports to developed economies are also ready substitutes for products produced by importing economies. Low cost and competitive prices mean extensive plant closings in developed economies. Unemployment in developed economies rises as a result.

Worldwide economic downturn translates into rising unemployment in most of the developed economies. Compounded by China's rapid exports to them, further increases in domestic unemployment help breed resentment against China's trade practices.

Brewing resentment translates into disputes. Frequencies of fault-finding against China keep rising. The public's negative impression against China's trade policies correspondingly increases with time. There have been more product recalls for exports from China than from any other economy. It has become a cause labeling Chinese products as unsafe.

Another area of dispute is the process of products standardization. In China, product standardization has been less rigorous than in developed economies. Environmental regulations have also been less stringent in China than in richer importing countries. In addition, cheaper factors and lower labor cost all help contribute to reduced costs and more competitive export prices. Producers of similar products in more developed economies can no longer compete as effectively against Chinese exports.[27] Incidents of trade disputes between importing nations and China keep climbing. Frictions have also become both more public and more voluble. In late 2009, the United States was contemplating raising the tariffs on China's tire exports. Days later, China announced its intention to investigate into unfair trade practice by U.S. automobile and poultry products.[28]

Conflicts between EU and China over the latter trade practices have also been on the rise. The issue at hand is "perceived abuse of trade defense instruments."[29] EU demands freer access to the Chinese market and Chinese prefer market economy status instead of being labeled as a nonmarket-based system. The EU and the United States have requested the WTO for dispute investigation and settlement against China. The dispute is the former's charge that China restricts the exports of key raw materials either not as readily available outside of China or are significantly less costly in China. Industries in China therefore have access to cheaper materials than their competitors outside China. That is not a level playing field, and the EU and United States have filed grievances against China at the WTO.[30] In 2009, a total of 118 grievances were filed against China at the WTO. The United States led the way with 23 cases, affecting $7.6 billion worth of Chinese exports.[31]

A Concluding Note

China's gradualism approach to reform opened up its economy to global interactions, not suddenly as wide open as transitional economies in Eastern

Europe but judiciously and cautiously. The government's role was pervasive. Every step widening the scope of either foreign investment or foreign trade was circumspectly measured. Its foreign investment and foreign trade policies have been instrumental in propelling China to the forefront of the world's economic arena. Successes in the theater of international economic relations have correspondingly helped expedite structural reforms within. China's success in its foreign trade policy has been unprecedented in the annals of world's economic history. Given a population of more than 1.3 billion and a host of highly motivated entrepreneurs, the potential for continual expansion of its foreign trade is nearly immeasurable. Successes aside, however, the central administration is concomitantly aware of the limitations to sustained growth and the need for flexible new policy measures. Paralleling successes, challenges similarly abound. And government has exhibited no intention of discontinuing its presence in mapping out the future of China's economy.

In brief, China's foreign economic relations have transited from a system that was command to directed, and from centralized to coordinated. The government's relationship with microeconomic entities is not laissez-faire. Politics is still in command, though less authoritarian than the Mao era. To the extent microentities abide by the parameters defined by the state, they are free. Government presence in economic affairs varies from being controlling to being directive or merely tangible. With foreign trade, the major domain where the state's presence is still pervasive includes foreign exchange, tax rebate, subsidies, and export and import credits.

This year concludes the policies outlined in China's 11th FYDP (2005–2010). China's growth path has been on the drawing board for the 12th FYDP that is expected to be presented to and accepted by the central administration during the second half of 2010. Whichever direction China charts for its policies relating to foreign economic relations will decidedly impact the future of China and the rest of the world's economies.

CHAPTER 6

A COMPARATIVE PERFORMANCE STUDY

THIS COMPARATIVE PERFORMANCE ANALYSIS WAS PERFORMED on a macrolevel based on the determinants of economic growth in China and other transitional countries. China's reform approach is compared on an economical and political basis with that of Poland, Ukraine, and Romania. The primary thesis is that during the reform approach of each country, the contraction of political freedom and/or civil liberties in each transitional economy equates to an increase of economic growth and vice versa. Thus, a negative correlation exists between the two determinants: political freedom/civil liberties and economic growth. This negative relationship is most prominent during the initial stages of reform. This analysis focuses on the affect of an economy to attract foreign investment in terms of capital inflow based on that of political freedom and civil liberties. Capital inflow, as measured by foreign investment and foreign trade, thus in return, affect economic growth.

The political and economic corridor to reform in the last few decades is rather distinct for China compared to the other former communist nations in this study. During the early stages of systemic transformation, there is a significant relationship between China's tight political controls with the liberalization of its economy. The other transitional countries were chosen for comparison because their assent to economic and democratic reform is inimitable. During systematic transformation, China reformed its economy but not its political system. Since 1980, China has and still is a communist country with little to no political freedom. Poland, to some extent, reformed both at once. It increased its economic freedom, while increasing its political freedom. Romania launched its political reform in terms of establishing its independent form of communism, long before instituting economic reform. Ukraine continues to lag at both. Both its economy and political sphere remains with little to no freedom. Given these variations, several political and economic factors will be analyzed. The methodology is to identify the impact of the similarities and irregularities in these countries based on their economic growth. A brief overview of post–World War II history of each country and reforms are introduced for background information.

Post–World War II China

On October 1, 1949, The People's Republic of China was established. The National People's Congress adopted a Constitution in September 1954, proclaiming the sole leadership and supremacy of the Chinese Communist Party (CCP). The power within the CCP was vested in the Central Committee, however, from 1949 to 1976, true power rested with the CCP's leader Mao Zedong.

Mao Zedong and the CCP developed a four-pronged approach to China's post–civil war recovery and reconstruction. The four-pronged approach consisted of: (1) socializing unprotected assets, (2) implementing the Agrarian Reform Law of 1950, (3) establishing the central government authority over economic administration, and (4) revitalizing the productive forces of a nearly bankrupt economy. The plan to abolish private ownership was announced in 1953 and dubbed the "social transformation." Four areas were to be socialized: agriculture, peasant handicraft industry, small commercial entities, and larger privately owned industrial enterprises. The CCP's plan for socializing the means of farm production relied on increased production and savings from the farming sector. The most efficient way to increase production in the agricultural sector was through collective farming. Revenues from increased production then were reallocated to the financing of rapid expansion of the industrial sector. By 1953, 96.3 percent of farms were successively collectivized. The CCP's five-year plan consisted mainly of state control over all aspects of agricultural and industrial production. From large commercial industries to small rural handicrafts, the CCP began to increase control over all enterprises leaving them with no option but to surrender to the state.

Social transformation through the four areas of production was completed ten years before the expected end date. Mao used this ammo and sought to complete full socialization of China. This began Mao's "great leap forward," which consisted of increased production of grain by 79.5 percent, doubling the production of steel, and transforming cooperative into collective farms. This movement's estimated completion was approximately one year.

Mao's policies cast a spell till 1978 even though he passed away in 1976, and his protege who took over as his successor continued his approach. Then Deng Xiaoping took over. This also marked change in the Party's policy and China's economic policy through reform measures, pursing modernization, and advocating regulated decontrol, while maintaining applicable macro-coordination. Deng's goal was to decentralize all aspects of China's economy while keeping China's communist political structure. Political control over economic reform was of prurient interest to Party leaders. Economic reform was not intended to compromise the CCP's authority. The Party therefore rested on four fundamental principles: (1) reform should not deviate from the nation's objective of constructing a socialist state, (2) reform must follow the working principle of governance by decisions arrived at through the process of people's democratic dictatorship, (3) the Communist Party must carry out the reform process, and (4) Marxist-Leninist doctrines and the thoughts of Chairman Mao would be upheld throughout reform. The CCP initiated economic reform on five fronts: agriculture, price reform, foreign investments, foreign trade, and enterprise.

Agriculture reform consisted of three major areas: decentralization, commodity circulation, and reducing state controls. Zhao Ziyang, secretary general of the CCP until 1989, first experimented with agricultural reform. At the time, Zhao was the Party's first secretary general of Sichuan Province. His reform measures in Sichuan Province consisted of production contract arrangements. This practice allowed for commune members to enter into contractual agreements with the commune to which they belonged. Individual farm households could take lease of part of the commune land, thus allowing the farm household to operate independently. The contract specified the amount of grain the independent farm household must deliver to the commune administration. After fulfilling the contract by delivering the quantity specified in the agreement to the commune, the farm household could sell the excess produced products on the open market or sell to the state at free market prices. This contract production delivery system was quickly implemented as a national policy.

Deng's address in 1978 to Party leaders signified China's need for change in their legal foundation. Deng's prurient interests of these necessary laws consisted of enterprise laws, people's commune laws, and foreign investment laws. Issued by the executive, the new laws, decrees, directives, and regulations indicated China's aspiration for economic reform. These new laws and decrees encompassed aspects of authorization or governing procedures for systematic decentralization, as well as defining the legal status of private industrial or commercial enterprises.

New policy measures were the legal foundation for price reform in China. Vital to the price reform process was the decentralization of administrative, managerial, and responsibility systems. The central administration delegated well-defined price adjustments for less essential goods and services to be under the authority of provincial, regional, and local administrators. However, the central administration maintained tight control over the direction, pace, and scope of price adjustments for services that could be affected at the macrolevel. The pricing commodities and service chargers were scheduled into three tiers. The central government had control over tier one, consisting of the most important goods and services and controlling the pace and sequence of price adjustment. Price determination was under the management of the state's Department of Prices and State Council's parallel offices located in tier two. Tier two was also controlled by the central government as well. There were three pricing possibilities that existed within the second tier: (1) variable prices, (2) restricted market prices for select productive resources, and (3) negotiated buying and selling prices. Tier three therefore, was controlled by delegated state authorities, determining the pace and size of price adjustment. For any commodity outside tiers one and two, prices are set by producers. However, producers can only determine prices within the predetermined range set by the state authorities.

MODERN DAY CHINA

Hu Jintao assumed the position of General Secretary of the Communist Party of China in 2002 and a year later became President of the People's Republic of China. Chinese leaders have stated "searching aggressively for a new set of principles and policies" to ensure its survival amid an increasingly market-oriented pluralist society and a mounting identity crisis.[1] The 16th Party Congress meeting in November 2002 implied seeking intraparty democracy while maintaining a one-party system. The major measures considered were to expand power sharing among the party elite and establish divisions within the party. Expanding power sharing among the elites in implemented policy measures left important decisions to full membership of the Party committees, instead of only the standing committee.[2] Some ideas on establishing divisions of powers within the party were proposed, but still it remained unclear whether they will be implemented.

China's 17th National Party Congress sought administrative reform and restructuring as a result of the heated debate among party members on the diminishing public sector and growing private sector–led economy. The new reform shifted from abolishing command economy ministries and agencies to fine-tuning policy-making and supervisory roles of the national government. China's economic policy has resulted in a quasipublic and quasiprivate market economy. China's emerging market economy has taken the role of the government in a new direction.

POST–WORLD WAR II POLAND

Under Soviet influence, the Polish Worker's Party (PPR) headed by Wladyslaw Gomulka was introduced as the formal government in Poland in the late 1930s. Following the Soviet model, Poland constructed its government into three separate branches: legislative (or *Sejm*), executive, and judicial. All the three branches would eventually be controlled by the Communist Party. The Council of State formed the executive branch, which was viewed as a collective presidency. However, the Council of State had authority over the ministers on issues of law and other certain policies. The judicial branch was under the persuasion of the government as well, mainly deciding high-profile cases.

With the formation of a coalition government, the PPR established itself in key positions in the army and police force. Once successively securing its presence, the PPR began to force opposition parties out. Gomulka wanted to establish a communist agenda in line with Poland's civilization. Eventually, Gomulka was removed from power by the Soviet Union and Boleslaw Bierut succeeded him. Bierut later combined the Polish Socialist Party (PPS) with the Polish Workers Party (PPR) to form the communist Polish United Workers Party (PZPR).

Communist Poland, in theory, was structured with three separate branches, but the functioning of the government was under the sole control of the Communist Party. The dominant part in the coalition, the National Unity Front, mostly was made up of members of the Communist Party. Members of smaller partiers included the United Peasant Party and the Democratic Party.

Central planning for the economy was under the direction of the Planning Committee in the Council of Ministers. The Planning Committee functions were to map out sources of revenues and expenditures, set production quotas to state enterprises and communes, apportion the factors of production, and decide the budget and funding for each ministry. In addition, the Planning Committee set wage payments as credits to the state budgetary instead of being based on worker productivity.

Poland's central planning modeled closely that of the USSR. In 1950, six-year development plans were initiated calling for rapid expansion in the heavy industry sector. The unpopularity of the communist government led to public outrage. After the death of Joseph Stalin, Stalinism was publicly criticized and Poles began criticizing and losing confidence in their own government. In response, Gomulka was the only one who could restore the public's confidence. Gomulka took charge under his own conditions: any reforms and policies pertaining to Poland must be free from external obstruction.

Gomulka officially returned to office in 1956. This marked a prospect for Poland to initiate new reform measures. This would ultimately put Poland in a position for economic freedom and development. However, the anticipated economic reform and straying from Soviet communism never happened. Some reform measures, such as decollectivizing farms and expansion of political freedom did occur, but not to the extent economic reform was pertinent to Poland's interests. Gomulka's promises for reform proved false; although some reform policy was initiated, it was half-heartedly put into action. Instead of promises of political and economic freedom, Gomulka actually did the opposite. The Communist Party took over all aspects of life in Poland and also its economy. Industry was taken over by mandating the private enterprises to register with the state. Registration required a high percentage of gross income to be allocated to the state. Unlike other communist countries, Poland allowed for small enterprises with less than fifty workers to remain private. Agriculture was taken over by the state through land redistribution and collectivized farming, and providing incentives for those who joined state collective farms and economic drawbacks for those who did not. However, the majority of Polish farmers were able to remain separate from the state's collectivized farms. Services such as health care, education, financial institutions, communication, and transportation came under government control.

Fixed prices and artificially low food prices led to an economic crisis. By the late 1960s, agriculture became stagnant, which made it necessary to import more high-priced food. By December 1970, the economic crisis was undeniable and the Communist Party introduced massive increases in the prices of food and basic goods. Demonstrations against the price rise led to the removal of Gomulka from power. Edward Gierek assumed the role of head of the party.

Gierek offered "customer satisfaction." He created new economic programs that resulted in large-scale borrowing from the West to import foreign goods and technology. He also implemented a wage increase, which in return led to inflation. With such a high demand for consumer goods, his system proved inefficient. As a result, foreign debt accumulated. Massive strikes and protests left the Communist Party to compromise with the public and allow the right of the Polish people to associate in free trade unions, abolish party supervision of industrial enterprises, and increase minimum wage. The association of free trade unions allowed for the formation and rise of an independent trade union opposing the Communist Party called "Solidarity." Growing membership in Solidarity led to the government ban on the party movement in 1982. The communist government in Poland slowly started to lose their grip on the Polish government as public opposition grew from the downward economy. Solidarity was legalized in 1989 and participated in semifree elections. The results of the 1989 election eventually led to the end of the communist government in Poland. After the formation of the new government, many small parties began to appear.

After the fall of Communism, Poland introduced economic reform and ushered in a liberal democratic government. In order to move from the command model of the planned economy, Poland initiated a shock therapy program in the early 1990s allowing for the economy to transform into a market economy. The shock therapy plan sought to increase market competition and force state enterprises to adjust and behave more like private firms. Poland has seen an increase in privatization of small and medium-sized state-owned enterprises, and an increase in private companies due to new laws and reforms. Reform measures consisted of introducing an open market while keeping the status quo of Poland's political structure.

Modern Day Poland

Poland's legislative government is made up two chambers of parliament: the *Sejm* and the Senate. Members of parliament are popularly elected. The president is also popularly elected and acts as head of the state. The prime minister is responsible for appointing members to the council of ministers, and administering the government. The *Sejm* has a dominant role in the legislative process and only the *Sejm* has the right to control the council of ministers.

Article 11 of Poland's 1997 Constitution allows the creation of a quasi-institutionalized party system. Financing of political parties were to be made open to the public as well. Major political parties have been established in the Polish party system including the Solidarity government and the Social Democracy of the Polish Republic (SDRP). Both have continued restrictive economic policies. As of the 2007 elections, parties in the government have become institutionalized. Presently, there are five major political parties represented in the *Sejm*: three leftist parties, one center-left, and the remaining on the right. Poland's party system has evolved from a volatile, underinstitutionalized system to a medium level stabilization since 2007.

In an effort to decentralize both pubic authority and public finance, on January 1, 1999 the *voivodship* (regional) councils became responsible for the development of regional economic policies. On September 23, 1999 the "Branches of the Government Administration" Act was passed, holding ministers responsible for overall sector policy and strategy while relieving their accountability for the work of specific ministries and central offices. As part of the decentralization process, the Interim Law was passed by parliament in December 1998. The Interim Law allows local and regional governments to have the opportunity to operate freely, matching financial resources to the tasks delegated to territorial self-government entities.

Post–World War II Romania

On August 23, 1944 King Michael, assisted by the Social Democratic Party (later becoming the Communist Party), overthrew Antonescu's government. The Communist Party eventually forced King Michael to appoint Petru Groza as Prime Minister. Manipulation by Groza led to the Communist Party's overwhelming victory in the 1946 elections. Securing their role in the government, Groza and the Communist Party began to forcefully remove and eliminate all opposing parties. Under the sole control of the Communist Party, the Romanian People's Republic was born and institutionalized with a new Constitution in April 1949. Groza and the Communist Party ignored the newly guaranteed rights written into the new Constitution.

Romania's communist government followed the standard Soviet command economy centralizing all aspects of the government and maintaining complete control. The state nationalized all industrial enterprises, dictating the factors of production. Collectivized farming allowed for state ownership over the agricultural sector. Created in 1948, the State Planning Commission (SPC) was responsible for planning all economic activity. The SPC took control of all financial institutions. Consumer income and purchasing power was dependent on the state's planned budget.

With Stalin's influence, Groza was replaced by Gheorghiu-Dej in 1952. Gheorgiu-Dej quickly asserted his power over Romania's government, taking control over the Communist Party and the National Assembly. Also, a new Constitution patterned after that of the USSR was adopted that same year.

The death of Joseph Stalin in 1953 ultimately led to rough relations between the Soviet Union and Romania. Tensions between the two nations became more strained resulting in Romania's ejection of all Soviet troops from its soil. Although Romania was a member of the Soviet bloc, Gheorghiu-Dej formed closer ties with the former Yugoslavia's Tito and China's Mao. The decreased influence of the Soviet Union allowed Romania to commence bilateral communications with the Western world.

Ceausescu took control over Romania in 1954. Romania's relative autonomy allowed for Ceausescu to apply his personal will and economic policy. During the 1960s, Ceausescu followed his own agenda, improving ties with China and refusing to join the Warsaw Pact's invasion of Czechoslovakia. The former signifies Romania's intent on becoming an independent nation. Ceausescu led Romania to closer economic and political ties with the Western and other nonaligned nations. Fearing an invasion from Soviet forces, Romania aligned itself with China and improved relations with Western Nations.

By the early 1970s, Ceausescu began appointing family members and faithful followers to high-ranking government positions. Appointing unqualified family members to the Politburo, along with his risky economic policy, resulted in a $10 billion debt by 1980. Ceausescu attempted to pay-off Romania's foreign debt ahead of time, but this policy led to draining Romania of all of its assets. Starvation and malnutrition ensued and became a common state among Romanian citizens. By the end of 1989, Ceausescu's irrational policies and dictatorship came to an end.

After Ceausescu's reign, several former communist leaders who opposed Ceausescu's policies formed a National Salvation Front (NSF). This new government nullified some laws from the Ceausescu era and voided the Romanian Communist Party (RCO) in national affairs. They also abbreviated the official name from Socialist Republic of Romania to just Romania. The NSF became a political party and demanded outlawing the Communist Party and the resignation of Iliescu. Iliescu attempted to transform the previous NSF to the Provisional National Unity Council (PNUC) in February 1990. Iliescu remained interim president until he appointed Theodor Stolojan as Romania's new prime minister in September 1991. Stolojan formed a coalition government comprised of members from both political parties. He balanced the need for economic and social reform against rapid decreases in the standard of living.

Modern Day Romania

Romania declared sovereignty in its new Constitution in 1991. Romania's national legislature is a bicameral parliament consisting of a Chamber of Deputies and the Senate. Romania's parliament remains volatile with parties splintering, reforming, and collating new parties continuously. There are currently five political parties represented in the Romanian parliament. Article 53 of the 1990 election law allows limited state financing through state subvention. By 1992, Nicolae Vacaroiu was appointed as the new Prime Minister, he and the ruling parties sought to eliminate smaller parties by enacting changes for the national elections. Social unrest continued until early 1993, but soon subsided.

In January 2007 Romania joined the European Union (EU). However, to gain full membership, Romania must conform with EU standards. Thus, Romania has sought to decentralize its public administration structure. Romania's public administration is structured into a three-tier system: central, county, and local. The central level of government consists of the President of the Republic and the Parliament. The parliament controls the independent agencies; such agencies include the Competition Council (monitoring fair competition) and the Ombudsman (mediating administrative disputes). The second tier (county level) constructs local public authorities on operating public services. The Prefect, who is to supervise the administrative activity of the County Council, making sure all regulations and laws are followed, represents the central government at the county level. As of 2006, the Prefect position is a nonpolitical position. The local level or the third tier consists of communes, towns, and cities, considered public legal entities deemed "territorial administrative units" made up of a mayor and local council members.

Although reform measures have been put in place to weaken political influence at the local level, there has been an increase in political migration of the elected mayors. The allocations of financial transfers from the state budget for local governments have been influenced by political/party affiliation. The decentralization process has been slow and unequal. Romanian local public officials are left with covering expenses for public services while the central government controls the organization and functioning. However, in 2005, a government decision (no.521) obligates central authorities to consult the associations of the municipalities when adopting measures that would affect them and provide mandatory consultation procedures. Due to the political influence the county councils had on the locally elected officials, new regulations on local public finances were adopted (Law 273/2006). The regulations addressed four principles as to how local finances need to be managed: financial autonomy, consultation, proportionality, and solidarity.

Post–World War II Ukraine

In 1922, during the Lenin era, Ukraine became an official member of the USSR. As part of the Soviet Republic, the Ukrainian government adopted the communist economic policy. This policy was based on a command model mainly used during wartime. As a result, the industrial production, especially the iron ore and coal sectors, suffered devastating decreases. Lenin installed a moderate approach dubbed as the New Economic Policy (NEP). However, this approach was short-lived as Joseph Stalin's reign over the Soviet Union emerged. Stalin's approach to economic integration began with political subjugation of the new republic. Sovietization of Ukraine began with Moscow's tight control over the mass media and isolated Ukraine from the outside world.

By the end of World War II, the Soviet Union gained control over the portions of the region lost to other countries. Germany occupied Ukraine during 1941–1944, but Ukraine was quickly recovered by Moscow. The Soviet Union had three objectives for Ukraine. First, there was to be no

Ukrainian government independent of the USSR. Second, programs promoting Ukrainian culture were to be abolished. Third, Ukraine's economy was not to be separate from the USSR's economy. In order to secure control over the Ukrainian government, Moscow replaced Ukrainian officials with faithful Communist Party members. Starting from the top, officials in the highest offices were removed and replaced with Russian natives. All decisions concerning Ukraine were either made in or approved by Moscow. Ukrainian officials had no say in the policy of their government, but were to only assist with the administration of directions coming from Moscow. Ukrainian culture was absorbed by forced USSR propaganda promoting ideology and values from all state-owned media outlets. Along with other aspects of life in Ukraine, the Soviet Union took full control over Ukraine's economy. Under the Soviet planned economy, Ukraine's economy was planned with the primary interest in benefiting the USSR. All orders concerning Ukraine's economy came from the Communist Party's Politburo in Moscow.

The agency responsible for integrating Ukraine's economy was the USSR's Central Planning Committee (CPC). The CPC initiated five-year plans according to the Politburo's long-, medium-, and short-term objectives. After approval from the Communist Party's Central Committee, the five-year plan was submitted to the USSR parliament for legislative approval. Upon approval from the USSR parliament, the plan was set in motion by the CPC implementing their policy through the respective agencies and units in the Ukrainian government. Ukraine's own CPC held very little power and its primary focus was to see that the plans were carried out. Moscow gained control over Ukraine's industrial sector from the first five-year plan. The CPC moved nonnative workers into industrial centers for ethnic integration and for the rapid production demanded from Moscow. In addition, it sealed Ukraine's industrial economy by making it dependent on Moscow's market. On the agricultural front, the CPC issued increases in grain production quotas for private and state farms. Moscow forcefully took over the Ukraine's agricultural sector, and eventually all farms and farmers were either employees or property of the state or collectives.

Modern Day Ukraine

August 24, 1991 marked Ukraine's independence. Ukraine's political liberalization revamped its whole structure of government. Its political structure is broken into three branches: executive, legislative (Supreme Rada), and judicial. The executive branch consists of a president, prime minister, and cabinet. Currently, there are six main parties in Ukraine's Supreme Rada. Attempts at reform in Ukraine have been slow due to inefficiency and corruption of the government. In 2007, Ukraine saw attempts to form a new democratic government and move toward a free market economic policy with the "Orange Revolution." However, attempts at privatization have been unclear. Since many of the political parties are coalitions, there is a high rate of party fragmentation. Some coalitions have members on the right and the left, making it hard for a clear consensus to be reached on economic policies. Ukraine has attempted to become a more liberal democratic society, while still wanting to hold on to socialist ideas on economic reform. The former President Viktor Yushchenko a member of the opposition block "Our Ukraine"; Yushchenko has failed to gain a runoff spot for the 2010 Ukrainian presidential elections. Yuschenko is most notably known for his informal leadership of the "Orange Revolution" and the leader of "Our Ukraine-People's Self Defense bloc," a party represented in Parliament. Viktor Yanukovych was sworn into office as Ukraine's president on February 25, 2010.

Former President Viktor Yushchenko had promised economic reform and to rid the government of corruption. However, economic reform and progress have been sluggish in Ukraine. According to an article published in the *New York Times*, the uncertainty about privatization is already contributing to reduced investment and low growth.[3] The issues surrounding the clarification of privatization and property rights have been hindered by ideological disputes between the coalition governments in parliament.

Framework for Analysis and Methodology: The Data

Data were obtained from two primary sources in order to complete the performance study. The data for the economic variables were derived from one main source as well as a few secondary sources for completion.[4] The majority of the economic variables were obtained from the World Data Bank[5] using the World Development Indicators (WDI) dataset. The WDI dataset covers 331 development indicators for 209 countries from 1960 to 2008. The WDI dataset presents economic and social measures derived from the World Bank and has more than 30 partner agencies.[6]

Political, social, and freedom indices were retrieved from the Freedom in the World Comparative and Historical Data set presented by Freedom House.[7] Freedom House assesses global political and civil liberties as experienced by individuals in 193 countries. It monitors and tracks expansion and impediments in freedoms and summarizes each pair of scores in an index known as freedom status. Freedom House does not directly rate the actual governments or the government's performance, instead, it focuses on individuals to act spontaneously both politically and civilly including political participation, freedom of expressions, association, and other activities without the interference from the state. The methodology is derived from the Universal Declaration of Human Rights, which applies to all countries irrespective of demographic, geographic, or economic differences.[8]

Other sources include the International Financial Statistics from the International Monetary Fund as well as the World Economic Outlook Database.[9] Data was also obtained from the *Chinese Statistical Yearbooks*.[10]

This study will employ economic and social data as a secondary analysis of the determinants of economic growth for the countries China, Poland, Romania, and Ukraine for the consecutive years from 1980 to present. The primary intention for analysis is to explain the tremendous economic growth in China, while political growth remains stagnant. The selection of the comparison countries Poland, Romania, and Ukraine was based on their differing post–World War II communist experiences, as well as their varied economic and political transformation since 1980. The limited data poses only a slight restriction to the analysis since reliable economic data is scarce for some of the countries during their communist years.

THE VARIABLES AND INDICATORS DEFINED

The primary hypothesis is to identify the determinants of economic growth based on a variety of economic, political, and civil indicators for China, Poland, Romania, and Ukraine.

Principally, do political rights and civil liberties affect economic growth by affecting the environment for foreign investment and foreign trade? Several hypotheses have been suggested throughout the economic literature in regard to the actual dependent variable for economic growth. Several dependent variables will be evaluated because due to significant covariance that exists between indicators such as gross domestic product (GDP) and gross national income (GNI). GNI is the current term used by the World Bank in place of the more familiar term "gross national product" (GNP).[11]

The GDP indicator is measured in current prices and is the sum of a country's overall economic output. It is the gross value of all goods and services within a country at purchaser prices converted at market exchange rates to current U.S. dollars. The current exchange rate method is used as an indicator of the countries relative economic strength. GDP is equal to GNI less net receipts of primary income.[12] GDP is determined by the private consumption plus gross investment plus government spending plus the difference of exports and imports.

$$GDP = C + Inv + G + (X - M)$$

GDP growth rate will be explored as an indication of any movement in a country's production compared to the previous year. The World Bank reports GDP growth as the annual percentage growth rate of market prices based on constant local currency.[13]

GDP growth rate for year n = [(GDP in year n) − (GDP in year n − 1)]/ (GDP in year n − 1)

GNI is the total value of a nation's income for its resident people including the value of all production within a country plus net income from abroad. Unlike GDP, GNI measures only its residents' income no matter where it is earned while GDP measures all production within a country no matter who produces it. Two separate methods of calculating the GNI will be utilized in the study. Both the GNI per capita Atlas method in U.S. dollars and the purchasing power parity (PPP) method will be analyzed. The Atlas method uses a three-year average of exchange rates accounting for exchange rate fluctuation. The World Bank prefers this method for comparing and classifying the relative size of a country's economy. The PPP method better describes the purchasing power of an average domestic producer or consumer within a country. As such, the World Bank favors the PPP method when describing poverty and the overall well-being of the economy.[14]

The statistical covariance between GDP and the two measures of GNI exists because of the obvious interrelation between the two measures but also because the measures do not always increase or decrease together. If a country services a large national debt, it may reflect a decrease in the GNI, but not necessarily a decrease in GDP. Yet, if a country or its residents reduce foreign assets, it may also be reflected in a decrease in the GNI, but not necessarily the GDP. Thus, the hypotheses will run all three measures as dependent variables. The determinants of each match should be fairly consistent within each country but not necessarily across all countries.

Another part of the analysis more tailored to China will employ another dependent variable: foreign exchange reserves (FOREX). This variable is of special interest for China since its foreign reserves have skyrocketed in the last two decades. The foreign exchange reserve is the foreign currency deposits and bonds held by a country's central bank to back its liabilities.

Independent variables can be categorized into economic, political, and social/civil indicators. The economic indicators include foreign direct investments (FDIs), imports and exports of goods and services, military expenditures, and energy consumption. Political indicators are summarized in the political freedom index and the freedom status average. Social and civil indicators include poverty, the Gini coefficient, and the civil liberties index.

FDI is the net inward and outward long-term private investments in an operation operating in a foreign economy. The World Bank defines this investment as at least 10 percent of voting stock.[15] Since FDI is in direct relation with imports and exports of goods and services, the covariance will be controlled. FDI net inflows will also be explored and should more accurately describe China's experience with its great success in attracting foreign investors. World Bank defines net inflows as the sum of equity capital, reinvestment of earnings, other long-term capital, and short-term capital.[16] It is more simply stated as new investments minus disinvestment. The hypothesis expects to see FDI emerge as an intervening variable in which several of the other independent variables are filtered through FDI while some may also have direct paths to the dependent variable(s). As an intervening variable, it is expected to see that the enormous growth in FDI related to the economic reforms in China precipitated by the lack of political and social reforms. In contrast, it is also expected to see growth in Poland with both economic and political reform but little growth in Romania and Ukraine.

Imports and exports of goods and services are the value of all goods and other market services received from and provided to, respectively, the rest of the world. The World Bank measurement includes the value of merchandise, freight, insurance, transport, travel, royalties, license fees, communication, construction, financial, information, business, personal, and government services. Excluded are wages, salaries, and income such as from property, investment, and labor.[17] Military expenditures are also derived from the World Bank Development indicators and measured as a percent of GDP including all current and capital expenditures in the armed forces for both military and civil personnel. For some countries, this data is estimated by the World Bank.[18] Energy use is measured as kg of oil equivalent per capita.[19]

The political indicators are obtained from the Freedom House ratings on Political Rights and Status of Freedom. Political Rights are rated on a scale from 1 (high) to 7 (low). A country rated high ensures free, fair, and competitive elections with competitive political parties or other political groups or interest groups. Minority groups can either participate directly or informally in the government. A country in the middle of the scale has aspects that have undermined freedom including civil war, heavy military or royal involvement in politics, unfair elections, and one-party dominance. Some aspects of quasiinfluence exist. Citizens in countries on the low end of political freedom have little or no freedom as a result of extreme oppression usually marked by extreme violence or warlord rule.[20] Freedom status is an average of political rights and civil liberties and then rated as "Free," "Partly Free," and "Not Free."[21]

The social/civil indicators include the Freedom House rating of civil liberties. As with the political rights index, countries are rated on a scale from 1 (high) to 7 (low) for civil liberties. A country with a high level of civil liberties ensures the freedom of expression, assembly, association, education, and religion. They will also maintain political and/or judicial due process and allow free economic activities and free economic opportunities. A country with a middle rating depicts possible censorship, political terror, and prevention of free association. Countries on the low end of civil liberties allow for virtually no freedom and a high level of political terror.[22] Poverty rates were obtained from the World Bank using the poverty headcount ratio at the national poverty line as a percentage of the population.[23] Because poverty rates vary from source to source and are incomplete across time, the final independent variable is the Gini coefficient as a measure of household income equality. Based on a Lorenz curve, the coefficient represents the difference between the distribution of income and a perfectly even distribution. That is, it is an indicator of how wealth (or lack thereof) is distributed within a country. A Gini coefficient ranges from 0 to 1 sometimes multiplied by 100 with 0 representing complete equality and 1 representing complete inequality. Globally, most countries range from .2 to .7.

ANALYSIS I: CORRELATION ANALYSIS

Analysis I identifies and assesses the effects of the political decisions on economic growth in China, Poland, Romania, and Ukraine from 1980 to 2010. The data analysis resulted in two forms, which will be discussed separately below. In this section, all the variables are examined through cross-tabulation, breakdown, and correlation analyses. These findings establish the basic patterns of relationships among all the variables in the analysis. The main purpose of the statistical manipulation is to find the clues for performing regression and causal analyses. The regression and causal analyses will be presented in the next section.

An excerpt of the correlation matrix for selected variables is presented in Table 6.1.[24] This table summarizes correlations of the key political and economic indicators. With but a few exceptions, all the relationships are in the expected directions. However, they deserve elaboration.

GDP has soared in China since economic reforms have transpired. As reported by World Bank, GDP has grown from $189 billion in 1980 to over $4 trillion in 2008.[25] That is a 22-fold increase and double-digit annual growth rates for most years since reform. Poland has also shared a substantial growth of over sevenfold. Romania and Ukraine have less significant growth and even had several years of significant decreases on the heels of instituting their economic reforms. The bar chart in Figure 6.1 illustrates the enormous growth for China's GDP compared to the other countries. China's initially timid but steady growth coincides with the experimentation with SEZs until the decision to expand widespread reforms.

Table 6.1 Correlation Matrix for Selected Variables by Country

China	GDP	FDI	FOREX	GNI	GNI, PPP	GINI	POL	CIVIL
FDI	.955**	……	……	……	……	……	……	……
FOREX	.963**	.911**	……	……	……	……	……	……
GNI	.999**	.951**	.960**	……	……	……	……	……
GNI, PPP	.993**	.955**	.931**	.994**	……	……	……	……
GINI	.836**	.886**	.883**	.828**	.881**	……	……	……
POL	.573**	.660**	.428*	.554**	.638**	.820**	……	……
CIVIL	−.279	−.097	−.303	−.294	−.209	.106	.527**	……
FREE	.000	.000	.000	.000	.000	.000	.000	.000
Poland								
FDI	.953**	……	……	……	……	……	……	……
FOREX	.966**	.941**	……	……	……	……	……	……
GNI	.995**	.935**	.971**	……	……	……	……	……
GNI, PPP	.955**	.879**	.983**	.969**	……	……	……	……
GINI	.754**	.699**	809**	.627**	.692**	……	……	……
POL	−.674**	−.722**	−.776**	−.724**	−.828**	−.751**	……	……
CIVIL	−.646**	−.708**	−.724**	−.706**	−.583*	−.685**	.956**	……
FREE	−.542*	−.635**	−.683**	.000	.000	−.662**	.965**	.942**
Romania								
FDI	.939**	……	……	……	……	……	……	……
FOREX	.982**	.955**	……	……	……	……	……	……
GNI	.999**	.940**	.981**	……	……	……	……	……
GNI, PPP	.980**	.936**	.984**	.979**	……	……	……	……
GINI	.449*	.504*	.498*	.440*	.576**	……	……	……
POL	−.278	−.374	−.514**	−.314	−.437	−.761**	……	……
CIVIL	−.313	−.519*	−.539**	−.363	−.491**	−.827**	.972**	……
FREE	−.347	−.484	−.564**	—	−.514**	−.804**	.987**	.956**
Ukraine								
FDI	.888**	……	……	……	……	……	……	……
FOREX	.917**	.971**	……	……	……	……	……	……
GNI	.998**	.889**	.919**	……	……	……	……	……
GNI, PPP	.869**	.825**	.898**	.883**	……	……	……	……
GINI	−.395	−.274	−.401	−.405	−650*	……	……	……
POL	−.228	−.077	.073	−.229	.146	.256	……	……
CIVIL	−.844**	−.822**	−.810**	−.863**	−.820**	.540	.228	……
FREE	−.542*	−.975**	−.856**	−.521*	−.430	.176	.218	.747**

*Significant at the .05 level.
**Significant at the .01 level.

GDP has been selected as the primary dependent variable. As expected for all four countries, GDP is highly correlated with the other economic indicators such as FDI, FOREX, GNI Atlas method, and GNI PPP. All bivariate correlations of these variables are positively significant at the .01

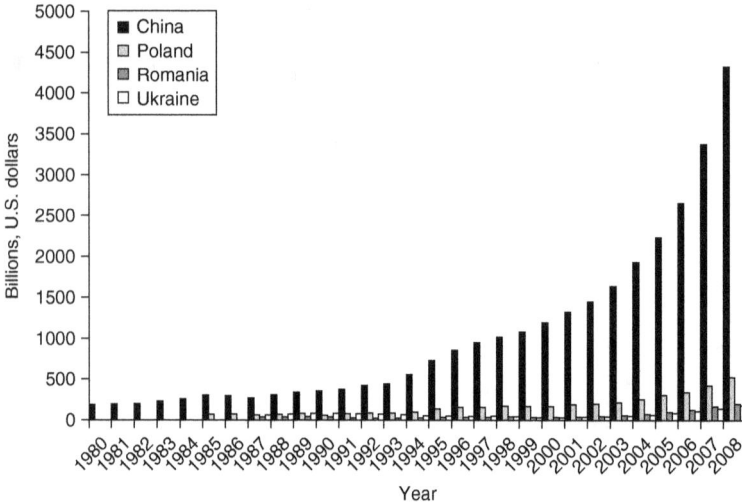

Figure 6.1   GDP for China, Poland, Romania, and Ukraine.

level with the values ranging from .869 to .999. The pattern is consistent for all economic variables reported in Table 6.1. Each of the relationships is discussed below.

Since the GDP is a measure of all economic activity with a country's borders, it is expected to be highly correlated with the GNI of its country's residents and foreign investments. As expected, the correlation between GDP and GNI is above .99 for each of the four countries meaning that as GDP increases, GNI correspondingly increases. The argument is that the variables are codependent as the two measures comprise aspects of each other. Although GNI subtracts payments to the rest of the world, they would be equal if all economic activity in a country were owned by its citizens. Consequently, both variables will be treated as dependent variables for the regression analysis.

GDP is also highly correlated with FDI. As with GDP and GNI, FDI is also a characteristic captured in the GDP measurement and the correlations are significant at the .01 level for all four countries. The relationship describes a positive movement indicating that as FDI increase, so too does the GDP. The lowest of these relationships is .888 for Ukraine with the highest .955 for China. Net FDI in China has skyrocketed. As Deng Xiaoping opened up China to foreign investment, FDI has grown at a healthy rate from 1980 until the early 1990s. With accession in the World Trade Organization (WTO), China's net FDI tripled in one year in 1993 and doubled again in 2007. It continues at an unprecedented rate with only a slight dip in late 2008 and 2009 as a result of the global slowdown. China's FDI continues as the leader among the developing nations with actual used value of $94.320 billion in 2008. Since the relationship between GDP and FDI is significantly high, FDI will be treated as a mediating variable in a path analysis in which imports and exports are filtered. Figure 6.2 describes FDI inflow for each of the four countries.

Corollary to the relationship of the key economic indicators, there is a strong positive correlation between GDP and FOREX. The correlation coefficients between GDP and FOREX range from .917 in Ukraine to .982 in Romania. The coefficients for all four countries are significant at the .01 level. The theory is that large reserves allow a government to provide a favorable economic environment by indicating the country's ability to repay foreign debts. Of course, the costs can also be high as fluctuations in the exchange markets result in gains and losses. China's $2+ trillion reserve is highly dependent on the health of the U.S. dollar. Should the U.S. dollar weaken, China would suffer a significant loss. Figure 6.3 indicates the growth of the foreign reserves of the four countries. Notice the historic growth in China's foreign reserves.

The bivariate correlations between GDP and the other social-political variables deserve some attention. Some unexpected relationships evolved. The social-political variables include the Gini coefficient, political freedom, civil freedom, and freedom status.

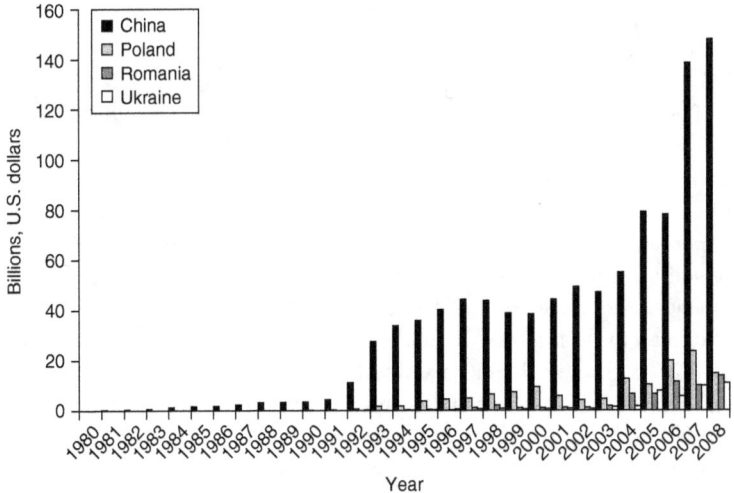

Figure 6.2 Foreign Direct Investment, Net Inflow.

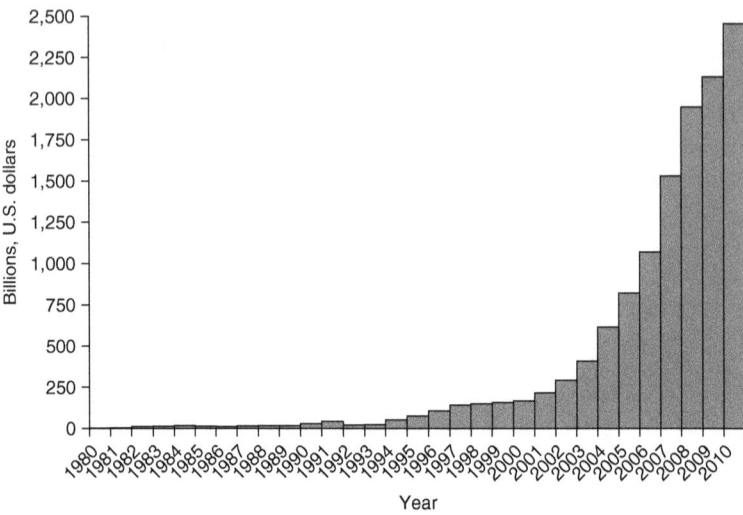

Figure 6.3   China's Foreign Reserve.

GDP and the Gini coefficients are positively significant at the .01 level for China and Poland and at the .05 level for Romania. However, the GDP and Gini coefficient is negative and not significant for Ukraine. A positive correlation is actually counter-intuitive. A positive value indicates that as the economic growth of a nation (as measured by GDP) increases, so too does its inequality. As stated previously, Gini is a measure of a nation's wealth and income with values ranging from 0 to 1 (sometimes multiplied by 100), where 0 reflects complete equality and a 1 reflects complete inequality. Thus, a positive relationship is indicating a country's overall economic growth but with increasing economic inequality of its citizens. China's economic growth has skyrocketed for the nation at large but not shared by all of its citizens. Basically, it is the old adage "the rich get richer and the poor get poorer." The assumption is that the economic elite are tied directly to the political elite. As economic reform began in China, the Gini coefficient of inequality hovered around 29 and 30. By 2001, it has reached the 40s and is currently in the mid-40s. Similarly, the .754 correlation for Poland's GDP and Gini is also very high. Poland's Gini coefficients have been increasing from a value of 23.1 as reform began to the mid-30s today. Poland's experience is reflecting that the farming sector is still quite high, and although income, trade, and foreign investments have all increased, its distribution has not increased as rapidly. The situation in Romania is slightly different. Romania's economy is still developing at a slower rate than most of its neighbors. Its GDP and Gini coefficient is .449 and is significant at the .05 level. Romania's Gini coefficient has ranged from the low-20s in the early reform years to 32 in 2007. The correlation coefficient for GDP and Gini in Ukraine is −.395. This value is not only negative but it is not significant either. Ukraine's Gini coefficients have been trending downward over the last few decades but there is a lot of inconsistency throughout. This is not surprising since Ukraine's economy is still struggling and is still reliant on social programs. Its more productive economic activities are still more agrarian and elementary. Although not significant, the negative relationship indicates that the workers are receiving a more sizable share as they become more productive.

The argument for the freedom indicators and GDP is that economic growth occurred under tight political control. Basically, controlled political decisions granted economic freedom leading to the tremendous economic growth in China. Since freedom indicators are measured from a 1 indicating freedom to 7 indicating no freedom, the expected correlations with GDP should be negative. This trend seems to hold for Poland, Romania, and Ukraine. Political rights, civil liberties, and a country's freedom status are all negatively correlated with GDP in all countries except China. Only civil liberties are negatively related in China. Additionally, China's freedom status remains unchanged as "not free" over the thirty years since reform began, and as such, does not produce a correlation with GDP.

The freedom indicators include political rights, civil liberties, and freedom status. The correlation of China's political rights with GDP is .573 and is significant at the .01 level. Since rights are ranked from 1 (free) to 7 (not free), the positive correlation indicates that worsening political rights accompanied growth in the economy. This is in fact our main thesis: China's economic growth has been spurred by economic inducements in an extremely controlled political environment providing a stable arena for foreign investments. This theory is furthered by the fact that there has actually been a decrease in China's political status indicating that political rights went from bad to worse in the years during economic reform. China now receives the worse rating indicating the absence or virtually nonexistence of political rights as a result of the extreme oppression.[26]

Political rights in Poland have moved in the opposite direction. Poland began reform under a very oppressive political system and rapidly moved to a freer society. Poland received the best score for political freedoms early in 1996. Poland's political rights rating and GDP is −.674 and is significant at the .01 level. Because the political rights indicator is ranked from 1 (free) to 7 (not free), the negative correlation is interpreted as increased political freedoms accompanied by an increase economic growth. To a lesser extent, this is also true for Romania. Romania has also significantly moved to a freer political system since reform. In just three short years starting in 1990, Romania's political rights indicator moved from 6 (almost absent political freedoms) to 4 (moderate freedom with some lingering oppressive behaviors). By 1996, Romania's score was and remains a 2 (approaching freedom with characteristics such as political corruption or violence). The correlation for Romania's political rights and GDP is negative, –.278, but not significant. The same is true for Ukraine. The correlation for Ukraine's political rights and GDP is also negative, –.228, and also not significant.

Civil liberties can also play a significant role in enticing foreign investments. The Freedom House index of civil liberties measures freedoms including expression, assembly, association, education, religion, rule of law, and a free economy with equal opportunity. A rating of 1 indicates freedom while a 7 indicates no freedom.[27] Of the four countries in this study, China's rating on its civil liberties is the anomaly. China's score on civil liberties has lingered at 6 and 7 since reform began. A score of a 6 indicates a highly restricted civil and economic system where business activities and discussions are discouraged. A score of 7, the worse rating, represents a system with virtually no civil or economic freedom. As with political rights, civil liberties in the other countries have much improved. Poland's score began at a poor rating of a 5 (evidence of censorship and political terror) but was reduced to a 3 immediately with its initiation of reform and has been at a 1 (free) since 2004. Both Romania's and Ukraine's ratings have trended downward since reform to a respectable rating of a 2 today (indicating some deficiencies but a relatively free civil and economic system).

The correlations between civil liberties and GDP are negative for all four countries. Because of the inverse coding of civil liberties, a negative relationship indicates that economic growth was accompanied by increased civil liberties. While initially a negative relationship was not expected for China, an in-depth look into the measurement reveals the explanation. First the correlation is negative but not statistically significant (–.279). Very little movement in the rating has occurred both before and after reform. The initial economic reforms in 1976 resulted in a slight movement of the civil liberties index from a 7 (worst) to a 6 (very poor). The rating then moved back to a 7 from 1989 until 1997 when it again moved to 6. Thus the negative correlation reflects a slight improvement of the index accompanied by economic growth, however, the former has barely moved. Principally, any slight improvement in civil liberties (even if only in the business dimensions of the index) with any degree of economic growth will result in a negative correlation.

Encapsulating both political rights and civil liberties is the overall freedom status. A country's ratings on each dimension of the political rights and civil liberties indices results in an average rating of free, partly free, or not free. Coded as 1, 2, or 3, respectively, China's rating is again an anomaly. China's freedom status is rated as not free and has been so before and since reform. Because of the stagnate value of 3, the correlation table indicates no measurable correlation. Appreciably, China's drastic economic growth has occurred under highly restricted political rights, highly restricted civil liberties with basically no movement in overall freedom, or lack thereof.

Poland, Romania, and Ukraine have all moved from not free to free and, therefore, negative correlations with economic growth (more freedom accompanied by economic growth). However, the movement of the freedom status for each country was gradual. Poland was the first to achieve a free status in 1990 whereas Romania and Ukraine moved only to partly free in 1991 and only recently (1997 and 2006, respectively) to free.

Gross National Income

Gross national income (GNI), formally referred to as gross national product (GNP), is composed of all domestic production (GDP) plus the net flows of income and dividends from abroad.[28] GNI was explored as a possible dependent variable measuring economic growth from both domestic and international sources.

The correlation coefficients between GDP and GNI are nearly perfect. Each correlation for all four countries is over .99. This is not surprising because they are measuring aspects of the same economic growth. More purposely, the correlations for each of the variables presented in Table 6.1 and all other correlations conducted in our research produced the same relationships with GNI as they did with GDP. This confirms our expectation that either GNI or GDP are acceptable dependent variables.

Foreign Direct Investment

As discussed in chapter 4, the opening up of China's economy began with the drive to attract foreign investors to China. Slowly introduced in the special economic zones (SEZs) and then accelerated to other districts and regions, FDI soared. The magnitude of China's growth dwarfs the impressive growth of Poland's, and the more moderate growth in Romania and Ukraine. While investigating FDI in terms of net and percent of GDP, our main focus is FDI net inflow. Our hypothesis expects to see FDI emerge as an intermediate variable in which the other independent variables are processed both directly and indirectly through FDI.

As expected, the correlations between FDI inflow and the economic variables are high. Almost all are over .9, positive and significant.[29] Of particular concern is the correlation between FDI and exports. A strong correlation is expected due to the premise that as foreign investment increases, exported goods would also increase. While this is especially true for China and Poland, it is less so for Romania and is insignificant for Ukraine.[30] Similarly, the argument is made that FDI is also highly correlated with imports. The pattern for FDI and imports is the same as with FDI and exports. That is, there is a strong correlation in China and Poland, more moderate in Romania, and weaker in Ukraine.

Of more interest in this research is the relationship between FDI and political rights and civil liberties. Variations exist for each country. In China, political rights and FDI are significantly related while civil liberties are not. The lack of political rights in China is highly correlated with the surge in FDI. The argument is that the stable political environment and guaranteed economic relationships with foreign investors have resulted in huge growth in FDI. However, the correlation with civil liberties is not significant in China. Poland, on the other hand, had significant correlations between both political rights and civil liberties with FDI. Both variables indicate that FDI increased as political and civil rights increased. Alternately, only civil liberties and FDI are significant in Romania and Ukraine, indicating that FDI increased only as civil liberties increased. What will be interesting in the regression is whether these bivariate relationships will continue to be significant and continue in the same direction as they are regressed holding constant the effects of each other.

Analysis II: Regression and Path Analysis

Given the degree of interrelationships among several variables, especially GDP and GNI, and the inability of a correlation analysis to imply a causal order, this section carries out two analytical tasks that are related. The first goal is assessing the relative importance of the selected explanatory variables in influencing economic growth. The second goal is to specify the nature of underlying causal processes among the variables using path analysis.

Two separate measures of economic growth are specified as dependent variables. The first and primary indicator of economic growth is GDP. The second indicator is GNI. All independent variables are entered in a stepwise multiple regression with pairwise deletion of missing values with both dependent variables. The criterion for empirical significance is set at .05. A process of refinement and elimination based on regressions, correlation coefficients, and previous research resulted in approximately five of twelve independent variables remaining for the final analysis. When variables are conceptually or empirically redundant, the variable that is conceptually stronger is retained.

The variables that remained are then divided into background and intervening variables. The background variables include imports, exports, political rights, and civil liberties. Most of these background variables, whether directly or indirectly affecting economic growth, are processed through the intervening variable FDI.

Model I: GDP

The primary focus of this chapter is to explain the variance in economic growth as explained by political and civil liberties. The hypothesis is that the less political freedom and/or civil liberties, the faster the economic growth in transitional economies such as China, Poland, Romania, and Ukraine. More directly, it is hoped that the evidence will show that the enormity of China's economic growth has occurred under an exceedingly restricted political environment.

Several multiple regressions were conducted narrowing the number of independent variables resulting in a causal model presented in Figure 6.4. A total of fifteen variables were introduced. Based on covariance analysis and theoretical foundations, the final models include only the measures of imports, exports, political rights, civil liberties, and foreign direct investment. Model 1 defines economic growth as measured by GDP.

The amount of variance explained by the models differs insignificantly. The model for China explains over 98 percent of the variance in economic growth as defined as GDP. Poland's and Romania's models explain almost 90 percent. Contrasting is Ukraine's at 85 percent.

Several similarities exist for each country. FDI, exports, and civil liberties significantly predict GDP for all the four countries. Imports are directly significant in three countries, except Ukraine. Political rights are a significant predictor in China and Ukraine, but only indirectly in Romania and completely absent as an indicator in Poland. Since FDI is treated as an intermediate variable, its predictors are also similar in all countries except Poland in which political rights are nonexistent in both GDP and FDI.

While several similarities exist, there are significant differences that must also be addressed. These distinctions will be addressed country by country.

China's model includes all five independent variables. GDP is explained directly by imports, exports, FDI, political rights, and civil liberties. FDI also filters imports, exports, political rights, and civil liberties. Ninety-eight percent of the variance of GDP is explained by this model. The equation for GDP is

GDP = $2.602E12 + -2.72 imports + .730 exports + .416 FDI$
    $+ .119 pol + -.361 civ$

As expected, the model is indicating that a negative relationship exists between imports and GDP and a positive relationship between exports and

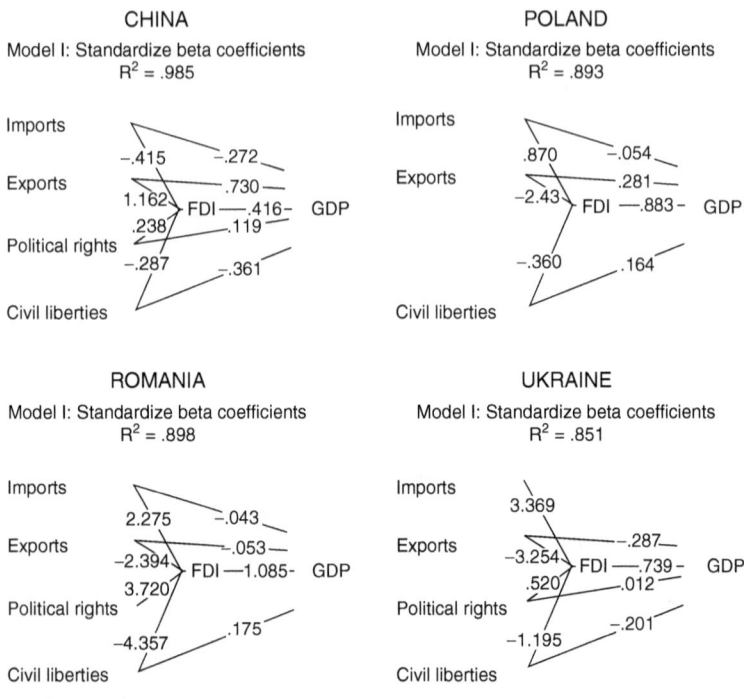

Figure 6.4   Path Analysis Predicting GDP.

GDP. Although imports are substantial, imports are typically attributed to domestic manufacturing leading to exported products. Also as anticipated, there is a positive relationship between FDI and GDP and between political rights and GDP, but a negative relationship between civil liberties and GDP. Because of the inverse coding of political rights, a positive relationship for political rights and GDP means that the lack of political freedom predicts economic growth. Correspondingly, the inverse coding for civil liberties means that a negative relationship signifies that even though there was only a slight improvement in civil liberties, it corresponds with the growth of GDP. The same relationships exist in the paths from imports, exports, political rights, and civil liberties to FDI.

This model supports our main thesis: China's economic growth has been spurred by economic inducements in an extremely controlled political environment providing a stable arena for foreign investments. The theory is furthered by the fact that there has actually been a decrease in China's political status, indicating that political rights went from bad to worse in the years during economic reform. China now receives the worst rating indicating the absence or virtually nonexistence of political rights as a result of the extreme oppression.[31] However, the civil liberties have only marginally improved, and as such, mostly in the economic measures of the indicator. As such, the slight, but very controlled, improvement of some of the economic freedoms has further led to economic growth.

The model for Poland explains 89.3 percent of the variance in GDP. As expected, imports, exports, and FDI are all included in the model and in the direction anticipated. What is distinctive in the model is the exclusion of political rights. Although the bivariate correlation was significant at −.674, political rights were excluded in both the direct path to GDP and the indirect path via FDI. A possible explanation is that political rights in Poland were rapidly obtained. By 1996, Poland scored as a free country, and as such, it becomes a moot point in its economic recovery that lingered for the decade following. Another possible explanation is that even during their communist era, Poland was less repressive and the people more independent minded despite the communist rule. Also unique in Poland's model is the positive relationship between civil liberties and GDP as a direct path, but a negative relationship to GDP via FDI. The positive relationship from civil to GDP may be representing the combination of two things. First, Poland's civil liberties index started out much better than the other countries in the study (a 4 and 5 in the early 1980s) and then rapidly improved to a 2 in 1990 where it stayed idle until 2004 when it was scored as free. It may also be reflecting that Poland's economy is more commercially oriented than the other postcommunist states, dominated by transactional activities and the service sector.

The variance in GDP explained by the model for Romania is 89.8 percent. Directly linked to GDP is imports, exports, FDI, and civil liberties. Indirectly predicting GDP includes imports, exports, political rights, and civil liberties. Excluded from the model is the direct link from political rights to GDP. To a lesser extent than Poland, Romania has also significantly moved to a freer political system since reform. From 1990 to 1996, Romania's political rights indicator moved from 6 (almost absent political freedoms) to 4 (moderate freedom) and then to 2 (approaching freedom). But unlike Poland's, the correlation for Romania's political rights and GDP was not significant. Also unlike Poland, political rights do predict GDP indirectly via FDI. Unique to Romania is the relationship of civil liberties to GDP and to FDI. The model indicates that a positive relationship exists between civil liberties and GDP but negative to FDI. Even though the bivariate relationships were all negative, the positive relationship to GDP is unexpected. This means that more freedom is associated with increased FDI but a decrease in GDP. An explanation may be that Romania's GDP growth has lagged and FDI has only trickled in.

Ukraine's model explains 85 percent of the variance in GDP. This model includes direct paths to GDP from exports, FDI, political rights, and civil liberties. It also includes indirect paths from imports, exports, political rights, and civil liberties via FDI. Excluded from the model is a direct path from imports to GDP. This is expected because the volume of imports is relatively small and not used to produce exported goods. On the other hand, exports tend to be more in the agricultural and handicrafts segments. Ukraine's model most closely mirrors China's in that the minimal level of political rights are associated with higher GDP and FDI. Although the bivariate relationships between Ukraine's political rights with both GDP and FDI were not significant, they were negative. However, both paths are now significant and positive in the causal model as political rights are both directly and indirectly leading to GDP. As to civil liberties, both the paths to GDP and FDI are negative. That is, the opening up, although minimally, of civil liberties leads to more conservative economic growth. Of course, in Ukraine's case, both GDP and FDI are substantially lower and civil liberties are marginally better than China.

ADDITIONAL CAUSAL MODELS

Several other causal models were explored using variations of GDP with and without FDI as an intervening variable. Again, most models were eventually reduced to the independent variables imports, exports, political rights, and civil liberties.

Model 2 emerged with GDP as the dependent variable and the four independent variables listed above. FDI was withdrawn from the equation. With only slight variations, Model 2 produced the same results for all four countries. The model for China is identical in that all four variables significantly predict GDP in all the same directions as Model 1. Over 96 percent of the variance of GDP is explained by a negative relationship with imports and civil liberties and a positive relationship with exports and political rights.[32]

Removing FDI from the equation, Model 2 for Poland explains almost 72 percent of the variance in GDP.[33] Political rights are still excluded as an insignificant predictor of GDP. The only difference in the model is that imports moved from a negative relationship to a positive relationship. This is probably attributed to the fact that imports were overshadowed by FDI in the previous model. The original bivariate correlation between imports and GNI was also positive.

Romania's model differs the most from any of the countries.[34] Imports also revert to a positive relationship, political rights enter in the equation as significant, and civil liberties revert from positive to its original bivariate negative relationship.

The model for Ukraine has one addition. Where imports had only an indirect path to GDP in Model 1, it now has a direct positive path in Model 2.[35]

Observing the original correlation analysis reveals that there is significant intercorrelation between GDP and GNI. As such, a causal model for GNI was also conducted. Unlike GDP, GNI measures only its residents' income no matter where it is earned while GDP measures all production within a country no matter who produces it. While GDP better suits the focus of our study, an inquiry into GNI seems appropriate. Two separate methods of calculating the GNI have been utilized in the study. Both the GNI per capita Atlas method in U.S. dollars and the PPP method were analyzed. The models produced the same causal models. Model 3 predicts GNI per capita with the independent variables imports, exports, political rights, and civil liberties as the independent variables and FDI as the intervening variable. Model 4 repeats the analysis excluding FDI from the equation. Both Models 3 and 4 also produce very similar results as Models 1 and 2. Models 3 and 4 for China are again identical to Models 1 and 2 in that the same variables are significant and in the same directions. The R^2 for both models is over 99 percent. The standardized beta coefficients for all direct and indirect paths vary only slightly across all models yet all are in the same directions.

Models 3 and 4 for Poland and Ukraine are also identical in paths with Models 1 and 2, respectively. Poland's Models 3 and 4 have the R^2 variances 87 and 78 percent, respectively. Ukraine's Models 3 and 4 have R^2 variances of .852 and 1.00, respectively. Only Romania's models differ. Model 3 differs from Model 1 in that political rights became a significant negative direct predictor of GNI and the direct path from civil liberties was removed (the opposite occurred in Model 1). While 91 percent of GNI was explained in Model 3, less than 48 percent of GNI is explained in Model 4. Model 4 predicts GNI with FDI removed from the equation. Romania's Model 4 paths look almost identical to Romania's Model 2.

CONCLUSION

The objective of this performance study was to explain the variance in economic growth as explained by political and civil liberties. The hypothesis was that the less political freedom and/or civil liberties, the faster the economic growth in transitional economies such as China, Poland, Romania, and Ukraine. A total of twenty analytical tasks are presented in this study. A correlation analysis and four causal analyses were conducted for each of the four countries, China, Poland, Romania, and Ukraine. The correlation analysis indicated several possible dependent variables measuring economic growth. GDP emerged as the principal dependent variable. GNI was analyzed to juxtapose to the models created by GDP. The independent variables used in the final causal models included imports, exports, political rights, and civil liberties. FDI emerged as an intervening or mediating variable.

The major finding of the present study is that the basic models explaining economic growth at the macrolevel do, with some modification, depend on tight political and civil controls. That is, whether economic growth is measured as GDP or GNI, the models differ only slightly across the countries. Tight political control, especially in the early years of economic restructuring, provided for a stable environment that attracted foreign investors, which in turn, led to higher economic growth. Contrasting the tight political control, the loosening of the tight civil controls, even marginally, encouraged further growth. This is most significant for China and Ukraine, both who have resisted opening up their systems the most. This is least significant for Poland and, to some extent, Romania. In fact, political rights were not significant in Poland, probably because of the rapid expansion of rights. Also, the granting of civil liberties in both countries has accompanied economic growth.

CHAPTER 7

SUCCESSES

PREAMBLE

After more than a quarter century of Mao's whimsical development strategy, China remained an economically stagnant and backward country. Reform was imperative and politics was still in command. The decision to reform was neither the studied recommendations from scholars nor the consensus of voters, it was by fiat. Comparable to when the regime first came to power in 1949, China had neither the knowledge nor the experience to effectuate a systemic transformation. Yet, status quo was no longer an option. Economic reform was to begin under secrecy and tight political control. As the leadership repeatedly stated, the reform process was likened to "crossing the stream by feeling the pebbles underneath." That is, very cautiously and tentatively.

Economic development was the main objective. Social calm and political stability were the premises. Phased release and orderly actualization of innate but hitherto repressed entrepreneurial spirit and inhibited productive energy of the masses was the pathway. Alternately stated, the leadership had a compass, but without a map. Deng and many of his first generation revolutionaries were victims of massive social disorder under Mao. Political stability and social calm, therefore, were to be preserved at all cost during reform.

Though China's reform began a decade prior to similar undertakings in Eastern Europe, it was able to avoid the pain of the so-called shock therapy approach, such as in Poland, or the reliance on foreign experts as governments of numerous Eastern European countries were obliged to. China took objective conditions into full consideration. Background forces inherent in China's history, culture, social fabric, value system, existing institutional arrangements, and the disposition of the masses in the late 1970s were all taken into due consideration. As a result, China adopted a gradualism reform path.

The patent desire and aspiration of the Chinese people were, among others, improved living standards and greater latitude for freedom. Alternately stated, the masses thirsted for at least some loosening of the state's grip that impinged on individual freedom. As we see today, greater freedom was granted; but it was greater economic freedom, not political freedom.

CHARTING THE PATH TO REFORM SUCCESS

The reform path that the Chinese leaders mapped was neither a thoroughfare nor an alleyway. The scope, pace, and depth of reform were well-defined and clearly delineated at every major juncture. All major reform measures began with carefully calibrated and narrowly delineated pilot projects. It was so on farm as well as in industry. Domestically and externally alike, only when the merits of experimental reform projects demonstrated success was the scope of reform permitted to expand and intensify. Successive administrations were not even distantly as dictatorial as Mao. Nevertheless, the dictum "politics in command" remains alive and well in China. Political decisions control the pace as well as the scope of reform. Economic reform does not presuppose parallel political reform. Political reform was not and is not on the cards. No one and no force was permitted to challenge the absolute leadership and authority of the Chinese Communist Party.

Domestically, reform secretly began with one experimental project in one agricultural commune in Sichuan province. On the industrial front, reform also began in Sichuan province but only six state-owned enterprises (SOEs) were given the permission to experiment with limited discretionary power for decision making.[1] The open door policy toward external economies was similarly gradual. Both foreign investment and foreign trade initially targeted the more developed economies in the Pacific Rim region.

Deng's reform scheme was to focus development efforts and to channel development opportunities where the returns would be the highest and the most rapid. Major urban centers along the seacoast promised the speediest actualization of latent productive potentials. Enabling development in a relatively small geographic area of China first with expansion later to other areas was foreseen and intended. The scheme was so that, in time, the "spillover effect" would be able to energize and mobilize the rest of the economy. Though gradual, beneficial externalities of reform rippled outward to larger circles of the economy. Though development had been unequal with respect to geographical regions, the intent of reform designers had been actualized. The avowed value of equal distribution of income characterizing socialism was thereby sacrificed for speedier aggregate economic growth.

With 1980 as the base year, Deng initially envisioned a doubling of average income by 1990 and then redoubling by the end of the century. Deng's aspiration was realized far beyond any reform architect dared to dream when the reform began.[2]

China's glaring successes have been of intense interest to academics and world leaders alike. Opening up to external economies served as the catalyst for awakening domestic productive energies. Reform in the realms of foreign investment and foreign trade were the major engines igniting the zeal of domestic entrepreneurship. Accomplishments on other fronts, however, also contributed appreciably to the country's overall success. Successes in the realms of foreign investment and foreign trade indeed served as the engine. An automobile, however, does not function on the merits of an engine only. The functioning of any powered instrument, however, depends also on other components that must at least be in modestly satisfactory working condition. Successes in one domain helped ferment changes in others, successively triggering chain reactions that in time reverberated to ever wider scope of China's entire economy.

PERFORMANCE

The ensuing section is a discussion of China's overall reform successes. Table 7.1 presents an overview of select macro data since reform began.

China's population was 975.4 million in 1979 when economic reform officially began. A year later, it grew to 987.1 million, a net increase of 11.7 million. That is, one year's population increase in China in 1979 surpassed Hungary's total population of 9.9 million in 2010. China's population is estimated to be 1.33 billion in the middle of 2010. Consequently, there are nearly 46 million more people in China since reform began. When analyzing China's economic growth during the past three decades, the increase in labor force needs to be duly noted.

The most pronounced success of China's systemic transformation is its economic growth rate. Its gross domestic product (GDP) by 1979 year-end was 406.3 billion Chinese yuan. Per capita income was 419 yuan. After a decade of reform, the GDP increased to 1.70 trillion yuan, a 305.5 percent increase. Mirroring Thomas Malthus's theory of geometric growth in population size, the annual growth rate of GDP in China between 1979 and 1989 was 30.6 percent. Taking into account population growth during the decade, the average annual growth in per capita income for the decade was still an impressive 26.3 percent. Two decades after reform began, China's GDP surged to 8.97 trillion yuan. The two-decade increase was a nearly implausible 2107.2 percent, averaging 110.7 percent a year. Per capita income, on the other hand, rose from 419 yuan in 1979 to 7159 yuan in 1999. That is, the average per capita income rose by 1608.6 percent, averaging 80.4

Table 7.1 Select Macro Indicators, 1979–2008

Year	GDP [billion Yuan]	Primary Industry [billion Yuan]	Secondary Industry [billion Yuan]	Tertiary Industry [billion Yuan]	Composition of Gross Domestic Product			Per Capita GDP (yuan)	Budgetary Expenditure [billion Yuan]	Budgetary Expenditure [billion Yuan]
					Primary Industry (%)	Secondary Industry (%)	Tertiary Industry (%)			
1979	406.3	127.0	191.4	87.9	31.3	47.1	21.6	419	—	—
1980	454.6	137.2	219.2	98.2	30.2	48.2	21.6	463	116.0	122.9
1981	489.2	156.0	225.6	107.7	31.9	46.1	22.0	492	—	—
1982	532.3	177.7	238.3	116.3	33.4	44.8	21.8	528	—	—
1983	596.3	197.8	264.6	133.8	33.2	44.4	22.4	583	—	—
1984	720.8	231.6	310.6	178.6	32.1	43.1	24.8	695	—	—
1985	901.6	256.4	386.7	258.5	28.4	42.9	28.7	858	200.5	200.4
1986	1027.5	278.9	449.3	299.4	27.2	43.7	29.1	963	—	—
1987	1205.9	323.3	525.2	357.4	26.8	43.6	29.6	1112	—	—
1988	1504.3	386.5	658.7	459.0	25.7	43.8	30.5	1366	—	—
1989	1699.2	426.6	727.8	544.8	25.1	42.8	32.1	1519	—	—
1990	1866.8	506.2	771.7	588.8	27.1	41.3	31.6	1644	293.7	308.6
1991	2178.2	534.2	910.2	733.7	24.5	41.8	33.7	1893	314.9	338.7
1992	2692.4	586.7	1170.0	935.7	21.8	43.4	34.8	2311	348.3	374.2
1993	3533.4	696.4	1645.4	1191.6	19.7	46.6	33.7	2998	434.9	464.2
1994	4819.8	957.3	2244.5	1618.0	19.8	46.6	33.6	4044	521.8	579.3
1995	6079.4	1213.6	2868.0	1998.0	19.9	47.2	32.9	5046	624.2	682.4

Year									
1996	7117.7	1401.5	3383.5	2332.6	19.7	47.5	32.8	5846	740.8	793.8
1997	7897.3	1444.2	3754.3	2698.8	18.3	47.5	34.2	6420	865.1	923.4
1998	8440.2	1481.8	3900.4	3058.1	17.6	46.2	36.2	6796	987.6	1079.8
1999	8967.7	1477.0	4103.4	3387.3	16.5	45.8	37.7	7159	1144.4	1318.8
2000	9921.5	1494.5	4555.6	3871.4	15.1	45.9	39.0	7858	1339.5	1588.7
2001	10965.5	1578.1	4951.2	4436.2	14.4	45.1	40.5	8622	1638.6	1890.3
2002	12033.3	1653.7	5389.7	4989.9	13.7	44.8	41.5	9398	1890.4	2205.3
2003	13582.3	1738.2	6243.6	5600.5	12.8	46.0	41.2	10542	2171.5	2465.0
2004	15987.8	2141.3	7390.4	6456.1	13.4	46.2	40.4	12336	2639.6	2848.7
2005	18321.7	2242.0	8736.5	7343.3	12.2	47.7	40.1	14053	3164.9	3393.0
2006	21192.4	2404.0	10316.2	8472.1	11.3	48.7	40.0	16165	3876.0	4042.3
2007	25730.6	2862.7	12479.9	10388.0	11.1	48.5	40.4	19524	5132.2	4978.1
2008	30067.0	3400.0	14618.3	12048.7	11.3	48.6	40.1	22698	6133.0	6259.3

Source: National Bureau of Statistics of China. 2009. *China's Statistical Yearbook 2009*. Beijing: China Statistics Press. P.37,38. (7-1 National Government Revenue and Expenditure and Their Increase Rates). The data in this table varies slightly from the World Bank and IMF data used for the analysis in chapter 6 due to the difference in source.

percent annually for two consecutive decades. No economy in the world has ever experienced such exceptional growth for such an extended period of time. The growth, however, did not appear to slow down substantially even though the world was in a firm grip of a deep recession during the final years of the 2000s decade.[3] Nevertheless, China's annual GDP growth rate for the three decades still managed to approximate 274.5 percent. Three decades after the reform began, China's per capita income had risen from 419 yuan in 1979 to 24,867 yuan in 2009. The annual per capita income increase between 1979 and 2009 for China's rapidly growing population was 194.5 percent. If this took place in an extremely underdeveloped economy with an exceptionally small population, it would still ring improbable. For this enduring growth rate to materialize in an economy whose population was already nearing 1 billion when reform began seems virtually impossible.

STRUCTURAL TRANSFORMATION

Four years after the communist regime came to power in 1949, the primary sector was still contributing 45.9 percent to the nation's GDP while 23.4 percent originated from the secondary sector. China's first Five-Year Development Plan (FYDP) began in 1953, ending in 1957. By the end of the first FYDP, the contribution from the primary sector to 1957's GDP decreased to 40.3 percent whereas industrial sector's output rose to 40.4 percent.

One year prior to the official beginning of the reform, only 17.9 percent of China's population resided in urban centers or townships. Yet, only 31.3 percent of China's GDP was derived from the primary sector whereas 47.1 percent originated from the secondary sector. China's economic structure was disproportionately tilted in favor of the secondary industries. Over investment and overproduction of unwanted industrial products abounded while basic consumer needs from the primary sector were still being parsimoniously rationed. Inefficiency and extensive waste of scarce resources were pervasive. One objective of systemic transformation was to restore balance among sectors of the economy in accordance with objective market conditions. Opening up to the outside and enlivening within, combined with decentralization and incremental profit motivation, the administration cautiously began the delicate balancing act of substituting the new by gradually phasing out the old in an organized and orderly fashion.

Reform invariably meets with resistance. China was not immune from it. Decentralization reduces the bureaucrats' authority and influence. Impediments to reform are either knowingly or unwittingly strewn along its path, delaying or derailing efforts at its initial stages. At the enterprise level, the time-honored "iron rice bowl" practice could be discarded. Surplus or less productive labor force could be pruned from their previously secure employment. Concern over possible unemployment also generated resistance to privatization and marketization of enterprise operations. Nevertheless, China was able to steadily move forward in its reform efforts and achieve overall successes in structural and systemic transformation.

Primary Sector

Several trends of structural transformation may be observed or derived from the data provided in Table 7.1. The growth rates in the primary sector between 1980 and 1985, both years inclusive, were −1.5, 7.0, 11.5, 8.3, 12.9, and 1.8 percent, respectively. Rapid gains in the primary sector between 1981 and 1984 paralleled ongoing agricultural reform measures being taken on farm during that period. That was also the period when farmers could leave the commune system and work independently under the "responsibility system." That is, after delivering the promised and contracted produce to the state, the farmer could sell the surplus on the free market for personal gains. However, growth rates on farms declined drastically from 12.9 percent in 1984 to 1.8 percent in 1985. That was the year when the reform focus diverted from agricultural to the industrial and manufacturing sectors. Alternately stated, no new reform measures were taking place on farm while liberalization in the secondary sector began.

Although small, there has been sustained growth in agricultural production since 1985. The growth rates hovered mostly between only 2 and 4 percent. A host of factors contributed to the relatively stagnant environment on farms. Movements from one geographic location to another were no longer strictly enforced as during the Mao era. Land fragmentation compounded by surplus labor on farms translated into gathering momentum for off-farm migration. It was particularly true for the younger generation who began flooding major urban centers in search of more rewarding employment.

More important, with decentralization and the "get rich quickly" fever, local officials in rural districts began concocting pretexts for imposing arbitrary service charges, fines, and fabricated taxes on farmers. Many farmers simply abandoned their farms to escape the tyranny. Industrialization, infrastructural construction, and urban encroachment also combined forces to infringe on crop acreage. The modest gains in growth by the primary sector were due primarily to more intensive application of yield-increasing factors.

Output growth on farm in some measure rebounded from 2004 forward. Growth rates between 2004 and 2008, both years inclusive, were 6.3, 5.2, 5.0, 5.0, and 5.5 percent, respectively. The modest recovery was due primarily to the central administration's avowed efforts at improving living conditions on the farm by the Hu–Wen administration. By March 2008, all agricultural, livestock, and special produce taxes were eliminated. At the same time, subsidies of one form or another were being channeled to the agricultural producers. Productivity increases on farms rebounded, enabling the underemployed and the disguised unemployed on farms to branch into nonfarming ventures.

The most noteworthy development is the substantial structural transformation that has been taking place in China since the reform began. As noted in Table 7.1, 31.3 percent of GDP originated from the primary sector in 1979. The primary sector's contribution to GDP was disproportionately small for the simple reason that rural population was still in excess of 80 percent of the total population.

Over the brief span of three decades, genuine strides have materialized, increasing production and productivity while the share of primary sector's contribution to GDP declined. Yet, aside from a brief surge in the primary sector's contribution to GDP between 1981 and 1983, the share of GDP derived from it kept maintaining a rapid and steady downward trend, from high of 33.4 percent in 1982 to 11.3 percent in 2008. The share of agricultural sector to GDP in the United States is less than 2 percent; but the U.S. decline occurred over more than two centuries. The comparison reveals the speed of economic growth and the restoration of sectoral balances that have been achieved by China during the past three decades.

Secondary and Tertiary Industries

Examined from the perspective of product composition, the contribution of the secondary sector to total GDP hovered around 40 percent between 1979 and 2008. When reform began, 47.1 percent of China's GDP originated from the industrial sector. Nearly thirty years later, the rate was only at 48.6 percent. Alternately stated, amidst phenomenal GDP growth over the three decades, the share of industry to the economy's total GDP has unexpectedly remained relatively stable.

Given the rapid decline in the primary sector's relative importance to the nation's economy during these three decades, expectation would lead to nearly parallel decreases in the industrial sector's relative importance. Additionally, the expectation would be that corresponding increases in the service sector would increase. It is the rise in tertiary industry in an economy that normally suggests structural maturation. Yet, China's tertiary sector has been on the rise in importance without corresponding decreases in the relative importance of the industrial sector. Tertiary sector's contribution to GDP in 1979 was 21.6 percent. By 2008, 40.1 percent of GDP originated from the tertiary sector. That is, the share of primary sector to GDP declined by 20 percent while that of the tertiary sector rose by 18.5 percent.

It would appear as if the rise in the service sector comes almost exclusively at the expense of the primary sector.

A host of factors have contributed to the distinctive development pattern in China. China's rapid growth has been powered by the growth of its industrial sector. More specifically, it is the phenomenal growth of China's export industry within the manufacturing sector that has been powering China's economic ascendancy on the world stage. Growth in the service sector generally accompanies rising productivity in the industrial sector. In China, however, it has been the unprecedented growth in both productivity and production in industry that helped fuel the growth in the service sector. The share of the industrial sector in the nation's total GDP did not decline as expected because the market for low-cost exports from China kept growing, obliging the sustained expansion of the industrial sector via increased production.

As the development and reform processes continue in China, the relative share of the industrial sector to China's economy is unlikely to decline any time soon. China's export sector will continue to grow for years to come. More important, though not yet enunciated, the likelihood is that China's 12th FYDP will focus more on meeting the rising demand in the domestic markets. For instance, it is expected that China will budget 7 trillion yuan, approximating $1.03 trillion for urban and infrastructural constructions during the 12th FYDP period of 2011–2015.[4] By 2006, China was already building the world's largest solar power plant, with a 100 megawatts capacity. Three years later, China signed a multibillion contract with First Solar (FSLR), a publicly held U.S. energy company, to build a solar power plant in Inner Mongolia capable of yielding two gigawatts.[5] Accompanying similar sustained construction and industrial expansions, demand for service will correspondingly rise, fueled primarily by rising demand in financial services, wholesale, retail, and real estate services. China's rapid expansion in the industrial sector has enhanced its productive capacity and deepened its industrial base. To date, China has become the largest producer of steel, coal, cement, television sets, and textile products. It ranks second in the world in power generation and fifth in crude oil production.[6]

On the other hand, China's rapid growth in its industrial sector has not been consistently rational. One major factor contributing to it is that the state's role remains prevalent in China's sustained growth path. That is, China's economic system is still on its journey to being fully market-based and market-driven. Till the present, the state keeps mediating the balancing act of maximizing overall benefits on the one hand or minimizing detrimental consequences on the other. As an example, a glaring incongruity is China's rapidly growing public debts amidst its immense foreign reserve.

One major factor contributing to this quandary of deepening public debt is the government's massive spending schemes intended to prevent the rise in unemployment. That is, unwarranted budgetary disbursements for construction or industrial projects are authorized to keep unemployment from rising.

IMPROVED FUNCTIONAL EFFICIENCY

The command system fossilized the subjective pricing system, froze productive incentives, constricted the distribution systems for factors as well as products, and neutralized the dynamic function of a viable financial system. It was against the backdrop of the command system's waste and inefficiency that the motto of "enliven within, opening up to the outside" became the rallying call for reform. "Enliven within" began with the removal of the central government's omnipresence in all spheres of people's lives. Phased decentralization in administration, investment and production decisions, and price determination all contributed to enlivening within. Decentralization of the responsibility system revived the atmosphere for entrepreneurship and reactivated the spirit for profit motives. From the smallest farm to the largest SOEs and financial institutions, the concepts of scarcity and value began guiding microentities in their decision-making processes. A brief sketch on improved efficiency in select domains in the economy is presented below.

AGRICULTURE

China has been a rural-based society for tens of centuries. Land ownership ranks high among cherished values. Agricultural productivity soared in the early 1950s when peasants received titles to land that had been confiscated from the landlords. But in the second half of the 1950s, agricultural productivity plunged when their land became "owned by all the people." Farmers were herded into collectives and communes. The farmers lost more than the land that they had just been allotted. They lost their freedom and their individuality.

Domestically, "enlivening within" began on the farm. Land ownership still belonged to the state. Nevertheless, with the contract responsibility system and the land-leasing program, the farmers' individuality and their incentive reemerged. The farm reform measures helped release the long suppressed productive energy of hundreds of millions of farmers. Human resourcefulness replaced plan directives in factor procurement and product distribution. Combined with phased liberalization of the pricing system, factor allocation as well as product combinations became the domain of the producer instead of the state. Productivity and production kept rising over the decades despite massive off-farm migration of the underemployed and disguised unemployed.[7]

Wen Jiabao succeeded Zhu Rongji as the PRC's new Premier in March 2003. Wen aimed at sustained reform on four fronts when he assumed the post of Premier. The four fronts were: SOEs, financial markets, government structure, and agriculture.[8] On March 5, 2008, Premier Wen reported to the First Session of the 11th Congress that

> ...Our (initial) point of departure was to strengthen the foundation of agriculture. (We) regarded increasing production and farm income as our primary task, adopting a series of all-encompassing measures affecting system, policy and budgetary outlays for agriculture. (We) eliminated agricultural, livestock and special produce taxes altogether, annually reducing the farmers' burden by 133.5 billion yuan. At the same time, (we) established a system subsidizing agriculture, giving direct subsidy to grain producers, to special-quality products, to farm equipment purchasers... comprehensively increased (budgetary) expenditures for agriculture and villages.[9]

The system of taxing agricultural producers was altogether eliminated on January 1, 2006. The income gap between the farm and nonfarm sectors keeps widening. The living standards of farmers have nevertheless risen substantially since reform began. More important, agricultural producers have regained their freedom in being masters of their own decisions and destiny. The result is that productive efficiency keeps increasing, with fewer producers producing more. There has not been a food shortage problem as during the decades under the command system. On the contrary, China's total exports of surplus agricultural produce have been on the rise. The positive consequence of reform on agriculture's functional efficiency is incontrovertible.

Industry

No private enterprise existed before reform began. The state owned the enterprises, managed them, and reaped the surplus. Productivity was low. Innovations and initiatives were either absent or scarce. After three decades under the planned system, China's industrial sector trailed far behind Japan and the four Asian Tigers. "Enlivening within" meant reducing and then removing the constraints that inhibited individual creativity, resourcefulness, and ability at the workplace. In time, reform required the nurturing of appropriate environment for fermenting productive energy and fervor.

Administratively, reform measures redefined the productive relationships among the state, the enterprise and the labor force. Departing from past practices, enterprises were to function as business concerns expected to turn a profit, actively divorcing politics and government interventions from business decisions. On the part of the state, the new slogan was "close supervision" of strategic SOEs and loosening grip on smaller ones.

Reform began with SOEs in the Sichuan province.[10] Enterprise directors and managers in the six factories were granted limited flexibility in decision making. Comparable to the responsibility system on the farms, these enterprises pledged to deliver the assigned production quotas. Production over and above the quotas belonged to the enterprises. Benefits from the sale of the surplus accrued to the management and workers. The political slogan of "crossing the river by feeling the pebbles underneath" was put into action. The outcome of the experiment was successful. Beginning in 1985, the scope of decentralizing management responsibility to enterprise level kept broadening.

The central administration was aware of the overall efficiency of the private sector over that of the state. Nevertheless, to appease the more conservative elements in the Party, ownership remained in the hands of the state during earlier stages of industrial restructuring.[11] In transitional economies in Eastern Europe, reform moved swiftly into privatizing SOEs. In China, the pace of ownership transfer was controlled. While the management supervised the operation of the SOEs, ownership remained in the hands of the state. With permission given for private enterprises to reemerge, the SOEs began experiencing the pressure of competition for the first time. Given the option of profit sharing and minimizing reinvestment in depleted or obsolete capital goods meant profits for management and workers at the expense of the asset owner, which was the state.

All SOEs were then mandated to render their respective assets transparent and corresponding rights defined in preparation for the process of privatizing nonstrategic enterprises. SOEs of varying sizes became shareholding companies. Ownership rights of nonstrategic SOEs were then transferred to the private sector over the subsequent years either through buyouts or public offering of company shares. Large, strategic SOEs remain state-owned, but boards of directors were instituted to oversee the operation and performance of these SOEs on behalf of the state.[12]

FISCAL AND FINANCIAL DOMAINS

There was no fiscal or financial independence before reform began. The central administration received all the revenues and disbursed all the expenditures according to the FYDP. Provincial and regional administrations served only as agents of the central government. Administrative decentralization in the fiscal domain began in 1980. The central administration discontinued the system of centralized revenue collection and disbursement. Provincial and regional administrations continued collecting revenues within their respective jurisdiction. However, lower-level administrations remitted only a predetermined percent of the revenues to the central administration. The residual revenue remained with the local administrations. The decentralized revenue system enhanced local administrations' attentiveness in revenue collection and disbursement. Increased responsibility in budgetary expenditures, thereby, improved fiscal efficiency for all administrative units.

Decentralization in the financial sector began in 1983 when The Bank of China officially became the country's central bank. Its focus then was on the more conventional functions of regulating money supply, charting monetary policy, and supervision. State-owned special purpose banks were granted autonomy from the Central Bank to function as commercial banks. Private banks, credit institutions, trust funds, investment banks, stock exchanges, and a host of other financial institutions began emerging, competing with the state sector. However, the state's banking sector still dominates in terms of asset capitalization. Functional efficiency in the financial sector has witnessed substantive improvement since reform began.

Nevertheless, the performance of China's state-owned banks has been mixed. As in most of the economies in transition, political connection, bribery, influence-peddling, and corruption have been prevalent. A Chinese saying "ensnare fish in muddy waters," loosely translated, means getting whatever one can before it becomes difficult. Combining connections with briberies, loss-incurring SOEs have been able to secure loans from state-owned banks with the knowledge that such loans would not be repayable. Individuals with connections also were able to secure credit lines for activities such as real estate speculations and purchasing of undervalued SOEs. One citation suffices to illustrate the anomaly that exists in the state sector of the banking industry.

> The banking system faces several major difficulties due to its financial support of SOEs and its failure to operate solely on market-based principles... Currently, over 50 percent of state-owned bank loans now go to the SOEs, even though a large share of loans are not likely to be repaid. Ernst & Young estimates that the level of nonperforming loans by Chinese banks in 2002 was $480 billion... Three out of the four state commercial banks are believed to be insolvent... Corruption poses another problem for China's banking system because loans are often made on the basis of political connections.[13]

The expectation is that, upon the completion of the transitional period for China's membership into the WTO, the growth in foreign financial institutions in China will help accelerate the continual reform of the sector in the years to come. That is, with the progression of time, China's financial system will be able to function as efficient conduits for mobilizing and allocating financial resources efficiently.

Macro Overview of Functional Efficiencies

To expedite the functioning of the centralized command system under Mao, the government appropriated all means of production, suppressed the pricing system's feedback mechanisms, reduced the number of circulation channels for both factors and products, and disregarded the objective measures for evaluating benefits or losses. Factor immobility, especially in the realms of labor and financial resources, translated into overall passivity and underperformance. The resulting structural rigidities, functional inefficiencies, and sectoral imbalances joined forces rendering the Chinese economy stagnant and listless.

Reform over the decades decentralized decision-making processes, divorcing ownership from enterprise operations. Macro coordination has replaced micro management. Respective rights and responsibilities of the central and regional administrations were redefined. Bureaucratic delays have been reduced and administrative efficiency has improved. Lower-level administrations and micro producing entities have both been granted the latitude to pursue self- interest. The result has been substantive growth in value maximization and opportunity cost minimization. Replacing central planning with market coordination has restored the pricing system as the efficient and objective measure of scarcity or abundance. Surplus capacity in heavy industry in the past in time kept declining while supply kept increasing in realms that traditionally experienced severe shortages.

Recognizing ownership rights and profit motivation have activated and energized entrepreneurial spirit and have helped actualize the potentials that have long been dormant in the productive forces of the nation. Freer mobility of resources effortlessly channels factors to where marginal value product could be maximized and wastage minimized. In the process, the aggregated dynamics translate into increased productivity, creativity, and actualization of potentials. Composition of outputs has been duly rationalized and is well aligned with objective conditions of the market. Commodity circulation channels not only have been unclogged but also have been widened, multiplied, and rendered smooth. Technical improvements and technological advances have upgraded China's ability in the product mix, adequately meeting increased demand domestically as per capita income keeps rising. Exports surged and foreign reserve soared, propelling China onto the world stage that demands attention as well as scrutiny.

On the financial front, though irregularities continue plaguing the majority of state-owned banks, the theoretical framework has at least been established for more efficacious allocation of financial resources. Objectifying flexible interest rates has helped refine the productive function of financial resources. The central bank's ability to regulate money supply and maintain financial stability and been enhanced. In brief, instruments for managing the nation's fiscal and monetary policies are now in place. With continued efforts at systemic restructuring and accompanying readjustments, both the refined instruments and their improved efficiency will be able to better promote macro compatibility on the basis of increased micro flexibility.

Since reform began, China has made the transition from being a developing country to one that is already moderately industrialized. The economic system and structure have been radically transformed from a state-determined one to one that is far more rationally and efficiently coordinated by market forces. The composition of exports has been upgraded from basic value-added manufactured goods to quality electronics, communication equipments, and computational apparatuses. The level of scientific accomplishments has been elevated to a new height, with orbiting an astronaut being the crowing showcase as of late. It successfully isolated itself and successfully weathered the Asian financial crisis of 1997. It has been more successful than other major economies in mitigating the adverse effects of the financial crisis that have gripped the world since late 2008. On the microlevel, the phenomenal increases in the number and the scale of private enterprises have surpassed the estimates of even the most optimistic of prognostics. Rapid rise of the service sector in the economy is also indicative of the success of China's economic reform. On a more tangible level, the average income rose from 419 Chinese yuan in 1979 to 22,698 yuan in 2008. Life expectancy increased from 68.6 years in 1990 to 71.4 in 2000 and now to 73.1 by 2008.

GLOBAL INTEGRATION

China has just overtaken Japan as the world's second largest economy. Reform enabled China to project its presence and relevance onto the world stage. Membership in the UN, the World Bank, and the International Monetary Funds and then the World Trade Organization increasingly pointed to China's readiness to be an active participant in the world community. The 2010 World Expo in Shanghai, following upon the heels of the 2010 summer Olympics in Beijing, all point to the reality that China is open to the outside world.

China has joined the major league as a vital player on the world stage of politics and economic affairs. It is also perceived by the governments of many developing nations, especially on the African continent, as an ally and a champion of their causes. Even world powers have to include China in their equation for bilateral or multilateral deliberations. Earlier, what China did affected mostly the Chinese people and the Chinese society. From hereon, what China does or chooses not to do will likely have a significant impact on world events and the course of world development. Visible tributes aside, more substantively, reform has brought China's economy out of its doldrums to a horizon bright with promises. From SEZs in the south to open cities northward, from rural to urban at the beginning and later channeling successes in urban centers backwards to rural, the ripples and depth of reform keep extending. At the same time, China's status on the international scene keeps augmenting, in some ways causing discomfort to traditional superpowers of the world. The guesswork now is whether or not China will in time replace the United States as the world's leading economy.

A Comparative Overview of the Performance of Select Economies in Transition

Recent decades have witnessed numerous former command-type economies undergoing systemic transformation. Among all former or current communist regimes, China led the way in introducing substantive and wide-ranging systemic reform and structural transformation.

Former centralized economies from Poland in the north, Ukraine to its east, and Romania farther south all went through the transitional process more than a decade later. From Poland's 'shock therapy' approach to the less radical but nevertheless abrupt dismantling of the old system method, the majority of transitional economies in Eastern Europe experienced severe macro dislocations and disturbances.

The rapid growth rates in Poland have been the showcase for the merits of "shock therapy" approach to systemic transformation. China began reforming its economic system in late 1979. Its approach to reform was gradualism. The merits of gradualism approach in China were already manifest before Poland began its systemic transformation in 1990. Nevertheless, the majority of the economies undergoing transition in Eastern Europe followed more of the "shock" than the "gradualism" approach in the early 1990s.

Poland's prime minister Leszek Balcerowicz adopted the undiluted "shock" approach to reform in 1991 as recommended to him by experts from abroad. For Romania, former communist dictator Nicolae Ceausescu fled Bucharest in late December 1989. The provisional government headed

Successes

Table 7.2 Select Macro Data for China, Poland, Romania and Ukraine, 1980–2008*

Year	FDI ($100 million)				GDP ($ billion)				GDP Growth (%)			
	C	P	R	U	C	P	R	U	C	P	R	U
1980	0.57	0.10			189.40				7.8			
1981	2.65	0.18			194.11				5.2		0.8	
1982	4.30	0.14			203.18				9.1		4.0	
1983	6.36	0.16			228.46				10.9		6.1	
1984	12.58	0.28			257.43				15.2		5.9	
1985	16.59	0.15			306.67	71.00			13.5		−0.1	
1986	18.75	0.16			297.83	73.89			8.8		2.4	
1987	23.14	0.12			270.37	63.88	38.07	64.10	11.6		0.8	
1988	31.94	0.15			309.52	68.82	40.42	74.70	11.3		−0.5	2.6
1989	33.93	0.11			343.97	82.21	41.45	82.70	4.1		−5.8	3.9
1990	34.87	0.89	0.0001		356.94	58.98	38.30	81.50	3.8		−5.6	−6.3
1991	43.66	2.91	0.40		379.47	76.43	28.85	77.46	9.2	−7.0	−12.9	−8.4
1992	111.56	6.78	0.77	2.00	422.66	84.33	25.10	73.94	14.2	2.6	−8.8	−9.7
1993	275.15	17.15	0.94		440.50	85.85	26.36	65.65	14.0	3.8	1.5	−14.2
1994	337.87	18.75	3.41	1.59	559.22	98.52	30.10	52.55	13.1	5.2	4.0	-22.9
1995	358.49	36.59	4.19	2.67	728.01	139.10	35.48	48.21	10.9	7.0	7.2	−12.2
1996	401.80	44.98	2.63	5.21	856.08	156.66	35.33	44.56	10.0	6.2	4.0	−10.0
1997	442.37	49.08	12.15	6.23	952.65	157.08	35.29	50.15	9.3	7.1	−6.1	−3.0
1998	437.51	63.65	20.31	7.43	1019.46	172.00	42.12	41.88	7.8	5.0	−4.8	−1.9
1999	387.53	72.70	10.41	4.96	1083.28	167.94	35.60	31.58	7.6	4.5	−1.2	−0.2
2000	383.99	93.43	10.37	5.95	1198.48	171.32	37.10	31.26	8.4	4.3	2.1	5.9
2001	442.41	57.14	11.57	7.92	1324.80	190.42	40.18	38.01	8.3	1.2	5.7	9.2
2002	493.10	41.31	11.44	6.93	1453.83	198.21	45.82	42.40	9.1	1.4	5.1	5.2
2003	470.77	45.89	18.44	14.24	1640.96	216.81	59.51	50.13	10.0	3.9	5.2	9.4
2004	549.36	127.16	65.17	17.15	1931.64	253.02	75.50	64.88	10.1	5.3	8.4	12.1
2005	791.27	103.09	64.82	78.08	2235.91	303.98	98.91	86.14	10.4	3.6	4.2	2.7
2006	780.95	198.76	113.93	56.04	2657.88	341.67	122.64	107.75	11.6	6.2	7.9	7.3
2007	1384.13	237.00	94.92	98.91	3380.00	424.79	169.00	142.72	13.0	6.8	6.0	7.9
2008	1480.00	148.00		109.00	4330.00	528.00	200.07	180.35	9.0	4.9	9.4	2.1

*C, China;P, Poland; R, Romania;U, Ukraine.
Source: http://data.worldbank.org/indicator

by the National Salvation Front in 1990 was in reality a reorganized political party with extensive connection with the Communist Party of the past. As a result, Romania was plagued by political discord and social unrest during earlier years of the 1990s. Ukraine on its part gained independence from the former USSR in 1991. From Prime Minister Valentyn Symonenko in 1992 onwards to Viktor Yushchenko in 2001, Ukraine had ten prime ministers in nine years. There was not a consistent approach to systemic reform for nearly a decade.

In varying degrees, political repression and economic deprivation characterized all four nations prior to the inception of their respective drives for economic restructuring. The background forces at play in the four countries prior to reform, however, differed.

Growth of an economy depends on the productiveness and productivity of a political entity. The rate of growth in a less developed economy usually can be faster than in a more developed one. Assumed therein is that the unrealized productive potentials in a less developed economy is more abundant than in a developed one. Under the centralized system, suppressed productive forces are understandably plentiful. That was true for all four economies under consideration.

Data presented in Table 7.2 are complete for China from 1980 through 2008. Reform in Poland began in 1990, followed a year later by Romania and Ukraine. The relevant data for Poland, Romania and Ukraine in the Table, therefore begin with the year 1991.

GDP GROWTH

Poland is heralded as the best performing economy in the EU since the current recession began in 2008.[14] When reform began, it sustained a 7.0 percent decline in GDP growth the following year. It has not experienced a GDP decrease since, although the sum of 2.6 and 3.8 percent gains in growth in 1992 and 1993 still meant a negative growth when compared with the GDP of the year prior to the inception of reform.

Performances in Romania and Ukraine were not as encouraging during the early years of their reform efforts. After nearly a decade of reform, Romania's GDP had no real growth to show when compared with the last year of Ceausescu's communist administration. There already was a GDP decline of 12.9 percent during the last year of Ceausescu's reign. Between 1992 and 1999, the hardships experienced by the newly unemployed and those on fixed income do not reveal themselves in the quasimarket system's GDPs. It is only in the twenty-first century that there has been a consistent upward movement in Romania's GDP growth rates.

Ukraine's efforts at systemic transformation were the most futile among the four economies under consideration. It suffered eight consecutive years' GDP decreases since reform began in 1992. GDP decrease was 22.9 percent in 1994 alone. The average annual growth in GDP between 1991 and 2001 was a negative 6.6 percent.[15] After nearly two decades of reform, Ukraine's GDP per capita is still below $800. Its best single year performance on the growth front was in 2004 when it scored a 12.1 percent gain. That was also the sole year when there was a double digit GDP growth rate for all these three transitional economies in Eastern Europe.

As noted, China officially began its current reform in the beginning of 1980. Not only was there not a single year when China experienced a negative growth during the past three decades, fifteen of these years scored double-digit gains in growth rates. Even when the world economies are mired in a tight grip of economic recession, China managed to maintain its annual growth rates above 8.5 percent between 2008 and 2010, both years inclusive.[16] Uninterrupted growth characterizes China's economy since reform began. Its sustained economic growth rates have no parallels in the history of world economies.

Foreign Direct Investment

The volume of investment flows into a country is indicative of, among others, political stability, returns on investment, growth potentials, and incentives such as tax holidays and tariff exemptions status provided by the host country. For any developing economy, foreign injection has always been a catalyst to growth. It not only helps create jobs, contributes to a host country's revenue but also serves as a conduit to a local economy's growth and maturation in foreign trade. China, Poland, Romania, and Ukraine were all intent on creating a favorable environment for inducing foreign investment.

Poland
As evidenced in Table 7.2, the sole Eastern European economy from which data for FDI were available between 1980 and 1990 was Poland. Despite Poland's relative proximity to Western Europe, total FDI flowing into Poland for the ten-year period between 1980 and 1989 was a minuscule $115.0 million. That is, the average annual FDI entering into Poland for that ten-year period was only $15.0 million.

Poland ranks the highest in terms of inducing foreign capital inflows among the three Eastern European economies under consideration. Poland was the first of the three countries to oust the communist regime. It was also the first to introduce systemic restructuring. Initial foreign investments flowing into Poland, as seen in Table 7.2 were tentative. Social tension was still high in 1990 and 1991. The volume of FDI began to swell after four years of attempts at systemic transformation. FDI in 1993 alone surpassed the sum total of that from 1980 to 1989. By 2008, FDI in Poland was $14.8 billion. When compared with the previous year's $23.7 billion, it was a sharp decline. The current slump in FDI is attributed mainly to the worldwide recession, especially in EU nations with whom Poland has the most of economic relations.

Romania
Growth in FDI in Romania was slow for a dozen years after the end of the communist regime. Frequent changes in central administration since 1991

and inconsistencies in reform policies failed to generate confidence in major investors from abroad. It was not until the mid-2000s that some semblance of stability and consistency emerged. It was until then when Prime Minister Adrian Nastase managed to pass significant legislations and implemented substantive reforms as Romania earnestly sought membership into the EU. It succeeded at becoming a member of the EU in 2007. As data in Table 7.2 indicate, real surge in FDI began materializing in 2004. Romania has since scored significant gains in FDI.

Ukraine
As evidenced in Table 7.2, with a population of more than 46 million, Ukraine has had little foreign capital inflow until the middle of the first decade of the twenty-first century. That is, for nearly fifteen years after gaining independence, foreign investors did not find the environment appealing for initiating significant projects therein. It was not until 2005, which was fourteen years after gaining independence, that Ukraine was able to turn the corner in inducing foreign investment. FDI in 2004 was a paltry $1.7 billion. A year later, it bounded to $7.8 billion, a 355.3 percent increase. Despite the recent global recession, FDI continues rising in Ukraine, increasing to $9.8 billion in 2007 and $10.9 billion in 2008. Whether the momentum for attracting FDI can be sustained or not depends on the government's ability to generate greater assurances for prospective foreign investors and when economic recovery in the region can take place.

China
When divided by its population in excess of 1.3 billion, the per capita FDI is not as significant. Nevertheless, China has been the most fertile grounds for FDI in recent decades. With a humble beginning of $57 million FDI in 1980, China has continuously been able to adjust the scope targeting foreign capital in search of investment opportunities. The average annual growth in FDI for the first decade of its reform was a nearly fictional 5,942.6 percent. Growth rate for all major economic variables tends to be fast at the beginning for a growing economy. For the second decade of reform, however, China's annual growth rate for FDI still scored an imposing 104.2 percent. For the nine-year period 2000 through 2008, the annual FDI growth rate was a modest 28.2 percent.

Both China's FDI and exports have achieved phenomenal successes. By the end of July 2010, the total foreign exchange reserve for the world economies as a whole was $10 trillion. Among the four economies under consideration, Ukraine had $28.8 billion, Romania $43.6 billion, and Poland $86.5 billion. Japan, which China has surpassed as the world's second largest economy and whose rapid economic recovery and growth hinged most heavily on its foreign exports, is numbered two in the world, with a foreign reserve of $1.1 trillion. China, on its part, had a foreign reserve of $2.5 trillion, accounting for 24.5 percent of the world's total.[17]

On a less optimistic side for China, the prediction for FDI in China for 2009 and 2010 was that there would be substantial decreases due to the prolonged worldwide recession. As China's rapid growth in the export sector depended heavily on the growth in FDI, it may be expected that at least the growth rate in China's export will correspondingly decrease in the near future. The challenge that China faces in inducing foreign capital inflows during the next few decades will be from India. India has a relatively small cadre of highly trained and competent high-tech personnel with whom the large foreign investors from abroad are intensely interested in. Growth in FDI in China will continue. Nevertheless, unless China succeeds cultivating a comparably competent R&D specialists within a short period of time, the more capital intensive investments from the developed economies will likely tilt in favor of India. Corollary to that scenario is that the growth in China's export will also likely begin to decline unless China upgrades the composition and quality of exports to the rest of the world markets.

A Comparative Overview of the Four Economies' GDPs

China was the first country among centralized economies to initiate systemic and structural reform. Its GDP in 1979 was $175.6 billion.[18] A decade later, it grew to $344.0 billion, a 95.9 percent increase. That is, the annual growth rate approximated 10 percent. By the year 1991, all three Eastern European economies under consideration were undergoing reform. Poland's GDP in 1991 was $76.4 billion whereas those for Romania and Ukraine were $28.9 and $77.46 billion, respectively. Between 1989 and 1991, China's GDP grew by 10.3 percent more. Another decade later, China's GDP had reached $1.3 trillion while those for Poland, Romania, and Ukraine were $190.4, $40.2, and $38.0 billion. The annual growth rate for China for the decade was 24.9 percent. For Poland and Romania, the growth rates were 14.9 percent and 6.0 percent, respectively. For Ukraine, there were no GDP gains for the entire decade. In actuality, the annual negative GDP growth was 5.1 percent.

China's combined GDP growth for the next seven years (2001–2008) was 126.8 percent. For that of Poland, Romania, and Ukraine, it was 177.3, 397.9, and 374.5 percent, respectively. That China's annual GDP growth rates have been slower than that of the other three economies in transition is because it has already entered the beginning of the fourth decade of reform. As seen in the seven-year period (2001–2008), Poland's annual GDP rates, though still rapid, already is notably behind that of Romania and Ukraine. The explanation is the same as above. Namely, growth tends to be the fastest during early stages of sustained drive for economic development. Whether Poland's annual GDP growth rates for the next decade can remain as high as that of China's third decade of reform remains to be seen.

When economic restructuring began in China 1979, China ranked tenth in the world in terms of GDP.[19] As of middle of August 2010, China overtook Japan as the second largest economy in the world. By the beginning of August 2010, according to both the World Bank and IMF, Japan's GDP was $5.07 trillion, trailed by China, which had a GDP of $4.91 trillion. According to *Bloomberg Business Week*, August 2, 2010, GDP rose an annualized 4.9 percent, less than the 5.5 percent median forecast in a Bloomberg survey of twenty-one economists.[20] According to The National Bureau of Statistics of China, "The gross domestic product (GDP) of China in the first half of 2010 reached 17.284 trillion yuan (US$2.55 trillion), a year-on-year increase of 11.1 percent, which was 3.7 percentage points higher than a year earlier."[21] By August 16, 2010, the international media announced that the second-quarter GDP growth rate of China over took Japans, the once unconceivable became reality.

Needs that Yet Accompany Successes

Aside from overall successes, there have also been notable improvements on other fronts. In his most recent report to the 17th People's Congress, President Hu noted vastly energized productive endeavors, improved safety net on farm, absence of inflationary threat, rise in per capita income, growing standing in international affairs, technological and military advances, and legal system development.

Nevertheless, incongruities and challenges remain. Despite unprecedented growth, factor productivity remains low. Per capita income has been steadily on the rise, yet unequal distribution of economic opportunities and income has left the majority of population on farm farther and farther behind their counterparts in urban centers. There is a basic frame for rule by law but democracy and political reform have not kept pace with economic liberalization. With increased integration into the world economy, competition has become a growing challenge. Exposure to foreign economies has indeed benefited China substantially over the decades; nevertheless it has also rendered the economy more susceptible to international disturbances. Despite significant gains on the technical and technological fronts, China remains technologically mediocre when compared with the more developed economies in the West. In brief, with successes, new or previous predicaments spring forth revealing anomalies and challenges side by side. China wishes to keep the growth momentum. The need for sustained efforts at reform and adjustment remains unabated.[22]

CHAPTER 8

ANOMALIES AND CHALLENGES

CHINA'S REFORM APPROACH HAS BECOME COMMON KNOWLEDGE. After three decades of reform, it has recorded unprecedented successes. The world perceives China as an awakened dragon, being projected onto the world stage as an economic, political, and military giant. General interest in China's affairs in the past has evolved into concern and apprehension. Instead of being seen as a mass of muscles with minimal constructive energies, China is seen to have transformed itself into an astute participant in the world of business and political affairs. The world sees China's systemic transformation as a success story.

All major economies and powers in world history had their eras. Upsurge emanates from an entity's deftness at seizing perceived opportunities, discarding incongruous elements from the old while adapting to the new. Downward movement is rooted in contentment with existing conditions without appropriate and timely adaptation to evolving conditions. The post-Mao leaders in China opted to adapt to changing dynamics in the globalization process. The deadweight from the old was Mao-style political dogmatism. The new was pragmatism. If it works, then shed the old and embrace the new.

Instead of Mao's penchant for "ideological purity" and idiosyncrasies, two of Deng Xiaoping's guiding principles were "seek truth from facts" and "fresh approaches to doing things."[1] The facts were that China was poor and that China was falling farther and farther behind its smaller neighbors in development. "Facts," therefore, meant tangible results rather than political hot air. However, facts also encompassed the background forces at play in China and in the world. Given the complex fabrics of the Chinese society and history, abrupt changes would invariably result in chaos. Sudden adoption of the market system would be a tacit admission of failure of the centralized system. "Fresh approaches to doing things" translated into the "one nation, two systems" notion. Elements of the new system were to be introduced on an experimental basis. Upon success, the scope of reform would be widened, and its speed accelerated and depth extended. The fundamentals of reform approach were enunciated and reform began. There have been some successes, but unexpected failures were soon encountered.

Behind the veneer of dazzling successes, however, are anomalies and emerging challenges. In a dynamic evolving environment, new successes generate new challenges and at times anomalies. Economic successes abound in China during the past three decades. Nevertheless, anomalies likewise ferment while new challenges emerge.

China's economic growth has been powered by its exports, which in turn had been energized by growth in foreign direct investment (FDI). In other words, China's economy has been increasingly woven into the fabrics of external economic relations. Prosperity abroad sustains stable growth within. Disturbances from without likewise cause ripple effects within. The world economy has been in the firm grip of recessionary spiral for two-and-a-half years since late 2007. Yet China's GDP grew by 9.0 percent in 2008. According to the National Bureau of Statistics of China, the economy in 2009 grew another 8.7 percent, only a slight decline from the previous year.[2] Thus far, China still appears to be insulated from economic turmoil abroad. However, if a robust recovery is slow in arriving from abroad, then the long-term adverse effect on China's continual reform and development could be acute. Conversely, since the world economies have been interacting more actively with China, then economic downturn in China could also adversely affect world economic order. This has been made clear by the financial crisis in the United States in late 2007. It was the crisis in the United States that precipitated the current worldwide recession. Therefore, as China continues its path toward economic growth, it must timely remove existing anomalies and effectively meet evolving and emerging challenges for economic well-being and stability of all that have a stake in it. The ensuing sections highlight select anomalies that require constant vigilance on the part of policy designers in China.

ANOMALIES ON FARM

As the scope of systemic transformation in nonfarm sectors widened and deepened beginning in the mid-1980s, the rural sector became neglected by the central government. Problems began emerging. Grain surplus led to declining food prices and reduced farm incomes. Factor costs and the cost of living kept rising, eroding farm producers' purchasing power year after year. The more widespread and pernicious woes afflicting farm producers were not caused by the market but by humans.

Village and town mayors, as a rule, were party members. They had connections. They had power. They exercised their power. The atmosphere of "getting rich quick" was sweeping the nation. The rural officials readily exhibited their aptitude in that regard. Since the local administration was responsible for providing basic services and making necessary infrastructural investments, excuses abounded for exacting charges, fees, taxes, levies, duties, fines, and obligatory contribution of labor from farmers and rural residents. One analyst described the frustration of rural folks succinctly in these words:

> The relationship between rural cadres and the public has become increasingly tenser by the day. Incidences of armed conflicts have been frequent. The farmers accuse low-level cadres of taking life ("planned" birth control and forced abortion), taking money and are shameless. The low-level cadres on their part—in order to maintain numbers (income), to assure (their) performance, to safeguard (their) jobs, to get promotions (and) to preserve continual operation (of the local administration)—impose compulsory obligations, demand money and grain, some even resort to using police to make illegal arrests. Some places (the local officials) confiscate farmers' livestock and possessions as payment for "debts" (supposedly owed to the local administrations), to the point of maliciously causing deaths. Plentiful of farmers do not trust the Party organization's local officials.[3]

As early as in March 1992, in his annual report of government performances for 1991, Premier Li Peng outlined some of the urgent tasks for the years ahead: "(We must) effectively control agricultural factor prices, resolutely end arbitrary imposition of fees or collecting unwarranted charges, (and) realistically reduce burdens borne by farm producers."[4] A year later, the Premier reported to the First session of the Eighth Congress on March 15:

> The disparity between relative prices of industrial and farm products have been widening in recent years. The rise in farm income has been slowing. Especially (troublesome), there have been pervasive practices of collecting unreasonable fees, generating unwarranted revenues (by local administrations) and assigning (to farmers) uncalled-for obligations. The burdens on farmers have been excessive, impairing the state and farmers' relationship... (We must) implement effective measures and steadfastly help resolve the problem so that the burden on farmers be strictly limited to the parameters as defined by the state.[5]

In his annual government report on March 5, 1996, the Premier Li Peng continued repeating what he had reported the previous years. He said that "(We) must pay close attention to protecting the farmers' legitimate rights and well-being." He continued to emphasize the need for "adopting genuine measures to reduce the burdens placed on farmers, (concurrently) stabilizing the farmers' income, fostering, protecting and broadening their positive attitude."[6] That Li had to repeat and reemphasize the need for reducing the farmers' burdens and protecting their well-being was sufficient evidence that abuse by local officials in rural regions continued while the central government did little to carry out its pledges.

Wen Jiabao China's current Premier took office in March 2003. Wen aimed at sustained reform on four fronts when he assumed the post. The four fronts were: state-owned enterprises (SOEs), financial markets, government structure, and agriculture. Enterprise and financial reforms were difficult. They would involve bad credits being extended to loss-incurring SOEs and to borrowers with political connections. Those with political connections were known to be raiding the most competitive SOEs, buying them at disgracefully undervalued prices. Wen was either unable or unwilling to step on the toes of the political elite who were publicly known to be deeply involved in such shady activities. The most cost-effective reform was to focus on the rural economy. Successes in rural reform would benefit the vast majority of China's rural population without risking the ire of corrupt high-level officials. Wen made known his intention to labor diligently for the improvement of living conditions in rural China.

On March 5, 2008, Premier Wen reported to the First Session of the 11th Congress that taxes on agriculture, livestock, and special produce had been eliminated. Furthermore, a system of subsidies had been established for grain producers, quality products, and purchasers of farm equipments. He said:

> ...Our (initial) point of departure was to strengthen the foundation of agriculture. (We) regarded increasing production and farm income as our primary task, adopting a series of all-encompassing measures affecting system, policy and budgetary outlays for agriculture. (We) eliminated agricultural, livestock and special produce taxes altogether, annually reducing the farmers' burden by 133.5 billion yuan. At the same time, (we) established a system subsidizing agriculture, giving direct subsidy to grain producers, to special-quality products, to farm equipment purchasers... comprehensively increased expenditures for agriculture and villages.[7]

Official statistics for 2008 listed 54.3 percent of China's population as rural. This means that nearly 900 million Chinese reside in rural areas and townships.[8] The implication is that anomalies on farm must be eradicated and that living environment must be improved for more than half of China's population still residing on farm. A few anomalies are briefly highlighted below.

Townships

First, townships constitute the core of consumer goods market for agricultural producers. Farmers' purchasing power directly affects the economies of townships. In the Premier's March 5, 2008 report, a financial burden totaling 133.5 billion yuan had been lifted from the farmers. However, the burden that was removed from the farmers were the taxes that urban and township populations never had to pay but which the farmers had been paying all along.[9]

Farm Subsidy Programs

In order to meaningfully improve the living standards of the farmers, the government has initiated farm subsidy programs. Irrigation projects, rural roads, safe drinking water, and other infrastructural support systems in recent years have all benefited from the government's endeavors at improving living conditions on farm. Nevertheless, the intent to eradicate abuses by local officials still awaits actualization. During the second working session to remedy some of the anomalies, Premier Wen addressed the participants on April 9, 2009 as follows:

> ...Resolutely resolve characteristic problems infringing on the farmers' well-being. Strengthen supervisory system in the disbursement of budgetary outlays intended to benefit the farmers, thoroughly investigate siphoning or senseless spending of funds allotted to assist the needy...severely prosecute and punish (those) exacting unlawful fees, fines...intensify education and supervision of rural cadres, diligently solving exceptional problems involving the minority of rural cadres' callous and unjust behaviors.[10]

The Premier's observation reflected and confirmed the reality that abuses perpetrated by local cadres on farms remains a serious concern.[11] To meaningfully improve the living environment and standards of more than half of China's population, therefore, it is imperative that the government nurtures and intensifies its current efforts on behalf of the disenfranchised farmers.

Macro Disparities

Perceived perils trigger intent for solutions. Acknowledged failure of the command system generated resolve for reform. Appropriate reforms yield the desired successes. China has achieved unprecedented successes. Successes, however, may likewise breed complacency. New problems and challenges sprout paralleling successes. The prerequisite for continual success is for problems foreseen, challenges forestalled, and appropriate sustained reform measures being implemented. This section delineates some of the more pronounced macro disparities for consideration by analysts.

INVESTMENT AND DEMAND DISPARITIES

China's phenomenal gross domestic product (GDP) growth has been fueled by even speedier growth in exports. Export growth has become the focus of strategists. Corresponding to economic growth, savings have been on a sustained and steady rise. Motivated by swift returns on investment, savings pour disproportionately into investments in the export sector. Exports continue growing. Yet, growth in domestic consumption trails significantly below growth in income. Increases in supplies of consumer goods on the domestic market keep falling behind the increases in income, keeping prices of consumer goods needlessly higher than warranted. High relative prices on their part help reduce consumption on the one hand and generate more savings on the other. Increased savings in turn finds ready channels, leading to further increases in investment in the export sector.

Excess investment in a sector produces sectoral imbalances. Excess investment in heavy industry under Mao made the resulting anomalies evident. The same pertains to excessive investment in the export sector. On average, domestic consumption ranges between 60 and 75 percent of a given economy's GDP. The consumption to GDP ratio tends to be closer to the higher end while it tends to be lower in developing economies and economies in transition. One study reports that China's total consumption recently accounted for only 37 percent of its GDP.[12] Successes on the export front accelerate growth in foreign exchange reserves. Rising trade deficits in developed economies generate downward pressure on convertible currencies' worth. Relative devaluation of convertible currencies engenders upward pressure for the Chinese yuan. Yuan revaluation increases relative factor costs in China that in time will usher in episodes of decline in export growth. Excess investments in the export sector, combined with slow recovery of the current worldwide recession, will then result in underutilized capital goods and parallel reduction in employment in the export sector. Unless domestic consumption substantially increases, growth in GDP will subsequently decline. For China, 1 percent loss in GDP growth can lead to loss of millions of jobs. Reduced aggregate income causes further reduction in aggregate demand, a downward spiral can set in.

Concern over likely slowdown in GDP growth rate, the central administration has embarked on massive budgetary outlays investing in infrastructural improvement and in industries. The objective was, through increased investment expenditures by the government, rise in unemployment could be prevented or mitigated.

A twofold inauspicious outcome may ensue. First, returns on investment in infrastructural buildup are less than immediate. Job loss may indeed be prevented or reduced with aggregate income remaining relatively stable. In a transitional economy, increased investment yielding no proportionate increase in the supply of consumer goods exerts pressure on prices. Inflationary pressure builds up. Second, increased government expenditure in industries enhances productive capacity. In a developed market system, increased productive capacity is induced by expected increase in demand. In China, the increase in industries is for job loss prevention and not for expected increase in demand. Growth in domestic demand has been slow. Increased production consequent upon increased productive capacity results in oversupply of goods and insufficient demand.[13] Deflationary pressure follows. On the one hand, consumer surplus increases. On the other, resources that could otherwise have been deployed in the production of higher-valued goods and services are being wastefully allocated to producing excessive supply not warranted by demand conditions. Reduced aggregated value product comes at the expense of higher opportunity costs. Less than optimum aggregated value product compromises potential GDP growth. In time, state-directed investment policy would still lead to delayed increase in layoffs. Growth in domestic demand must be one of the pivotal priorities in the immediate future for two reasons. First, unless there is changing demand conditions abroad, growth in exports will decrease. Among the needed adaptations are quality improvements and upgrading the composition of exports. Technical and technological advances that can lead to the introduction of high-tech exports are needed. Second, China's population exceeds the combined population of the United States and the EU countries. Only when steady income increases from sustained economic growth and increases in domestic consumption occur can continual growth be pressed forward.

FINANCIAL–FISCAL INCONGRUITIES

Imbalance between investment and consumption, combined with disproportionate savings flowing into the export sector, compromise potential value productivity of financial resources. It in turn adversely reduces longer-term growth potentials. Increased share in less than ideal assets in time will adversely affect stability of the financial sector. The resulting macro disturbances will consequently hold an early maturing economy in a firm grip at the expense of mostly the low income segment of the population.

Compounding the above-outlined scenario is the mounting burdens being layered on state-owned financial institutions. To prevent the rise in unemployment, budgetary expenditures are being poured into nonperforming state enterprises. There was a budgetary surplus of 1.0 billion yuan the year prior to the inception of reform. Upon the completion of the first year of reform, there was a deficit of 6.9 billion yuan. For the calendar year 2008, the negative balance was 126.2 billion yuan.

On the external sector, China's foreign debts were $145.7 billion at the turn of the century. Five years later, it grew to $281.0 billion. Still three years later, China's foreign debt climbed further to $374.7 billion. That is, between 2000 and 2008, China's foreign debt was growing at a rapid rate of 19.6 percent.[14] If foreign debt incurred had been efficiently channeled to ventures of high-potential returns, then the mounting foreign debts are justifiable and constructive. It has not been so as a considerable part of the foreign borrowings ended up being bad credits extended to nonperforming investments. Presently, rapidly growing aggregate debts, with a substantial portion being allocated to nonperforming investments, helps fuel inflationary pressure. In time, it will exact a heavy toll on future generations via increased tax burdens.

Two additional factors can adversely affect the maturing process of China's emerging market forces. First, China's rapidly soaring foreign exchange reserves have sounded an alarm among developed economies with mounting trade deficits against China. It provides ready fodder for growing concern over China's export policy. Disputes over unfair trade practices against China grow in number and in intensity. At the same time, capitalizing on being classified as a developing economy, China keeps borrowing from abroad at concessionary rates. Developed economies are less than willing to grant licenses for exports of advanced technology to China. China's own skyrocketing foreign reserves have not been able to mitigate developed economies' concern in general or "export" concerns. In view of that reality, a substantial portion of imports financed by resources borrowed from abroad theoretically could, in time, have been developed and produced by domestic resources. With reduced foreign borrowing and increased expenditures on research and development domestically, two positive outcomes could materialize. One, increased expenditure on domestic human resources concurrently increases aggregate demand. Via the multiplier effect, the economy would then grow on a more solid basis at a more sustainable level. Two, increased domestic expenditures on research and development helps grease the wheels of technical and technological advances. In time, China's export growth will be able to continue on the basis of market-driven structural changes. A greater dividend from such an approach would be the much-needed upgrading of high-tech human resources on the domestic front.

The second factor that can conceivably detract from the maturation process of the market system in China is at least indirectly caused by its mounting foreign reserves. The growth rate of China's foreign exchange reserves has been climbing at a steady and swift pace.

Over time, excess foreign reserves can pose serious threats to macro stability. For example, China's value-added exports employ mostly domestic factors of production. More competitive rates for factors secured from the domestic market means foreign earnings must be exchanged for domestic currency. The central bank buys the convertible currencies from domestic entrepreneurs. Foreign currencies enter into the central bank's vault while the Chinese yuan keeps pouring into the economic system. A reduction in the supply of yuan is caused by an oversupply of foreign reserves in the central bank's holdings. That in turn reduces the bank's ability to more effectively implement monetary policies. Viewed from another perspective, demand for yuan keeps rising relative to foreign currencies. It exerts upward pressure on the yuan in value while concurrently eroding the worth of rapidly rising supply of foreign currencies. Revaluation of the yuan renders Chinese exports relatively less competitive, with that of imports simultaneously more attractive. In time, increase in imports of either factors or products that could otherwise have been supplied by domestic sources thereby applies pressure to reduce the domestic demand for labor. A rise in unemployment can occur. It may also reduce the effectiveness of the policies for reducing unemployment. In sum, this possible scenario is the result of the rapid increases in the central bank's holdings of foreign currencies.

A second reason as to why excess foreign reserve can cause undesirable macro disturbances is rooted in expectation or speculative activities. Revaluation of the Chinese yuan relative to hard currencies had been anticipated since the late 1990s. The administration resisted pressures from the developed economies to alter the official exchange rate in favor of hard currencies as it had a direct bearing on the growth rates of China's export sector. For years, anticipation and speculation mounted. The question was not whether but when the yuan's value would have to rise relative to foreign currencies. The longer the established exchange rates remained, the greater the anticipation and the busier the speculative activities in foreign exchange markets. Demand for the Chinese yuan kept rising over time while supply for major convertible currencies steadily rose as well. The central bank ended up with increasingly more foreign reserves while drawing down the supply of Chinese yuan. The market-dictated result would be appropriate interest rate hikes. Yet, in order to prevent a rise in unemployment and to maintain high growth rates, such increases have been less than adequate. Meanwhile, the growth rates in the money supply consistently exceed that of GDP growth. M1 in 2000 was 16 percent while that for M2 was 12.3 percent. In 2008, the growth rates for M1 and M2 were 9.1 and 17.8 percent, respectively. For more than two decades, money supply invariably exceeded that of GDP growth rates every single year, sustaining inflationary pressures without relief in sight. Low interest on its part keeps fueling investment flurries, causing excess productivity capacity without corresponding increases in domestic demand. The central bank on its part has raised reserve requirements more than a dozen times in recent years. The phenomenon of monetary overhang persists, keeping inflationary pressure on without viable relief in sight.

A third reason that bulging glut in foreign reserves can seriously threaten macro stability in due time follows upon excess money supply in the system. Investment opportunity did not exist before reform began. Micro entities had neither the knowledge nor the experience in investment decisions. That is, investment by the private sector has been a relatively novel experience for enterprises and households alike. Banking, stock, and bond markets have only recently been introduced into the economic system. China lacks a well-developed, smooth functioning financial system. Deficiencies in rationalized allocation of financial resources arise from two fronts. First, nonperforming loans by state-owned banks continue. The ability of a supervisory agency monitoring financial markets' operations is still in its nascent stage. Irregularities in financial transactions have not been lacking. Second, with excess money supply in the economy, people look for promising investment opportunities utilizing household and enterprise savings. Seasoned speculators create a euphoric image of investment opportunities in stock markets. Stock prices keep rising without concurrent increases in productivities. Excess money supply from the private sector finds its way effortlessly into stock and bond markets, expecting continual upward movement in stock prices. Comparable to the collapse of the housing market and the near meltdown of the financial markets in the United States in 2008, a bubble is rapidly forming in China's financial system as well. In sum, effective policy is needed in order to reduce excess foreign reserves and to mitigate the quandary of excess money supply in the economy. One effective and constructive long-term solution that remains is to give a meaningful nudge to expand the frontier of domestic consumption.

Administrative Variances

Deng Xiaoping repeatedly stated that the centralized system was too rigid, stifling the creative energies of micro entities. Aimed at enlivening the entrepreneurial spirit of the masses, decentralization was the answer. From planned price decentralization domestically to opening up to economies abroad, decentralization also included administrative decentralization. Fiscal decentralization became part and parcel of the central administration's decentralization program. In time, privileges and responsibilities of the central administration and the provincial or regional administrations became more clearly defined. On the fiscal front, lower administrative units were individually responsible for generating and collecting tax revenues within their respective jurisdiction. Corollary to that privilege was that the same administrative units were responsible for budgetary disbursement.

Population sizes and densities differ from one region to another. So do economic foundations and pivotal economic activities therein. Some provinces and regions are substantially better endowed in industrial bases, soil fertility, resource deposits, infrastructural foundations, and climatic and geographic amenities than others. The differences, therefore, speak of relative fiscal potentials as well as developmental and social needs among the lower level jurisdictions. As an example, Shanghai, Beijing, and Chongqing are three municipalities that, like China's twenty-six provinces, are the first level administration directly reporting to the central government. The 2008 population in the three municipalities numbered 18.9, 17.0, and 28.4 million, respectively. Yet, the populations in the provinces of Qinghai and Tibet for the same year were 5.5 and 2.9 million, respectively. Shanghai is a municipality within the geographic boundaries of Jiangsu province. Beijing and Chongqing are two municipalities in the provinces of Hebei and Sichuan. Only six provinces in China have population sizes that are greater than the combined population of these three municipalities.[15] On the revenue and expenditure sides, however, the predicament for many lower level administrations emerges. The revenue for the three municipalities in 2008 was 23.6, 18.4, and 10.4 billion yuan. The respective revenues from per resident of the three municipalities were 12,493, 10,840, and 2,034 yuan. On the provincial level, the revenues for the six provinces listed above were 9.5, 27.6, 23.6, 10.1, 33.1, and 10.4 billion, respectively. The respective revenues generated per capita resident of the six provinces, therefore, were 1,356, 3,558, 2,078, 1,070, 3,468, and 1,280 Yuan, respectively.[16] The disparity in per capita income per resident of the three municipalities and the six provinces is self-evident. The revenue generated per resident of Shanghai was more than ten times that from the province of Henan, which was still higher than the 867 yuan per capita revenue generated from citizens of Tibet.

From the perspective of what each of the municipality or province can accomplish with the revenues generated from their respective jurisdiction, the poor provinces or municipalities do not come even close to what the better endowed jurisdictions can do. With decentralization, each administrative unit became responsible for providing most of the social services that used to be provided by the central government.

For comparison purposes, the per capita expenditure on residents of Shanghai by the municipality was 13,738 yuan in 2008. In the province of Henan, it was 2,525 yuan. The total expenditure by the Henan provincial administration was twice its revenues generated that year. That poorer provinces and jurisdictions do receive special budgetary allotment is clear. Even taking subsidies from the central administration into account, substantial disparities remain.

ADMINISTRATIVE DEFICIENCIES AND SOCIAL DISQUIET

Administrative decentralization means henceforth individual jurisdictions can now exercise autonomy from the central government. Aside from revenue collection, each local jurisdiction is also responsible for providing social and economic needs of citizens within their jurisdictions. Among the many needs are education, health care, social safety net, general services, agriculture, water conservancy, forestry, and environment protection.

Select services among diverse jurisdictions are given a numerical comparison. For example, the 2008 per capita expenditure by Guangdong province on education was 737 yuan. For Shanghai and the province of Sichuan, it was 1,727 and 454 yuan, respectively. Per capita expenditure to provide a social safety net in Beijing was 1,235 yuan. For the province of Shandong, it was 303 yuan. And for health care, the per capita expenditure in the province of Henan was 154 yuan. In Beijing, it was 856 yuan. The picture that emerges from contrasting these statistical disparities is that serious inequalities exist among diverse administrative jurisdictions in terms of fiscal privileges and responsibilities. This somber inequality exists even after having taken into account the subsidies that are being allotted to the less well-endowed provinces and regions.

With reform comes an opportunity. The getting rich mentality swept across the landscape. However, in rural regions that cover more than half of China's population, revenues could not adequately meet expenditure needs. Before reform began, basic services were provided by the central administration. With administrative decentralization, revenue sources for many lower level administrations were inadequate while needs were more than considerable.

Compounding the scenario is that promotions to higher appointed positions depend on success. In an era where success is measured by tangible returns, aspiring local cadres must be resourceful. The vast majority of China's population, especially those on farm, quickly learned to be resourceful. As alluded to earlier, rising factor costs and slow growth in product prices caused widening income disparity between urban and rural population. Fees, charges, taxes, fines, and a host of other creative revenue sources mushroom at the expense of the masses. With unjustifiable and at times unexplainable financial burdens being placed on their shoulders, complaints and petitions pile up at the central administration. Unable and at times unwilling to be weighed down by complaints and petitions streaming in, administrative abuses on the local level most often went unresolved.

Localized demonstrations and at times violent confrontations with authority occurred. On many occasions, security forces were deployed to quell the demonstrations. The fabric of social calm keeps tearing.

Another by-product of administrative decentralization is the proliferation of enterprises producing low-end manufactured or value-added products. Inducement for investments in export destined manufacturing nurtured increases in low-end exportable products. Provinces and regions vie for shares in export markets, duplicating investments in low-tech content industries. As competition for value-added exports grow, especially from economies like India, Vietnam, and other developing economies in the Pacific Rim the excess capacity in China's export sector may be eliminated from the global market. In brief, the potential opportunity cost of the current investment trend in decentralized administrative regions would then be high. If this materializes, then pressure will mount in the labor market that would in turn cause a chain reaction adversely impacting larger segments of the economy and society.

Administrative decentralization in itself is an essential component of systemic transformation. The anomalies that bud forth in the process nevertheless bring to light the fragility of social and political fabrics that presently exist. It concurrently suggests flaws in the legal system weak on effective and timely enforcement. A question may be raised consequent upon administrative decentralization. Is a wholesale administrative decentralization in the best interest of fostering economic growth and maintaining social and political calm?

Wrinkles in the Banking Industry

The smooth functioning of an economy presupposes a well-developed and organized financial system. It is the rationalized functioning of financial flows that can assure an efficient allocation of financial resources to accompany the real flow. Productive forces coursing through a well-oiled financial system lead to maximization of value product and minimization of loss and waste. Flaws in the system can precipitate hemorrhaging of vital forces from a healthy economy. Major flaws, if unchecked, pose serious threats to economic stability and public trust.

Evolvement of a modern financial system in China has been a recent development. Before reform began, all liquid assets belonged to the state. All assets were concentrated in the Bank of China and a few special purpose banks. In 1983, the Bank of China became the central bank. Instead of functioning as a clearing house for the state's financial transactions, it began assuming the traditional role of a central bank. In theory, the special purpose banks became independent commercial banks, reaping successes or bearing loss on their own.

With deepening of the reform process, with the exception of select SOEs deemed pivotal to national interest, other SOEs became financially independent from the state budget. Predicaments arise when SOEs incurred losses or become insolvent, which was not a rare occurrence, especially during earlier years of reform. Allowing the insolvent SOEs to bankrupt would mean further increases in unemployment, which had already become a growing social ill. The dilemma was acute since nonperforming SOEs abounded. The articulated objective in decentralization was "separation of state from enterprises." It nevertheless was easier envisioned than realizable. Key SOEs incurring losses could still expect budgetary assistance from the state. For the other nonperforming SOEs, the solution was to turn to state-owned financial institutions.

With political connections, pressures would then be exerted on state banks to extend mostly unrecoverable loans to the nonperforming SOEs. The borrowers are state-owned enterprises. So are the lending financial institutions. More explicitly stated, it is the state lending to nonperforming state institutions. On paper, the net worth of state banks still includes credits extended to nonrecoverable state institutions. In reality, traces of past practices of the state directing or interfering in enterprise operations remain. As a result, financial bubbles are in the forming in the economy.

Nonperforming SOEs are not the sole beneficiaries of nonseparation of state from enterprise performance. As alluded to earlier, expenditures exceed revenues in numerous administrative regions. A convenient solution is resorting to borrowing from state banks. With correct connections, the banks would once again be directed to extend the loans fully realizing that the probability of repayment would be less than slim. Prolonged relationships between state banks and nonperforming loans as they exist in China are the seed for a financial crisis being sown. As observed by a financial expert in China, "Presently the problems proliferate in the financial domain. They manifest themselves primarily in unrecoverable and flawed credits, financial bubbles and speculative fevers in the stock market."[17] For some time, bank insolvency can be cushioned by China's immense foreign reserves. Nevertheless, if and when the bubble does burst, then macro disturbances follow upon financial chaos. The current momentum of growth and restructuring efforts could suffer an incalculable setback.

HOUSING MARKET BUBBLES

Rapid economic growth compounded over the years, combined with repressed growth in consumption, means rapid increases in savings. According to the National Bureau of Statistics of China, China's fixed asset investment in urban centers rose by 33.1 percent during the first 10 months of 2009 alone.[18] As early as middle of 2007, savings of urban households had already exceeded 1.5 trillion yuan.[19] At an exchange rate of one U.S. dollar to 7.3 yuan by 2007 year-end, the household savings in urban centers had already reached the equivalent of $2.1 trillion. Sustained economic growth was anticipated. Household savings were to rise. There was no real estate market and there were no money and capital markets. Bank rates were low and the fever of "getting rich quick" ran high. Investment opportunities for mounting savings had limited opportunities. The social class that became rich by less than honorable means recognized a potential gold mine.

> A 1978 survey of housing conditions in 192 cities found that their combined population had increased by 83 percent between 1949 and 1978, but housing floor space had only grown by 46.7 percent. In 1978 there were only 3.6 square meters of living space per inhabitant in these cities. By 1981, living space in urban housing had increased to 5.3 square meters per person, and by 1985 the figure was 6.7 square meters... Despite this progress, scarcity of housing continued to be a major problem in the cities.[20]

All real estate properties had been nationalized during early years of the Mao era. When reform began in 1979, all land and building structures were state assets. Land-leasing programs began. The industrial and service sectors in urban centers remained under the umbrella of the old system. Eventually, real estate development companies began emerging in major cities. Nanning Real Estate Development Company of China Real Estate Development Group was founded in late 1981.[21] However, there was no enterprise savings since all enterprises were still "owned by all the people." There was also no meaningful household savings. The title "Real Estate Development Group" means there were a number of development companies. Yet, during early years of reform, the enterprises were enterprises and not companies. Who were authorized to form these companies while no companies as such existed at that time? Also, where did the initial investment come from? These are some of the preliminary unanswerable questions.

The formation of the earliest real estate development company in modern China was approved by the State Council on January 16, 1981.[22] Since its formation was sanctioned by the State Council, it also meant that partners of the enterprise had "connections." On another front, population densities in major urban centers have always been high. There was no vacant land to be found in locations of choice in major cities. Real estate development had to resort to the state's exercising of its eminent domain rights. Municipal authorities exercised the eminent domain privilege in the name of development. What motivated the authorities to develop which part of a given city was less than transparent. With some compensation, households in blocks after blocks of the city were ordered to move. Tens of thousands of inhabitants in select districts were relocated or displaced. Often, the cost of the newer housing units exceeded the compensation given. The variance between compensation and cost for a new housing unit was a function of how feverish the housing market was at a given time.

Similar to other major reform measures, experimental sites for marketizing the housing industry included several southern cities that included Hainan, Beihai, Guanzhou, and Shenzhen. A mortgage system was established in these experimental cities.[23] The phenomenal urban transformation in Shenzhen impressed Deng immensely during his 1992 southern inspection. His observation quickly became the ignition point for the housing market. Housing bubbles quickly formed. However, during Premier Zhu Rongji's southern inspection the following year, he recognized the nearly bursting bubble of housing market in Hainan. He ordered an immediate cessation to bank lending.[24] As real estate industry has been an integral and pivotal ingredient in economic growth, a nationwide mortgage system came into existence by 1997.

In the early 1980s, household savings in urban centers comprised of mainly cumulative savings of several generations. Given the high population-to-housing-floor space ratio, early phase of real estate development meant partly in housing units and partly in structures such as hotels, public service buildings and the like. No bubble was in the forming. As the economy entered into the decades of rapid growth, however, both enterprise and household savings correspondingly rose. The population had few investment options.

> Chinese citizens have poured their life savings into speculative real estate. This is not just misallocation; it is an inescapable capital trap. China's citizens have few options for investing their immense savings. Chinese households are prodigious savers: China boasts a savings rate of 38%, fully ten times that of the U.S. But Chinese savers have few choices on where to invest their money: they can either leave it in a savings account which draws 2.25%, less than the inflation rate of 3.1%, or invest in real estate or domestic stocks.... The money pouring into property has created a worrisome asset bubble in housing, which rose 12.4% year-on-year in May, according to China's National Bureau of Statistics.... Chinese authorities' attempts to cool the housing market have so far yielded little result. With no other choice of where to put their savings other than domestic real estate and the volatile Chinese stock market.[25]

The average household saver possesses neither the knowledge nor the experience of investing. Leaving money in the bank means either minimal or even slightly negative returns. What the average saver is inundated with is the news of rapidly rising housing costs. Fanned by the media, the fever to invest in housing progressed from zeal to frenzy. Despite the still low person-to-floor space ratio, the housing market has been more than saturated for years for two main reasons. First, housing prices keep rising. Households that could not afford purchasing new and more spacious housing units till now can no longer afford the current housing prices. Urban citizens who have not yet purchased new housing units lacked the means for housing purchases. The simple explanation is that the mass off-farm migration that crowds urban centers does not translate into rising demand for housing units. The Central Bank of China issued a communiqué granting permission to commercial banks to extend mortgage loans to credit-worthy patrons. It was through state intervention from 1998 onward that the growth in the housing market accelerated.[26]

> With the institution of the mortgage system, the housing market boom accelerated. The peaks and troughs of real estate development followed political decisions. For instance, the year 1998 was a landmark year for China's real estate industry. The dividing line was the first six months and the ensuing six months. Many developers found (the housing development) environment inhospitable. They hurried retreated from the market. By the second half of 1998, however, policy began changing. A series of stimulus packages aimed at enlivening the real estate industry burst onto the scene. One of such policies was the practice of an enterprise providing housing facilities for workers. That is, persons in need of housing units must obtain them through the market. The units that could not be sold off before were snatched off the market in no time. At the same time, financial and tax policies concurrently created an atmosphere favorable to real estate development. Interest rates kept falling while down payment also saw substantial decreases.[27]

The total value of outstanding mortgages in 1998 approximated $51.7 billion. In 2003 it had reached more than $1.45 trillion, with China Construction Bank being the largest provider of mortgage lending.[28] The price for one square meter of housing space in Shanghai ranged between 3,000 and 4,000 yuan in 1999. The following year, it increased to between 6,000 and 7,000 yuan. By 2004, the cost soared to 20,000 yuan per square meter. The average monthly salary at that time was 2,000 yuan. Yet, the former Party Secretary General of Shanghai Chen Liang Yu insisted that "Shanghai's real estate market has consistently been on the right track. No bubble exists."[29] Lacking channels to invest, the average citizen with savings and borrowing capacity pours all his or her available resources into the housing market.

The mass media recognized that the housing bubble in China was directly linked to the municipal government of Shanghai. The February issue of *Finance*, a periodical published in China, pointed out that:

> The (municipal) government's role in Shanghai's real estate market is both pervasive and deep-seated. Some district administrations enter the primary real estate market directly; "selling" land use and thereby reaping colossal benefits. In addition, they vie to establish housing development companies. These companies then secure choice locales from the authority at cut-rate prices. The same companies control all stages of development—from land development to demolition of existing structures, and from building construction to marketing—thereby securing monopoly profit.[30]

To what extent public servants are involved in housing market development is beyond the scope of this manuscript. Nevertheless, that the authority's role in creating the housing market situation is present may be gleaned from two citations.

> The Chinese authorities have printed and instructed the banks to make loans for shopping malls, apartment buildings, office towers, and condo towers...their $585 billion (yuan) stimulus package was used to build entire cities that sit unoccupied. The 2.2 million-square-foot South China Mall, with room for 2,100 stores, sits completely vacant.[31]

And,

> ...an economist at the Chinese Academy of Social Sciences noted estimates from electricity meter readings that there are about 64.5 million empty apartments and houses in urban areas of the country! This number is five times larger than the roughly 12 million in total US public (3.89 million) and shadow (8 million as estimated by Morgan Stanley) home inventory available currently.[32]

Then, as the central administration contemplates property tax reform, sales of real estate fell by 70 percent in Beijing and Shanghai in the most recent months of 2010.[33]

One final irony that merits mentioning is that many average citizens in major urban centers purchase housing units not for occupancy but as an instrument for gambling.[34] Bubbles cannot sustain continual expansion. Otherwise the sole outcome would be a sudden burst similar to the mortgage market collapse in the United States and the subsequent financial crisis that followed in late 2007. China has just overtaken Japan as the world's second largest economy. The impact of a housing market collapse and a possible financial market meltdown in China would not be as severe as the one in the United States. Its potential adverse impact on its neighboring economies could be incalculable. The most severe loss would then be borne by citizens who have invested in the housing markets. Extensive default would then in turn impact China's financial institutions. The domino effect then would be a scenario that is best left to the imagination.[35]

STOCK MARKET BUBBLES

Financial instruments are created, develop, and adapt to changing market conditions for mobilizing and channeling financial resources. Interacting and interdependent instruments form an operational system. A smooth functioning system operates according to rules and regulations, effectively and efficiently coursing financial instruments for value maximization. In monetary terms, value is a function of consumer needs and wants. In less readily quantifiable terms, value is a function of overall social well-being and advancement as well. A well-oiled financial system serves to benefit society and its constituents. A flawed one detracts from the fundamental purpose of the system. The meltdown of the financial system in the United States that was caused by massive mortgage defaults and operational irregularities in the system precipitated adverse effects worldwide. A similar commotion in its financial system will inevitably yield similar tremors. Speculations abounded as to when China would overtake Japan as the world's second largest economy. It was not a speculation over if but when. On August 15, 2010, the *New York Times* issued a breaking news alert:

> After three decades of spectacular growth, China has passed Japan to become the world's second-largest economy behind the United States, according to government figures released early Monday. The milestone, though anticipated for some time, is the most striking evidence yet that China's ascendance is for real and that the rest of the world will have to reckon with a new economic superpower.[36]

No financial market existed in China prior to the current reform. The system that has been developed is in its nascent stage. Flaws and weak linkages exist among components within the system. The primary investment outlets for average household savers include banks, stock and bond markets, and insurance and trust funds. No commodity market has evolved in China. Nor have money markets, derivatives, futures, and foreign exchange markets. A host of resources that are freely traded via financial markets in developed economies are still in the hands of the government.[37] Channels for coursing private savings, therefore, are both few and still in their developing stages.

Average household investors in developed economies invest in listed companies that either possess a record of quality performance or have illustrated growth potentials, or both. In China, the predicament emerges as strong demand for investment opportunities is faced with few investment options. As previously mentioned, the overwhelming majority of household savers possess neither the knowledge nor the experience in making prudent investment decisions in a system that is fundamentally volatile. The novelty of a stock market in China has become a gold mine for feeding the greed of those with the means to exploit. On the part of average savers, the dream of getting rich appears to be realizable. Intermittently, returns on investments in housing appeared attractive. Among the drawbacks of investing in the housing market are large sums of down payments that are required, nonliquidity of the assets, maintenance costs, and potentially nonresponsible tenants. Alternatively, the stock market becomes more attractive.

Presently there are more than a hundred million share holders in China, surpassing even the 76 million in the United States in 2007.[38] China currently has two stock exchanges: Shanghai Stock Exchange and Shenzhen Stock Exchange. Both were established in late 1990. Within a year, there were a total of 1625 listed companies, with 864 in the Shanghai exchange and 761 companies in Shenzhen exchange.[39]

In theory, stock price should reflect share value. Without the unavoidable speculative activities, relative stability in share price should prevail. In China, this relative stability has been absent. The following historical data provide an overview of the tumultuous cycles in China's stock market that began when the two exchanges were first established in late 1990.

There are twelve cycles that may be identified by the peaks and troughs in China's stock market. (1) The base was 100 points on December 19, 1990. It increased to 1429 points by May 26, 1992, a 1,329 percent increase in half a year. The composite index then fell below 400 points by November 16, 1992, a 67 percent plunge. (2) Then, from 400 points in 1992, it soared to 1537 points on February 15, 1993. By July 29, 1994, it plummeted to 334 points. (3) From 333 points on August 1, 1994, the index rose increased to 1,053 points by September 13 that same year. That is, it was a 215 percent increase in approximately a 40-day period. Then, it fell to 513 points by January 1 of 1996. (4) From January 19, 1996, the index rose from 500 points to 1510 points by May 12, 1997. By May 15, 1999, it fell back to 1047 points. (5) Thereafter, the index climbed to a new height of 1756 on June 30, 1999, only to decline to 1361 points on January 4, 2000. (6) Nearly a year and a half later, on June 14, 2001, the market gained 65 percent reaching another new peak of 2245 points. (7) Nearly four months later, the index swiftly dropped to 1515 by October 22, 1001. (8) It decreased further to 1339 by September 13, 2004. It fell below 1000 to 998 points on June 6, 2005. (9) By June 2005, it breached the 1000 mark. Beginning with 1200 points from January of 2006, the index began trending upward once again, reaching another new high of 3300 points on April 6, of 2007.[40]

(10) Another round of speculative fever materialized during the latter part of 2007. Speculators inundated the stock market, rendering China's stock exchange as the world's second largest for a brief moment. Fearing the bubble could soon burst, the government intervened to temper the fever, causing violent fluctuations. (11) The market reached a historical high of 6124 points on October 16, 2007. Shanghai's Composite Index then plunged by 65 percent by 2008 year-end. In 2007, a "stock market frenzy" pervaded, as speculative traders rushed into the market, making China's stock exchange temporarily the world's second largest in terms of turnover. Fears of a market bubble and intervention by authorities caused large fluctuation not seen since the past decade.[41] And, (12) the moving average for the month of August was 2627 points for 2010.[42]

The volatility of the China's stock market may be viewed from yet another perspective. The P/E (price/earning) ratios for shares in the two exchanges in 2007 were 59.2 and 69.7, respectively. Severe downturns were experienced in subsequent years. However, the ratios declined precariously to 14.9 and 16.7, respectively, a year later.[43]

The virulent cycles speak eloquently of the speculative fever that has gripped the household savers since the inception of stock market exchanges. The inopportune reality is that the "get rich quickly" mentality has been more than contagious, especially among the younger generation. Recognizing the high risks associated with speculating in a still immature stock market system, the risks takers continue their dreams of striking rich quickly. Without adequate knowledge and experience, waves of massive wealth redistributions follow upon the heels of peaks and troughs of each of the cycles. The gainers get richer and the average investors get poorer with each round of the cycle.

One major contributing factor to the bulging stock market bubbles is the low quality of enterprises that have managed to gain permits for public listings. According to one study, the annual reports provided by 1,344 listed companies in 2006 revealed that (1) the stock holders' equity that was less than zero was in 3.9 percent of the companies; (2) the adjusted net asset per share was less than zero in 4.6 percent of the companies; (3) the net profit that was less than zero was in 18.2 percent of the companies; (4) profit after deduction of the nonrecurring items was less than zero in 27.1 percent of the companies; (5) cash flow was less than zero was in 19.2 percent of the companies; (6) net increase in cash and cash equivalent was less than zero was in 54.9 percent of the companies; and, (7) return on equity that was less than zero was in 15.1 percent of the companies. According to international standards for sanctioning public offerings, nearly 70 percent of China's listed companies would not qualify.[44] Yet, even shares from loss-incurring listed companies can find ready markets for the simple reason that the demand is high. The inexperienced persons trading in stock market still entertain the dream that "buy low, sell high" would either bring them a fortune overnight or help them recover the losses already incurred.

Yet another factor contributing to the market's flaw is the government's role in the stock market. As of 2007, of the seven state banks whose shares are listed on the stock market account for nearly one third of total market value of the entire stock exchange. These banks carry combined unrecoverable loans totaling in excess of 600 billion yuan.[45] Furthermore, in Shenzhen Stock Exchange for instance, the government holds a controlling interest in listed shares. The exchange is viewed as a mine for mobilizing capital for the state and there has been no indication that the government intends to privatize or see off the state's controlling shares.[46] In addition, as briefly alluded to earlier, many of the key resources are held by the state and not available for trading. Land and mineral resources, for instance, are important factors in economic activities. Yet, their allocation is not according to market conditions accurately reflecting relative scarcity or abundance but according to the governments diktats. Alternately interpreted, no objective valuation system exists for these key variables. The stock market, therefore, is unable to fulfill its broad function of efficiently allocating resources for value maximization.[47]

A final observation pertinent to the topic of stock and housing market bubbles is the central bank's monetary policy. Growth in the money supply should be the function of growth in GDP. In decision making, the central bank implements policies independent of political interference. Loose or tight monetary policies are intended for maintaining price and growth stability or for forestalling disturbances. In China, the supply of M2 consistently exceeds that of GDP growth by a significant margin. For instance, during the first year of the stock market's operation, the GDP grew by 9.1 percent in 1991, while money supply grew by 26.5 percent. The stock market composite grew by 1,429 percent. The GDP growth for 1994 was 13.1 percent. The money supply increased by 34.5 percent and the stock market gain went from 333 points on August 1, 1994 to 1053 points by September 13 that same year. And inexplicably M2 grew by 47 percent within a 20-month period between yearend 2008 and early August 2010.[48] That such a monetary policy is based on sound economic rationality is questionable at best. To what extent the central bank's modus operandi is influenced or dictated by political decisions is a subject worthy of further studies.

A more cogent issue concerning stable economic growth and social wellbeing is whether macro policies based on political decisions is in the best overall interest of the nation in the longer run. The issue of price stability aside, if monetary policy is being implemented primarily for influencing housing and/or stock market activities, then the average household investors are being preyed upon redistributing wealth from many to a few. In a time when augmented domestic consumption is a crucial factor for sustained economic growth in China, such macro policies merit reconsideration.

WTO Challenges

The WTO was founded on the principle of free trade among economies agreeing to abide by the rules and regulations of the organization. Accession into the world organization broadens China's frontier for market integration into the world economy. It means accelerated systemic reform. It also means needed adjustments in the state's role in economic affairs. A time table was set forth between the WTO and China for implementing the needed changes, including transparency in government policy pertaining to both internal and external markets. Two primary domains become subject to challenges consequent upon being admitted into the WTO: political and economic.

On the political front, the WTO may challenge China's policies and modus operandi pertaining to foreign trade and domestic commerce. Therefore, since the founding of the People's Republic of China in 1949, this is the first time that a foreign organization may monitor, question and contest China's trade and business policies if infractions of the WTO rules and regulations should occur. Second, beginning in 2001, during the five-year transitional period granted to China, the existing laws and decrees, directives and operational procedures that are incompatible with the WTO charter must be amended, abolished, or rendered more transparent. Laws for foreign and domestic economic relations must be in sync with accepted international norms, mitigating the influence of political decisions on economic affairs. If such laws do not as yet exist, then new laws need to be adopted and promulgated within that five-year transition period. Furthermore, during a twelve-year transitional period, as alluded to in chapter 5, if Chinese exports to a host economy pose a threat to domestic producers, then challenges may be filed with the WTO against China for unfair trade practices. Thus, it is also the first time that China has agreed to be subjected to WTO arbitration when occasions should arise.

On the economic front, numerous challenges face China as a member of the WTO. In the longer run, it is to the benefit of China's economy and to the Chinese society to become more fully integrated into the tapestry of world affairs. For the more immediate future, however, the markets for many industries and institutions will face challenges of varying degrees.

Articles of agreement to accession to the WTO require that existing trade barriers or restrictions are to be removed. That includes restrictions on foreign communication equipment imports, mass media, Internet services, and the like. Communication and mass media has always been a potent instrument for promoting government causes and ideology. With the entry of foreign capital, foreign technology, foreign organizational and operational knowledge in communication and mass media industries, the communication industry in China will face severe competition. The effectiveness and scope of influence of government owned and operated media, therefore, will inevitably be compromised.

On the technological front, China has made significant strides since reform began. Nevertheless, China's level of technology pales when compared with dynamic technological advances constantly being achieved by some of the more developed economies. The tech content of China's growing industrial exports is also low. As an example, the growth in exports of China's manufactured goods such as color TV sets, computing equipments, and DVDs has been notable. Many key components of these products, nevertheless, have either to be imported or licensed by patent holders abroad. In addition, the majority share of such exports is either produced by foreign capital firms or firms with foreign interest in China.[49] China's R&D capacity also pales in comparison with that in the developed economies, especially when contrasted with research facilities in the United States, Japan, and some of the EU countries. The explanation is simple. Returns on established high-tech companies are high. Profit margins for lower-level tech exports are significantly lower. Most of the R&D activities in developed economies are financed by earnings from advanced high-tech products. The financially less well-endowed tech companies in China are also less empowered in talents and facilities. With China's meteoric rise on the world stage there is also an increase in the degree of apprehension on the part of developed economies. Tech leaders like the United States, Japan, and EU countries are likely to be more reluctant to export high-tech components to China. In addition, with membership in the WTO, capital-intensive research firms in developed economies can more freely enter into China. They will be able to compete vigorously for talents in China with their advanced equipments and lucrative remuneration. With still relatively inexpensive labor cost, the products from these foreign firms can then market both domestically and internationally at highly competitive prices. Moreover, mergers, acquisitions, and similar tactics on the part of foreign capital can slice deeply into China's intent of fostering a high-tech research force that can compete more effectively with other economies. The pace of China's drive for fostering a viable R&D foundation is likely to be slowed down as a result.

Another front that can expect serious challenges from injection of foreign interest is China's banking and insurance industries. According to agreements with the WTO, China promised to permit financial institutions including banks, insurance, and investment firms wholly owned by foreign interests to freely enter the country by 2005. Presently, the four largest banks in China are the Industrial and Commercial Bank of China (ICBC), the Agricultural Bank of China, the Bank of China, and the China Construction Bank. ICBC is the largest bank in the world today in terms of capitalization. All state-owned banks are commercial banks, with shares owned by corporations, households, and foreign investors. It is the state's share of ownership in these banks that enthroned its stake in the management decision-making position. Though commercial in nature, the state's four largest banks are plagued by nonperforming loans that require periodic recapitalization by the government:

> At the end of 2004, 19.1% of ICBC's portfolio consisted of non-performing loans...In order to clean up ICBC's balance sheet (alone) and prepare it for overseas listing, the Chinese government orchestrated a series of capital injections, asset transfers, and government-subsidized bad loan disposals that eventually cost more than US$162 billion.[50]

Inexplicably, "In 2005, non-performing loans by ICBC (alone) totaled $154.4 billion."[51] That is, a year after the government's massive injection into ICBC in 2004 to clear up the nonperforming loans, only a year later the bad loans climbed right back to nearly the same amount as a year earlier. Yet,

> In 2006, the total amount of non-performing loans was estimated at 160 billion USD...The financial sector is widely seen as a drag on the economy due to the inefficient state management. Non-performing loans, mostly made to local governments and unprofitable state-owned enterprises for political purposes, are a big drain on the financial system and economy, reaching over 22% of GDP by 2000, with a drop to 6.3% by 2006 due to government recapitalization of these banks.[52]

The five-year transitional period granted to China by the WTO ended five years ago. Foreign banks are now permitted to conduct business in Chinese yuan, servicing domestic businesses and consumers. Entry of foreign banks and insurance companies that are well-organized, experienced, and efficient can pose serious challenges to state-owned domestic banks.[53] The challenge to the government is whether or not to continue subsidizing the state-owned banks by underwriting nonperforming loans extended mostly to nonperforming SOEs and local governments. The challenge is whether the state is prepared to oblige the less efficient SOEs to undergo the test of market forces by having them either privatized or be eliminated from the market by competing forces. The challenge is whether the state is intent on deepening reform for improved efficiency or be more concerned with the rise of unemployment consequent upon reorganization of nonperforming SOEs. With entry into the WTO, the challenge is whether economic rationale can prevail over political predilections.

The final topic that the current discussion addresses concerns the agricultural sector which China's farm producers are to face consequent upon China's accession into the WTO.

By 2008, 54.3 percent of China's population was categorized as rural, although only 33.2 percent of economically active population was classified as in tertiary activities.⁵⁴ In 2008, 306.6 million Chinese were engaged in tertiary economic activities. Total cultivated land area was 121.8 million hectares. The average cultivated land area per tertiary economic activity was 0.9 hectare.⁵⁵ Tertiary economic activities go beyond just farming. They also include animal husbandry, fishery, quarrying, forestry, and mining. Therefore, the average cultivated land area per farmer would be more than 0.9 hectare. Nevertheless, it points to a serious land fragmentation problem. Economies of scale cannot be realized, resulting in lower factor productivity and relative higher product prices.

Entry into the WTO requires a reduction in farm subsidy, a reduction in tariffs, and, as a result, significant increases in agricultural imports. The fronts of challenge to China's agricultural sector are bounteous.

All developed economies protect their farm sector within the prescribed rules of the WTO. Wherever and whenever reasons or pretexts can be found, imports of agricultural products are deflected. The world economy continues to grow while consumer preferences correspondingly modify. Health concerns give rise to product quality, safety, and varieties. China's agricultural exports are mostly routine items. Relatively low-quality produce from abroad are faced with increased and increasing standards for food imports imposed by developed economies. Instances of unsafe agricultural exports from China have raised the level of apprehension on the part of importing economies.

On the domestic front, better quality imports that can be purchased at more competitive prices implies possible decreases in demand for domestically produced farm produce. Income disparity between farm and nonfarm will rise. That can translate into a rising level of underemployment and disguised unemployment on farm. More off-farm migration then leads to an increased pressure on urban unemployment, which still is a somber social issue. Given the high percent of China's workforce remains agricultural, the challenge to the state is that accession to WTO requires more decisive and fundamentally more extensive policy measures to ensure the well-being of a large segment of China's society.

In brief, China's entry into the WTO does bring with it a host of practical challenges that an already heavily engaged central administration must face. The long-term benefits hold vast promises. Short- and medium-term complications arising from WTO membership are manifold. Managed well, stability and sustained growth will prevail. Otherwise serious disorder and disruptions can either help delay or derail the state's current drive for continual reform and development.

CHAPTER 9

CONCLUDING OBSERVATIONS

A GOVERNMENTAL SYSTEM IS A COMPLEX ORGANIZATION that is comprised of interacting, interdependent parts that continually evolve. The interdependent parts include: the social system, the political system, the economic system, the value system, and the belief system. These systems in a society create a culture that in itself keeps evolving. No system or society is ever perfect. Evolution over time, on its part, engenders a quasinewer system that can become either less imperfect or more flawed. In an ascending movement, new weaknesses and challenges also surface. Accompanying the new weaknesses and challenges are opportunities for sustained improvements or the prospect of degeneration.

Since its founding in 1949, modern China has evolved from a socialist system to a fully communist paradise. The path to the envisioned paradise was to suppress interaction and interdependence of all the parts within its system. As a result, each part became dependent on the state. There was to be no interaction between individuals or the state. Instead, it was to be a one way communication from the state to individuals. To ensure that the outcome would be as the state envisioned it to be, social, economic, cultural, and value systems were all further subsumed under a political system that was commandeered by an autocratic ideologue. The outcome of the three decades of efforts proved to be less favorable than anticipated.

Being the largest country in the world, China was falling farther behind its smaller neighbors. In the process, high opportunity costs in addition to immeasurable human costs had incurred. As a result, reform began. The avowed objective from Deng Xiaoping in 1979 to Hu Jintao in 2010 has been to establish a democratic socialistic system. The concrete manifestations of a democratic socialist system, however, have yet to be elucidated.

The approach to developing a democratic socialistic society is circumscribed within the parameters prescribed by the state. On the economic front, paced gradual decentralization, and supervised liberalization would in time lead to a relatively uninhibited interacting and interdependent economic system. Politics is still in command, as it was under the Mao decades. The intensity of command, however, is less intimidating.

The economic model Deng devised was "one nation, two systems." It was intended to portray China as one nation with two economic systems: state-directed and market-coordinated. Hong Kong was scheduled to be returned to China by 1997. Hong Kong was to represent the market-coordinated system without government intervention. The reform program in China itself was to be under the leadership of the state. Economic reform has indeed been directed by the state, progressively devolving into a market-coordinated and market-driven structure.

In reality, the "one nation two systems" model may perhaps be more appropriately ascribed to the two systems, of which one is economic and the other political. Economically, the system is market-coordinated, but is being shaped by political dictates. The political system remains under the tight control of the Communist Party. The "democratic" portion of the phrase "democratic socialism" in practice means ultimate authority residing in the majority decision of Politburo members of the Communist Party. Membership in the Politburo is not by election, but by nomination from the existing Politburo. There are no free elections. High administrative offices are generally held by high Party officials. Instead of the government being elected by and representing the will of the populace, the Party leadership dictates to the general public what the "will of the people" is or should be.

In China, the line between the Communist Party leadership and the government is a nearly invisible thread. The decision to introduce measures of systemic transformation originated from Party leaders. The timing, scope, and sequencing of reform measures also originated from the Party leaders. Therefore, the political decisions that are reached by the Politburo are invariably translated into state policies.

After nearly three decades of Mao's authoritarian reign when social, economic, and value systems all became fossilized under one political system, economic reform injected a breath of fresh air. Opportunities began appearing. Labor mobility became feasible. Enterprise management was empowered to make operational decisions independent of a centralized Plan and entrepreneurial spirit was encouraged and duly rewarded. Economic freedom is what was accorded. Creative energies were all channeled and directed toward maximizing economic returns. However, the "socialist" aspect of democratic socialism somehow faded into the background. Instead, the "getting rich quick" mentality pitches forward, supplanting the ideal of working toward the well-being of society as a whole. The present societal fabric is weaved with a liberalized economic system under the well-circumscribed supervision of state directives. So long as there is no apparent menace or challenge to the central authority, limited interactions socially and culturally are permissible. However, no large-scale organized defiance of either the Communist Party or the state would be tolerated.

Three decades of sustained rapid growth adds a new chapter into the annals of economic history. A new chapter in the discipline of developing economies is in progress. A possible lesson may be learned from China's experience with systemic transformation and economic development. The relevant question is: what are the likely ingredients for China's apparent successes?

China's rapid growth began with increased economic opportunities granted to select economic activities and geographic regions. Growth has been propelled by unparalleled expansion and growth in the export sector. That in turn has been energized and sustained by substantive capital infusions from abroad. The ensuing question presented here is: what might be the key variable that has made China a prime market for foreign investments?

The notion or theory that is being proposed in this brief treatise emanates from a cursory examination of a few historical instances. The thesis is as follows: at least during the early stage of systemic transformation or early phases of economic development, if rapid economic growth is the objective, then a stable social and political environment must prevail with a strong administrative leadership. Emphatically maintained herein is that under no circumstance does this thesis propose that economic values take precedence over social and political values.

As discussed in chapter 6, it is political stability and social calm that helps gain the confidence of prospective foreign capital. Statistical analysis provided in chapter 6 affirms that foreign investment and export growth are significantly related. The GDP growth is in turn highly correlated with export growth, especially in this era when the train of globalization process keeps accelerating.

There are differences in the degrees of relatedness among the four countries being compared. However, the amount of variance explained by the models differs only insignificantly. This may be explained by the background forces at play in each of the four countries. The background forces that need to be taken into due consideration when explaining the observed slight variances include the following: historical, cultural, social, political, and economic variables. Having these background forces taken into due account, then the slight variances may converge into or even approach proximate synchronization.

Tight political control has a direct bearing on the environment for foreign capital inflow. In turn, FDI and export capabilities directly impact GDP performance. The varying degrees of effect that political rights have on GDP growth in the four countries surveyed may be explained by the fact that the people of Ukraine and China have had less experience with self-governance. Ukraine had been under foreign dominance for centuries until it gained its independence in 1991. The people of China, on the other hand, had been under imperial rules for centuries. Tight political control has been a way of life for the people of both countries. Given where freedom is permissible, that is also where creative energies flow. Political rights are scarce. Economic freedom within the confines of prescribed boundaries and tight political controls, however, does translate into economic initiatives and performances.

The relative absence of relatedness between political rights, FDI, and GDP in Poland may be explained by the force of cultural values held by the people of Poland. Historically, Poland had been a proud country due to its military power in Europe two centuries back. Individualism and independence are cultural values that have been deeply engraved in the hearts and minds of the Polish people.

> Even when its statehood was denied (by foreign invaders), Poland always existed and survived in the hearts and souls of the Polish people. "While we live, she exists"—the beginning of the Polish national anthem eloquently attests to the will of its people for an independent Poland.[1]

Therefore, whether political rights are officially granted or not, they have always been taken for granted and are exercised in whatever manner achievable. Consequently political rights are not a significant predictor for the current development scenario in Poland.

Finally, the fact that political rights are a significant predictor in Romania, even though indirectly, may also be explained by some of the background forces that were alluded to earlier. Not as fiercely independent-minded as the Poles, the Romanians are nevertheless gifted in capitalizing on whatever rights that have been made available to them.

> For the nobles, in the wake of declining Turkish powers and the rising influence of the Habsburgs in the region, economic gains and political expediency typically guided their respective courses of action. Aligning themselves with the Turks, or pledging allegiance to the Habsburgs, the nobles" primary concern remain the maintenance or the increase of personal gains at the expense of the peasants.[2]

Political rights being a significant predictor only indirectly in Romania may also be partially explained by the fact that Romania has historically been a thoroughfare of commerce for neighbors to the west, north, and south. The economic initiatives of microeconomic entities have been more independent of given political environment, with more or less political rights granted. As a result, political rights for individuals affecting the country's economic performance indicate a less strong correlation than that in either China or Ukraine.

Economies that Succeed

There are prerequisite conditions for economies to perform well during the early phases of economic restructuring. Otherwise, undesirable consequences may ensue. The absence of political rights and civil liberties can lead to undesirable conditions. The first subsequent section presents four administrations where successes are evident. Four others will be presented later where little or no political rights exist but economic performance has been dismal.

The hypothesis suggested in this study emanates from a cursory review of four historical personages whose firm grips on their respective economies have helped restore these economies to respectable and international recognitions. The four instances cited below pertain to Taiwan's Chiang Kai Sheik, Singapore's Lee Kuan Yew, South Korea's Park Chung-hee, and Russia's Vladimir Putin.

Taiwan's Chiang Kai Sheik

Before the communist regime took over, China was in a state of civil unrest. The economy was backward and corruption was rampant. Poverty was pervasive and the central administration was both inept and unconcerned with the needs of the population at large. Chiang Kai Sheik's Nationalist government lost to the advancing Communist Red Army and took flight to Taiwan. Though separated by the Taiwan Straits, Chiang was well aware of the menacing threat that remained. The imperative for a fundamental change in the modus operandi was clear. Chiang implemented land reform and imposed martial law upon the Taiwanese society.[3] It lasted for thirty-eight years, to be lifted only by Chiang's son Chiang Ching-Kuo who became the president of Taiwan in 1978. For two decades between 1949 and 1978, political freedom was still moderately curtailed after lifting of the martial law.[4]

Singapore's Lee Kuan Yew

Singapore became an independent state in 1965. Lee Kuan Yew became the new nation's first prime minister, serving in that capacity for twenty-five years. He imposed no martial law. Nor was he categorized as a benign dictator. He was an educated individual and was respected for his honesty and integrity. Nevertheless, Lee ruled the tiny peninsula nation with an iron fist. Government corruption was not uncommon in Southeast Asia. Lee created the "Corrupt Practices Investigation Bureau," granting it with great power. This power was used to conduct searches and arrests, and investigate witnesses, bank accounts, and income tax returns of suspected persons and/or households. The practice of corporate punishment in the form of caning, inherited from the British colonialists, was retained and expanded. Corruption was eradicated from Singapore. Under his tight political rule, Singapore was transformed from an underdeveloped patch of a peninsular into one of the wealthiest states in the region. Though not a despot, Lee is recognized as a man of iron will. The third president of Singapore Devan Nair depicted Lee as a determined individual whose approach to pursuing his opponents amounted to "an abrogation of political rights."[5] Whether Lee is a hero or a villain, it was his strong-handed rule over Singapore that has earned the tiny nation of less than five million the respect and admiration of the international community.

South Korea's Park Chung-hee

When Park Chung-hee became the president of South Korea in 1961, the country's economy was still on the mend after the Korean War that ended in 1953. The army-general-turned president, unlike Lee of Singapore, was dubbed as an autocrat if not a dictatorial ruler. On the political front, Park relied on the Korean Central Intelligence Agency (KCIA) to silence his opposition. Park clamped down on personal freedoms under the provisions of a state of emergency dating to the Korean War. Constitutional guarantees of freedom of speech and the press were often curtailed. The KCIA retained broad powers of arrest and detention, and opponents were frequently tortured.[6]

Nevertheless, it was Park who imposed social calm. Replicating Japan's approach to economic recovery, Park helped rebuild South Korea's economy by adopting an export-led growth strategy. Korea became one of the "Four Asian Tigers" whose economic vitality and viability helped inspire the Chinese leadership to initiate its own reform.

Russia's Vladimir Putin

Vladimir Putin was not a household name till his ascendency to succeed Boris Yeltsin. A KGB-trained diplomat and administrator, Putin was Russia's second president from 2000 to 2008. After the disintegration of the former

USSR, Russia adopted a reform program that approximated the so-called shock therapy. With the exception of few key industries, all the other state-owned enterprises were privatized. Corruption was rampant. Large portions of assets previously owned by the state ended in the hands of a few. The once stalwart pillar of the Warsaw Pact was deeply mired in a quandary of going nowhere. Hyperinflation combined with rising unemployment led to crimes and abject poverty that dotted the vast landscape of the once proud world power.

Putin's meteoric ascendancy to the pinnacle of power in Russia came just in time. With an iron fist, Putin's administration injected fiscal discipline, restored social calm, reined in corruption that included the imprisonment of some of the wealthiest individuals whose ill-gotten fortune should have been allotted to the commoners through the privatization process. Nevertheless, domestically and internationally, concerns abound about the lack of human rights and freedoms. Also, "by the beginning of Putin's second term he had undermined every independent source of political power in Russia, decreasing the degree of pluralism in the Russian society."[7] However, on the economic front, confidence in Putin's ability to maintain social and political stability gained momentum. Foreign capital began streaming into Russia. During his two terms as president, the economy recovered, grew, and began blossoming. The general well-being of the average citizen improved drastically, winning Putin a continual high approval rating among the constituents. As a result, Russia regained its respectability in the international community.

From a cursory perspective, the four instances highlighted above would suggest that there is a positive correlation between the decisiveness of the administration and economic growth. Decisiveness and consistency in policy direction paints a picture of stability and permanence, whether the picture delights the beholder or not.

STRUGGLING ECONOMIES

A valid issue nevertheless must be raised. Historical evidences point in the opposite direction. That is, tight political controls and the absence of civil liberties have resulted in dismal economic performances. Equal instances of four historical figures may help shed light on this query.

ZAIRE'S MOBUTU SESE SEKO

Mobutu Sese Seko of Zaire, the former Belgian Congo, was President of the country between 1970 and 1997. He transformed the country into a one-party state, silenced political dissent, and restricted civil liberties. He ruled

Zaire with an iron fist. After two decades of his rule, the nation suffered from unrestrained inflation, substantial debt, and devalued currency.[8]

Three other governments that suppress political rights and deny civil liberties whose reigns continue even to this day are Zimbabwe (the former Rhodesia), Myanmar (Burma), and Cuba.

Zimbabwe's Robert Mugabe

Robert Mugabe won the multiracial election in 1980 as President of Zimbabwe. Shortly after he assumed office as the President, civil wars erupted between the ethnic groups of Shona in the north and Zanu in the south. Mugabe is a Shona. The government of Mugabe responded brutally, "torturing and murdering many ZAPU-supporters and suspects." Zimbabwe became a virtual one-party state where both political rights and civil rights do not exist.[9] By the end of 2008, Zimbabwe's economy was in shambles. Inflation was more than 231 million percent with an estimated 80 percent unemployment rate. And the people of Zimbabwe have claimed the dubious title of having the lowest life expectancy at birth.[10]

Burma's General Ne Win

The third country merits mentioning in this respect is the former "Union of Burma," better known as Burma. In 1962, a military coup brought Burma under the military dictatorship of General Ne Win. The Constitution was suspended and authoritarian military rule began. For nearly three decades, the Burmese economy deteriorated. Once a relatively well-to-do economy was turned into one that has become one of the poorest in the region.[11] The country's name was officially changed to Myanmar by the military junta in 1989. Since 1992, the country continues being governed by the military junta under the leadership of General Than Shwe. Opposition is routinely suppressed and demonstrations for democracy quashed.[12] Without political rights and deprived of civil liberties, "the economy has been in a state of collapse except for the junta-controlled heroin trade."[13] With a population of more than 55 million, the estimated GDP for Myanmar in 2009 was only $57.5 billion with a per capita income estimated at $1,110.[14]

Cuba's Fidel Castro

The fourth economy whose performance has been lackluster is Cuba. Fidel Castro declared Cuba a socialist state on May 1, 1961, a first in the Americas. It was followed by the Bay of Pigs invasion of 1961 and the Cuban missile crisis the following year. Castro ruled Cuba with his personal charisma and socialist ideology. A socialized economy began taking shape under Castro's long reign. State control over economic activities rendered the Cuban economy inefficient and stagnant. The once prosperous island paradise has since been miring in mediocrity for nearly half a century. Part of the economic woes in Cuba may be attributed to the long-standing embargo imposed on it by the United States. Yet, despite strong government intervention in the economy, the system itself has been instrumental in inhibiting it from actualizing its vast potentials.

Economies Further Defined

All eight economies briefly reviewed above experienced tight political controls. Individual rights and civil liberties in all eight are less than visible. Yet, the economies of the first four mentioned countries have succeeded, while those of the other continue to struggle. In itself it cannot be concluded that tight political control invariably can yield a successful transformational or developmental outcome. The proposed hypothesis of this study must include the necessary preconditions without the absence of political rights or civil liberties, or it could lead to undesirable consequences.

First, tight political control must be accompanied by a clear vision and direction. The vision must in turn be based on a feasible and fitting course of action that also includes the scope, pace, and sequencing of policy measures. The desired direction should preferably be where the majority of the populace desires to head for. Periodic evaluation and corrective measures, when needed, must attend the ongoing process of restructuring and development programs.

Second, with a clear vision and direction, steadfast resolve is imperative. For, disruptions to segments of the economy or society often occur and the comfort level for those with vested interest will suffer. If those with vested interests are both prominent and resourceful, then resistance to changes is inevitable. That explains how all the reform measures implemented by communist regimes in Eastern Europe during the 1970s and 1980s netted no consequential results that had been envisioned.

Third, systemic and structural reform measures can succeed if appropriate and timely institutions are also present. This is particularly true in the less-developed economies or in economies undergoing substantive changes where institutional deficiencies tend to be more prevalent. New policy measures without appropriate and timely institutional support or the required infrastructures can create bottlenecks on one hand and incur unnecessary opportunity costs on the other. Some of the more cogent institutions are briefly suggested below.

Adjustments and addenda to legal frameworks as well as the impartial administration of the legal provisions are indispensable for orderly and balanced mediation, which is just and proper under the new legal environ.

Sustained improvements in and adjustments to administrative practices in order to accommodate changing economic conditions are needed. Bureaucratic tendencies are in attendance wherever human institutions are present. As an economy grows, unless institutions have been established to administer and facilitate the changing policies, then progress toward the aspired to objective would be hindered or even derailed.

Financial resources are the bloodlines that course through the system defining an economy. As systemic and structural transformation progresses, the financial institutions that expedite and allocate scarce financial resources efficiently require fine-tuning. Leakages from the system materialize when and if financial irregularities occur at a persistent frequency on a large scale.

In longer terms, the scarcest resources are that of humans. Comparable to early stages of export growth, labor-intensive products may suffice to meet market demands. As the export sector develops, however, product mix must adjust or the growth would first decline and then cease. Similarly, educated personnel might be adequate during early phases of development. As the economy or the system matures, substantively better educated and/or qualified human resources become indispensable. If China possessed a highly educated and qualified cohort of research and development (R&D) personnel at this stage of its development, then the prospect of its sustained growth would be far more promising than it is currently. Therefore, the pace and scope of educational reform must closely accompany systemic and structural transformation for favorable results.

In a society where political forces greatly influence or govern economic policies, judicious and appropriate reforms in political institutions are necessary and inevitable. Transformations and changes, whether they are systemic or structural are, by nature, dynamic. When dynamic forces are constrained by static institutions, then either the former bursts the latter or the latter suffocates the former. No continual changes or development would be feasible. For reform architects, the maxim that timely or early changes are better than passive resistance or no changes needs to be duly taken into account.

One more institution of fundamental consequence that merits mentioning is that of social services. Changes or transformations imply leaving behind the former for what is to come. In the process, a considerable segment of society may be left behind due to metamorphosis. As had been alluded to, social calm and political stability are prerequisites for uninterrupted progression. Viewed from a more constructive perspective, the objective of change is to improve the well-being of society at large. Logically deducible is that, at minimum, every effort needs to be made to minimize human sufferings consequent upon changes. Commensurate quality improvement and spread in the scope of its social safety net must be made available in a timely manner to minimize the number of economic subjects that are being leaked through the social safety net.

The fourth prerequisite for transformational success pertains to the physical aspects of an economy. Upgrading the quality and the qualifications of institutions involving humans is indispensable. Economic development also depends on suitable progress in physical reinforcement. Evolving infrastructural support system is also vital in order to ensure sustained transformational successes. Other than the basic infrastructure such as reliable water and electricity supply and the like, improved or contemporary facilities must also be in adequate supply to accommodate increased economic activities. Therefore, facilities such as upgraded roads, modern ports, and air services, information and communication systems, transport, and marketing resources all need to evolve and develop alongside economic progress.

In sum, the few preconditions that have been outlined above are comparable to links in a chain. The effect of a missing or weak link can obstruct or halt reform progress. It may also alter the direction of reform altogether, which is particularly true when required institutions pertaining to humans should be either lacking or absent.

Quantitative analyses of China, Poland, Romania, and Ukraine's performances, as presented in chapter 6, suggest a significant relationship, of varying degrees, between tight political control and economic growth during early stages of systemic transformation. Of the reform approaches and policies of the four transitional economies, China's economy has been the most gradual, most clearly defined, and the most minutely circumscribed at any given stage of development. Perhaps as a result, China's overall reform environment, at least in the economic spheres, has also been the least chaotic, yet the fastest compared to the growth among the four countries analyzed in chapter 6. A cursory assessment of the prerequisites for orderly and sustained systemic transformation and economic growth as outlined above shows that China appears to have tended to most of them at a relatively adequate level.

China's efforts at systemic transformation and economic restructuring have seen unprecedented successes. As discussed in chapters 6 and 7, qualitative successes are phenomenal. Nevertheless, anomalies and challenges abound as well. China has succeeded because, at least in part, there has been relative social calm and stability. That in turn is due to the tight political control that the decision-makers have imposed upon society. The scope and pace of institutional reforms aside, there has been sufficient continuity and consistency along the way. The intent and direction for reform has been unwavering. Reform progress—though unhurried in some needed realms such as the separation of ownership from the functioning of some major SOEs and state-owned financial institutions—has been steady as a whole.

China's development successes may also be attributed to the leadership's awareness of the background forces that were at play when reform began. Ideological differences between conservative ideologues and reformers still persisted. Legal, institutional, and human resource limitations, therefore, needed to be taken into due consideration. Consequently the scope, pace, and sequencing of reform were only experimental in nature. As cumulative successes appeared, policy measures were implemented to promote concurrent institutional and legal reforms. More promising students were sent abroad for advanced studies so that improvement in the quality of human resources would be able to contribute in a more meaningful way to sustained reform efforts. As success became increasingly more evident, resistance to reform also began dissipating. Reform deepened, ushering China into the current development stage that has gained both the respect and wonder of the international community.

Reform successes aside, flaws have been glaring. Accession to the World Trade Organization (WTO) membership carries with it mounting challenges. A major cause for inadequacy in meeting the challenges from the outside, however, is not due to increased competitive pressure which inevitably increases with the globalization process. Rather, the challenges are real because flaws exist in the reform program. Reform programs have not kept pace with the dynamics that exist on the international forum. Alternately stated, reform has been overly preoccupied with short-term quantitative gains to the neglect of qualitative improvements that are imperative in order to be able to withstand the inevitable challenges that accompany increased interactions with the international community. As an example, accession to the WTO membership has necessitated new and accelerated reform measures in the legal arena in order to accommodate the WTO requirements. Such reform measures began to be undertaken only when pressurized by the need to comply with the WTO standards.

On another front, ideological resistance to reform has indeed been on a steady decline. Nevertheless, the political will to implement reform measures more comprehensively, objectively, and justly has been less than resolute. As a result, persistent abuse of power by the lower-level bureaucrats, pervasive corruption, absence of an unobstructed forum for airing genuine social concerns, less than impartial judgments in judicial affairs, massive capital flight, and undue political influence in economic decisions continue dotting the landscape of quantitative successes. A number of these reform shortcomings suggest that the rule of law has yet to take root.

The slogan that has been accompanying reform is to construct a socialist economy. Deng did state publicly that the approach to reform was to allow one segment of society to experience economic success before another. However, permitting a segment of society to get rich first cannot be at the expense of permitting a large segment of society to be left behind. The reality is that there has been considerable poverty in rural regions. Furthermore, public services such as health care, free education, and basic social security no longer exists. The level of open unemployment remains high. Without a steady income while losing basic public services translates into abject poverty. That is, millions upon millions of the population have been subjected to economic hardship that was unknown even when China's economy was still in a backward stage. Though the per capita income is still low relative to many more developed economies, China has already achieved the status of being the second largest economy in the world. It is timely that more substance be injected into the phrase of "democratic socialism" by broadening and refining the socialism aspect during the current phase of reform.

After three decades of reform and transformation, China has surpassed Japan's economy. It is at the same time that China has entered into a transitional period. It faces imbalances within and imbalances without. Imbalances within are exemplified in insufficient growth in domestic demand while unwarranted investments keep accumulating. The Gini ratio has been on a steady increase, reaching a new high of .47 earlier in 2010.[15] The rich have become richer and the poor are trailing farther behind. Successes may be attributed to tight political control during early phases of reform. Anomalies may also be attributable to the extent of the government's role on the micro levels. On the other hand, the external imbalances manifest themselves in excessive trade surpluses and unparalleled accumulation of foreign reserve. China-phobia has been on the rise and WTO challenges keep mounting. Quantitative gains have come at the expense of goodwill abroad. The unrelenting drive for quantitative success has tarnished China's image abroad in the long run.

Incompatibility between the lack of political rights or civil liberties and economic freedom do not tend to be evident during early stages of rapid growth. This is due to the fact that, during early stages of drive toward rapid economic growth, a constructive government role can and does help nurture entrepreneurial spirit. Irregularities do occur. Nevertheless, no inherent incongruities need to exist between the two. However, as market forces continue to build while the extent of the government's role does not correspondingly decrease, then the two systems tend to reveal fractures or even conflicts. The two systems whose incompatibility level keeps rising consequent upon successes in the economic arena are: one highly centralized political system and a continually more liberalized economic one. As it is, political forces have become more of an impediment to unobstructed actualization of economic potentials. As a result, among others, the chaotic conditions in the housing and financial markets, corrosion in ethical standards, and the inability of the less-privileged to obtain equal treatment before the law have become increasingly problematic. China, therefore, has reached a crossroad. Economically, growth has been phenomenal. The time has arrived for the focus to shift from growth to development and from quantitative to qualitative performances.

Figuratively represented, the existing conditions in China are comparable to the production function where stage three of production is rapidly being approached. That is, until the level and depth of fixed inputs are appropriated, marginal productivity would be negative. At the current stage of reform, a new prerequisite for sustained successes emerges. That is, the role of "rule by law" must increase while the role of the central administration needs to correspondingly decrease. Accelerated institutional reform must attend economic growth. Only then, can there be more equitable distribution of both economic opportunities and legal rights. Only then, can the productive potentials of the masses that have been left behind also begin blossoming.

A Summary Observation

Reform implies that aspects of a system or entity are in need of discarding what is not compatible with the desired "form." It means adopting or adapting to that which does synchronize with the desired outcome.

Here arises the question of values. Among others, there are political values and political systems, social values and social systems, economic values and economic systems, and cultural values and cultural systems. At issue is whether the relative weights that have been assigned to or embedded in each of the systems also represent the overall values that society at large holds. A ready example is when political ideology minimizes the long cherished values that are inherent in cultural, social, and economic systems and dictates to the other systems what is good or desirable. The importance of objective values may be now addressed to the current political, social, economic, and cultural condition. In China, quo vadis is then the logical question that will present itself.

From a historical perspective, the people of China have been ruled by imperial edicts for centuries. Imperial decisions determined economic relationships. Over time, economic realities shaped cultural and social values. People were unaware that possibilities other than those inherited from their forebears existed. For centuries, interaction of social, cultural, and economic values remained within the confines of administrative determinations as well as physical conditions. As a result, the value systems remained nearly fossilized in accord with imperial discretions.

In time, a primitive transportation system emerged, increasing the possibility of enhanced communications and interactions. Social and cultural interactions among regions enhanced the possibility of contrast and comparisons. Ideas, although less than modern, began emerging. Ideas in time yielded gradual but inevitable shifts in relative weights that had been assigned to diverse systems in society. Living within the boundaries of imperial edits was no longer the sole option. Seeds for the possibility of individualism, of self-determination, and self-worth were sown over the by generations. Interaction among value systems increased. The values imposed by administrative decisions began giving way to rising weights being appropriated by enhanced social awareness. The contour of society that was comprised of social, economic, cultural, and political values correspondingly began evolving and altering.

The scenario described above may be projected to modern day China. During the Mao decades, social, cultural, religious, and economic values were all cast aside. Mao-style ideological purity alone was to be valued. Absolute control of the state over every facet of society isolated the people not only from the outside world but also from one another. All focus must be trained on party directives and on "the thoughts of Chairman Mao." Consequently, the sole meaningful interaction that was permissible was from the central government to every individual of age.

Economic reform brought a much-needed breath of fresh air. The focus of creative energies, exchanges, and interactions shifted away from political ideology to economic gains. Relative weights of value likewise began shifting away from political to economic concerns. Modern communication and transportation systems meanwhile help expedite interactions and comparisons among segments of society and among geographic regions. More important, no longer isolated from the outside world, contrasts and comparisons not only with economies but also with societies abroad became routine. New ideas emerge. The relative weights of varied values correspondingly undergo adaptations. During early phases of reform, economic values in general stream to the forefront. After three decades of improved overall economic well-being, the relative weight for material gains might well remain stable. Human aspirations, however, invariably begin seeking options for enhanced total value. The more fundamental values of individualism, of choice, of freedom, and of the concrete expression of one's will and preference will surface. In other words, economic gains consequent upon increased economic freedom can effortlessly transit into aspiration for improvement in the political arena. Thus, meaning that China's economy has successfully developed to a stage when it might be opportune that the government's role needs decreasing as forces of the market continue waxing strong.

China's economic success has gained the attention of the world community. Its reform approach will be studied and analyzed for decades to come by scholars outside of China. The thesis of this study is that tight political control during early phases of reform could contribute to speedier economic growth. The comparative analysis provided in chapter 6 substantiates this tenet. In brief, it is also the tentative proposition of this study that accelerated institutional reforms are also indispensable in modern day China so that the country may continue along its path of sustained growth. Among the institutional reforms are the timely and appropriate modifications in the degree of the government's role in the objective value system of the masses.

NOTES

1 LEGACIES FROM MAO

1. The Commune Program was formally introduced by Mao in 1958 and was an integral part of the "great leap forward" movement initiated by Mao. The actual "socialist transformation" period preparing for and leading up to communization dated between 1953 and 1957, after the Land Reform program was concluded in China in 1952.
2. Muqiao Xue, *Almanac of China's Economy 1981: With Economic Statistics for 1949–1980* (New York and Hong Kong: Modern Cultural Company in association with Eurasia Press, 1982), 81.
3. Chu-Yuan Cheng, "Chinese Communists' Political Shift and Economic Readjustment," *Asian Outlook*, Vol. 21, No. 1, January 1986, 23.
4. Jans Prybyla, *The Political Economy of Communist China* (Scranton, PA: International Text Book Company, 1970), 345.
5. Xue, 86.
6. Bill Brugger and Steven Reglar, *Economy and Society in Contemporary China* (Stanford, CA: Stanford University Press, 1994), 39.
7. Xue, 86.
8. In evaluating the party history between the founding of the PRC in 1949 and 1981, the sixth plenary session of the 11th Central Committee meeting in June 1981 conceded that: "Before the "Cultural Revolution" there were already mistakes of enlarging the scope of class struggle and of impetuosity and rashness in economic construction. Later, there was the comprehensive, long-drawn-out and grave blunder of the "Cultural Revolution." Ibid., 81.
9. The data are provided and further detailed in subsequent chapters.
10. Raphael Shen, *China's Economic Reform: An Experiment in Pragmatic Socialism* (Westport, CT and London: Praeger Publishers, 2000), 30–31.
11. For instance, Mao's single-minded insistence on "accelerated socialization" culminated in 1959–1961's farm collectivization and communization process. The land that the farmers had acquired during the Land Reform movement in the early 1950s became "owned by all the people" by 1958. Massive crop failures throughout China resulted in widespread famines, during which tens of millions of people, mostly on farms, reportedly starved to death. However, in order to please Mao, report on overall farm production

during these years was widely exaggerated, necessitating being readjusted later.
12. Ever since 1949, the general public not only had to work long hours for at least six days a week, they must also attend countless meetings aimed at political indoctrination in the evenings and on nonworking days.

2 THE POLITICAL ECONOMY OF REFORM AFTER MAO

1. The "Gang of Four" were instrumental in fanning the fire of the "Cultural Revolution" that caused the deaths and imprisonment of hundreds of thousands innocent citizens while wreaking unprecedented havoc throughout China for numerous years.
2. "we firmly uphold whatever policy-decisions Chairman Mao made, and we unswervingly adhere to whatever instructions Chairman Mao gave." The Two "whatevers" refers to the statement that "We will resolutely uphold whatever policy decisions Chairman Mao made, and unswervingly follow whatever instructions Chairman Mao gave," (凡是毛主席作出的決策，我們都堅決維護；凡是毛主席的指示，我們都始終不渝地遵循). This statement was contained in a joint editorial, entitled "Study the Documents Well and Grasp the Key Link," *People's Daily* and *Hongqi (Red Flag)* and *Jiefangjun Bao* (February 7, 1977), "Two Whatevers," Wikipedia The Free Encyclopedia, last modified July 24, 2010 (accessed July 9, 2010), http://en.wikipedia.org/wiki/Two_Whatevers. The authors' translations of the Chinese words differ only slightly from the cited source.
3. The "Four Asian Tigers" include Hong Kong, Singapore, South Korea, and Taiwan. These regions were known for their high growth rates and rapid industrialization between 1960 and 1990.
4. The seven adjustment and reform periods since the founding of the PRC in 1949 are: (1) the reconstruction period of 1949–1951; (2) the land reform years of 1951–1953; (3) the 1953–1958's "socialistic transformation" period when farms were collectivized and private enterprises in urban centers became "jointly owned" by the state and the private; (4) the "great leap forward" years of 1959–1961, when the socialistic transformation was complete and private ownership abolished; (5) a period of adjustment and reform after the disastrous failure of the "great leap forward" movement, commending in 1961 an ending in 1966; (6) the "great Cultural Revolution" decade of 1966–1967; and, (7) the current reform years since 1979.
5. Muqiao Xue, *Almanac of China's Economy 1981: With Economic Statistics for 1949–1980* (New York and Hong Kong: Modern Cultural Company in association with Eurasia Press, 1982), 86.
6. The "four modernizations" are objectives to modernize agriculture, industry, national defense, and science and technology.
7. To Deng, the kind of democracy China needed was "socialist democracy" or "people's democracy," not capitalist-style democratic individualism. In his speech to the delegates participating at a workshop for party theoreticians on March 30, 1979, Deng stated: "Our objective is to create a political

environ that possesses centralized democracy and organized independence while maintaining unified collective will in conjunction with individual contentment and dynamism. Hsing Hsu, ed. *Chronicle of a Decade of Reform: 1978–1987,* 十年改革大事記: 1978-1987 (Beijing: Hsing Hua Press, 1988), 63.
8. Hsu, 9–10.
9. The Warsaw Pact was an organization formed in Warsaw, Poland, in 1955. It was comprised of the following countries: Bulgaria, Czechoslovakia, East Germany, Hungary, Poland, Romania, and the USSR. This organization's primary reason was for a collective defense under a joint military command.
10. Hu was a daring reformer in the political arena. He was also a vocal advocate for China's systematic reforms. Being the party secretary general, it was Hu who constructively provided direction and support to Premier Zhao Ziyang in reforming China's economy.
11. The first general party leaders were Mao, Deng, and their civil war comrades.
12. Haike 海克, "The Post Zhao Ziyang China 趙紫陽之後的中國," *Open magazine*, Vol. 218, February 2005. 39.
13. Mao and Deng were the representatives of the first generation party leadership. Hu and Zhao, who were not founding members of the CCP, joined the Communist Party during the civil war. They were considered the second generation leaders. Jiang Zemin, who was a latecomer into the party history, belongs to the third generation of Chinese communist leader.
14. Li Peng was premier of the People's Republic of China from March 1988 to March 1998.
15. He was a professor of finance in China's most prestigious of universities—Tsing-Hua University—and later on as the mayor of Shanghai before being tapped by the CCP to assume leadership roles within the party and the state.
16. For instance, the Constitution guarantees, among others, the public's rights to religious freedom, to freedom of expression, and to freedom of the press have not duly respected.

3 Reform Approach and Framework

1. For instance, Mao's penchant for emphasizing rapid growth rates in heavy industries had already left China's agriculture and light industries lagging disproportionately farther and farther behind that of heavy industry. The real need for China's consumers in the mid and late 1970s was more and better food and light industrial products, not steel or the like. Hua's continuation of Mao's growth approach.
2. On August 16, 2008, China's National Bureau of Statistics and National Development and Reform Commission confirmed with the World Bank that China's per capita income by then had already reached $1,740.

3. Xing Su 蘇星, *An Economic History of the New China* 新中國經濟史 revised edition 修訂本 (Beijing: The Central Party School Publishing House 中共中央黨校出版社, 2007), 503.
4. Yun Chen 陳雲, *Selected Writings of Chen Yun*《陳雲文選》, Vol. 3 第3卷 (Beijing: People's Publishing House 人民出版社1995年版, 1995), 248–249.
5. Xiannian Li 李先念, *Selected Writings of Li Xiannian 1935–1988*《李先念文選》*(1935–1988)* (Beijing: People's Publishing House 人民出版社1989年版, 1989), 343–378.
6. Weizhong Fang 房維中, ed. *Major Economic Events of the People's Republic of China, 1949–1980.*《中華人民共和國經濟大事記》*(1949–1980)* (Beijing: China Social Sciences Press 中國社會科學出版社 1984 年版, 1984), 668–670.
7. Hsing Hsu, ed. *Chronicle of a Decade of Reform: 1978–1987* (Beijing: Hsing Hua Press, 1988), 122.
8. Ibid., 133.
9. Ibid., 76.
10. Reducing the scope of plan-mandated target while increasing the range of plan-directed activities means gradually replacing commands with directives.
11. Macro coordination of economic activities by administrative units was to comprise of three categories: plan-determined, state-directed, and market-based. "Plan-determined" included essential raw materials and consumer staples. The prevailing practice of centralized purchasing and distribution for such items was to continue. State-directed commodities, on the other hand, were not mandated in terms of production and distribution. They were intended as reference quantities needed by the economy. It was then the decision of local governments and micro entities to evaluate the potential markets for appropriate investment and production decisions. And, finally, the market-based category of goods and services pertained to nonessentials. Goods and services in this category were neither mandated nor directed in terms of production and distribution. Reliance on supply and demand conditions via the market's pricing mechanism would henceforth be the sole coordinating instrument for their circulation. Over time, the scope of state-determined items kept declining, being progressively replaced by either state-directed or market-based coordination mechanisms. Function of the market's pricing mechanism thereby orderly and systematically began emerging, gradually replacing plan-determined pricing.
12. Xiaoping Deng 鄧小平, *Selected Writings of Deng Xiaoping*《鄧小平文選》, Vol. 2 第2卷 (Beijing: People's Publishing House 人民出版社1993年版, 1994), 128.
13. In early 1999, nine regional banks were established, whose functions are comparable to that of the branch banks of the Federal Reserve System in the United States.
14. Yun Chen陳雲, ed. 279; Or: China Institute for Reform and Development, *The Path to a Stronger China: China's Reform Stepping into Its 30th Year* (Beijing: China Economic Publishing House, 2008), 104.

4 Foreign Investment

1. The members of COMECON were the same as those of the Warsaw Pact: USSR, Poland, Hungary, Czechoslovakia, Romania, and Bulgaria.
2. Four Asian Tigers refers to rapidly industrialized nations of Hong Kong, Singapore, South Korea, and Taiwan from 1960 to 1990.
3. Tsuo Tsien Wang, ed. *China's Foreign Economic Relations* (Beijing: Foreign Economic Relations Educational Press, 1988), 5.
4. Xing Su蘇星, *An Economic History of the New China* 新中國經濟史, revised edition 修訂本. (Beijing: The Central Party School Publishing House 中共中央黨校出版社, 2007), 503.
5. Mengkui Wang王夢奎, *China's Economic Development: Retrospect and Prospect* 中國經濟發展的回顧與前瞻 *(1979–2020)* (Beijing: China Financial and Economic Publishing House 中國財政經濟出版社, 1999), 428.
6. The fourteen open cities were: Dalian, Qinhuangdao, Tianjin, Yantai, Qingdao, Lianyungang, Nantong, Shanghai, Ningbo, Wenzhou, Fuzhou, Guangzhou, Zhanjiang, and Beihai.
7. The Yangtze River Delta (長江三角洲), the Pearl River Delta (珠江三角洲), and the South Fujian Golden Delta (閩南三角地區).
8. Economic Construction Institute, ed. *An Evaluation of Economic Development Policy of the Chinese Communists* (Taipei: Economic Research Division: Economic Construction Institute, 1990), 282.
9. People's Republic of China State Statistical Bureau, *China's Statistical Yearbook 1996* (Beijing: China Statistical Publishing House, 1996), 629.
10. Dominique T.C. Wang 王泰銓, *A Compilation of the People's Republic of China's Most Current Laws and Decrees* 最近中華人民共和國法律、法規彙編, ed. (Taipei: Hanlu Book Company LTD 翰蘆圖書出版有限公司, 2002), 461–483.
11. The discussion describes various Articles (2, 4, 5, 7, and 9) of the Joint Venture Enterprise Law. For a full overview of the law, see Dominique T.C. Wang 王泰銓, *China's Foreign Economic and Trade Law* 中共對外經濟貿易法 (Taiwan: Wu-Nan Book Company Ltd. 五南圖書出版公司, 中華民國85年, 1996), 58–71, 527–552, 637–653.
12. Ibid., Article 5.
13. Some minor modifications of no substantive consequence were introduced into the Directives on January 15, 1986; December 21, 1987; and July 22, 2001.
14. Foreign Capital Enterprise Law, Article 1. See T.C. Wang 王泰銓, 476.
15. The distinction made between a foreign enterprise and a subsidiary of a foreign concern under Article 2 is that the former is a limited liability company having its own legal identity whereas the latter had no legal identity dichotomized from its parent company, Article 2.
16. The references refer to the Foreign Capital Enterprise Law, Articles 3, 17, and 19.
17. The references refer to the Foreign Cooperative Enterprise Law, Articles 4, 8, 17, 18, and 19.

18. Economic Construction Institute, 293, 294.
19. Nannan Lundin et al., "FDI, Market Structure and R&D Investments in China," *Örebro University & Research Institute of Industrial Economics*, April 2007 (accessed January 17, 2010), http://magasinet.oru.se/oruupload/Institutioner/Ekonomi%20statistik%20och%20informatik/Dokument/NEK/Seminarier/wpICSEAD.pdf.
20. Guilan Ma馬桂蘭, "An Analysis of the Trend and the Factors of FDI in China 我國FDI獨資化趨勢的動因分析.當代經濟下半月," December 29, 2007, http://www.gjmy.com/Item/8857.aspx.
21. "The Global Situation and Trend of Foreign Investment in China 中國吸引外資的國際地位及趨勢," Kuaijiren.com (accessed July 30, 2007), http://www.kuaijiren.com/content/23555-0.html.
22. Li Yao姚莉, "Adjustment Strategy for Dealing with Transnational Corporations' Investments in China 如何應對跨國公司對華投資戰略調整," April 9, 2008, http://www.jjx.org.cn, http://www.gjmy.com/Item/ 7804_2.aspx.
23. Changwen Zhang張昌文, "New Strategic Modification for Utilizing Foreign Investments 新時期國企利用外資的戰略調整," March 7, 2008, http://www.gjmy.com/Item/8877.aspx.
24. Qunyang Du杜群陽, "A Practical Analysis of Technological Externalities from FDIs' Research and Development 海外研發與FDI技術外溢的實證分析.國際貿易問題," January 3, 2008, http://www.gjmy.com/Item /8873.aspx.
25. Such as resource and energy conservation, improved infrastructure and services and stemming the tide of growing income and regional inequalities.
26. Youwei Dan但有爲, "Astonishing Upsurge in Foreign Direct Investment (in China), A 353% increase During the First Quarter 我國FDI增速驚人，首季增長353%," May 12, 2008, http://www.sinotf.com/GB/ Tradedata/1141/2008-5-12/225938afgbd.htm.
27. China Infodoc Service China (accessed Dececember 4, 2009), infodoc@online.be
28. Ibid.
29. Japan's excess reserve, which ranks second in the world, was $1.02 trillion in June 2009. Eurozone's foreign reserve as a whole, which ranks the third, was $716 billion. Unless serious efforts are made by the Chinese government to achieve a less conspicuous current account surplus, China could become a ready target for foreign governments to vent their frustration over China's trade practices on the international forum: "The latest news and statistics on China's business and economic climate," http://www.Chinability.Com/Reserve.htm.
30. Pokong Chen陳破空, *Treading Russia's Path toward Russian Ascendancy: Mystery Solved for China's Frenetic Purchases of Western Enterprises* 走蘇聯之路的俄式掘起: 中國瘋狂收購西方公司解密 (Hong Kong: N.H.K Books 吳興記書報社, 2005); and *Open Magazine*, Vol. 224, August, 2008, 22.
31. China Institute for Reform and Development, *Illustrious Theory, Substantive Implementation* (Beijing: China Institute for Reform and Development,

2008) and China Institute for Reform and Development, *The Path to a Stronger China: China's Reform Stepping into Its 30th Year* (Beijing: China Economic Publishing House), 234.
32. Guilan Ma馬桂蘭, "An Analysis of the Trend and the Factors of FDI in China 我國FDI獨資化趨勢的動因分析.當代經濟下半月."
33. Guoqiang Long隆國強, "An Analysis for Improving the Quality and Level of Utilizing Foreign Capital 論新時期進一步提高利用外資質量與水平（上）. 國際貿易," December 20, 2007, http://www.gjmy.com/Item/8860.aspx.

5 Foreign Trade Reform

1. Deeper down, however, for historical reasons, China always kept a guarded eye on foreign powers. The Opium War, the eight-nation invasion of China, and World War II taught China to be less than trustful of foreign powers.
2. "Foreign Trade 對外貿易," WebNet of the Bureau of Statistics (accessed September 17, 2009), http://www.gov.cn/test/2009-09/17/content_1419657.htm
3. Joseph C.H. Chai, ed. *The Economic Development of Modern China Volume 3: Reforms and Opening Up Since 1979* (United Kingdom and United States: Edward Elgar Publishing, 2000), 453.
4. Fureng Dong and Peter Nolan, eds. *The Chinese Economy and its Future Achievements and Problems of Post-Mao Reform* (UK: Polity Press, 1990), 255.
5. Raphael Shen, *China's Economic Reform: An Experiment in Pragmatic Socialism* (Westport, CT and London: Praeger Publishers, 2000), 120.
6. "Directives Over Some Questions Concerning Accelerating and Deepening the Structure of Foreign Trade《關於加快和深化對外貿易體制改革若干問題的規定》," Baidu.com, (accessed June 23, 2009), http://tieba.baidu.com/f?kz=151117887.
7. "The State Council's Decision for Continuing Reform and Improvement of the Structure of Foreign Trade," 《國務院關於進一步改革和完善對外貿易體制若干問題的決議》, January 1, 1991, http://www.chinalawedu.com/news/1200/22016/22037/22567/22570/2006/3/zh42711125197360028316-0.htm.
8. This does not mean the cessation of subsidies to all export activities. Subsidies to agricultural exports, for instance, would remain. Loss incurred by exporters, however, would no longer be covered by the central budget.
9. The "One Subsidy-Three Inbound Sources" means subsidy for a certain type of export-destined activities. That is, foreign concerns would supply resources, technology, or equipment. In accordance with specifications outlined by foreign capital, domestic enterprises then produce or assemble finished products accordingly for exports.
10. Category one comprised of twenty-one commodities, including items such as grain, tobacco, and cotton. And category three goods were made up of products such as bicycles, tires, and porcelain china.

11. People's Republic of China State Statistical Bureau, *China's Statistical Yearbook, 2007* (Beijing: China Statistical Publishing House, 2007), 59.
12. For instance, the GDP growth rate was 15.3 percent in 1984. It declined to 13.2 percent the following year and then decreased further to 8.5 percent in 1986.
13. "WTO successfully concludes negotiations on China's entry," *WTO News*, September 17, 2001, http://www.wto.org/english/news_e/pres01_e /pr243_e.htm.
14. Karen Halverson, "Article address," February 27, 2006 (accessed June 17, 2010), http://www.bc.edu/schools/law/lawreviews/meta-elements/ journals /bciclr/27_2/06_TXT.htm.
15. Marcia Don Harpaz, "China and the WTO: New Kid in the Developing Bloc?," *Hebrew University International Law Research Paper* No. 2-07 (February 1, 2007) http://papers.ssrn.com/sol3/papers. cfm?abstract_id=961768.
16. "The 21 Concessionary Items China Made for Entry into the WTO, 2001 當代二十一條: 中國加入WTO的主要讓步清單," *Open Magazine*, November 12, 2001, 48–49, http://www.secretchina.com/b5/node/105849.
17. For instance, Part 2 of Section 5 under Article 9 of the 1994 law stating that "enterprises with foreign capital were exempt from..." was deleted from the 2004 law so to comply with the WTO agreement. Also omitted was Article 11, which stated: "In accordance with the law, foreign trade operators are responsible for their own management, bearing the consequence of reaping profit for or incurring loss to themselves." Article 16 of the 1994 law dealt with trade domains where for various reasons the state could impose restrictions on certain imports or exports. That article contained seven categories of trading activities. Also under Article 16 of the 2004 law, however, eleven categories were included.
18. For specific articles of the law, confer The Standing Committee of the National People's Congress, *Foreign Trade Law of The People's Republic of China*, April 6, 2004, http://tradeinservices.mofcom. gov.cn/en/b/2004-04-06/8381.shtml.
19. *Open Magazine*, 48.
20. When Mao instigated the "Let the Hundred Flowers Blossom" movement in 1957, allowing a segment of society to vent their frustration at the regime, the response from the public was swift and intense. It alarmed Mao. He promptly turned off the switch for "blossoming" and trained his target on the "rightists." Countless "flowers that bloomed" ended in labor camps. The communist regime could not afford and would not again permit Western democracy type of freedom.
21. Table 4.1, Foreign Capital Inflow, 1979–2008, for growth in foreign investments.
22. Primary goods sector comprises of the following: food and animal products, beverages and tobacco, nonedible raw materials, mineral fuels, lubricants and related materials, and animal and vegetable oils. The manufactured goods category, on the other hand, consists of: chemicals and related products, industrial products, rubber, minerals and metallurgical products,

machinery and transport equipment, and miscellaneous products. People's Republic of China State Statistical Bureau, *China's Statistical Yearbook, 2009* (Beijing: China Statistical Publishing House, 2009), 728.
23. Composition of primary goods import and export corresponds to that of for exports.
24. People's Republic of China State Statistical Bureau, *China's Statistical Yearbook, 2009*, 733–736.
25. *China Statistical Yearbook, 2009*, 725.
26. As presented in China's Statistical Yearbook, the only economies listed under "North America" are the U.S., Canada, Greenland, Bermuda, and other.
27. Wangyu Shao 邵望予, "A Cursory Analysis of the Transformation Process of China's Foreign Trade Increases 試論中國外貿增長方式的轉變.中國論文下載中心," *中國論文下載中心*, June 20, 2008, http://www.studa.net/china/080620/10073999-2.html.
28. Mark Trumbull, "US-China trade dispute about more than tires," *The Christian Science Monitor*, September 14, 2009 (accessed July 2, 2010), http://www.csmonitor.com/Money/2009/0914/us-china-trade-dispute-about-more-than-tires.
29. Qingjiang Kong, "EAI Background Brief No. 416," December 4, 2008, 2 (accessed June 29, 2010), http://www.eai.nus.edu.sg/BB416.pdf.
30. Brussels, "EU requests WTO consultations on Chinese export restrictions on raw materials, *Europa Press Releases*, June 23, 2009 (accessed June 30, 2010), http://europa.eu/rapid/pressReleasesAction.do?reference=MEMO/09/287&format=HTML&aged=0&language=EN&guiLanguage=en.
31. Qingfen Ding, "China to see 'more trade disputes' this year," *China Daily*, March 6, 2010 (accessed June 27, 2010), http://www.chinadaily.com.cn/china/2010npc/2010-03/06/content_9546712.htm.

6 A Comparative Performance Study

1. Ling Lin 林凌, "Theory and Practice of China's Economic Reform 中國經濟改革的理論與實踐," *Wangfang Data*, 2007 (accessed July 27, 2010), http://d.wanfangdata.com/cn/periodical_ shkxyj200701033.aspx.
2. Ibid.
3. Judy Dempsy, "Economic Reform Lags in Ukraine," *New York Times*, July 25, 2005.
4. A cautionary note concerning references to specific values and data: To enable comparison of the four countries, data for the statistical analysis were derived from one source as much as possible. Therefore, definitions and values differ based on sources. This will be true concerning data referenced in previous and following chapters.
5. "World Databank," The World Bank (accessed June 6, 2010), http://databank.worldbank.org.
6. Data | The World Bank, "World Development Indicators (WDI) | Data | The World Bank," The World Bank (accessed June 6, 2010), http://data.worldbank.org/data-catalog/world-development-indicators.

7. "freedomhouse.org: Freedom in the World Comparative and Historical Data," Freedom House (accessed June 6, 2010), http://www.freedomhouse.org/template.cfm?page=439.
8. "freedomhouse.org: Freedom in the World 2010: Erosion of Freedom Intensifies," Freedom House (accessed June 6, 2010), www.freedomhouse.org/uploads/fiw10/FIW_2010_Methodology_Summary.pdf.
9. The International Financial Statistics database is found at "International Monetary Fund—Data and Statistics—BOP, DOT & IFS Data Browsers," International Monetary Fund—Data and Statistics (accessed June 10, 2010), http://www.imfstatistics.org/imf/. The World Economic Outlook Database is found at "IMF World Economic Outlook (WEO)—Rebalancing Growth, April 2010—Table of Contents," IMF—International Monetary Fund Home Page (accessed June 10, 2010), http://www.imf.org/external/pubs/ft/weo/2010/01/weodata/index.aspx.
10. People's Republic of China State Statistical Bureau, *China Statistical Yearbook 2009* (Beijing: China Statistics, 2009). See also National Bureau of Statistics of China 國家統計局, *Fifty Years of The People's Republic of China 新中國五十年* (Beijing: China Statistics Press 中國統計局出版社, 1999), 57. See also People's Republic of China State Statistical Bureau, *China's Statistical Yearbook 1996* (Beijing: China Statistical Publishing House, 1996), 629.
11. "The World Bank," The World Bank (accessed June 6, 2010), web.worldbank.org/wbsite/external/datastatistics/extdecstama.
12. Data | The World Bank, "GDP (current US$) | Data | The World Bank," The World Bank (accessed April 12, 2010), http://data.worldbank.org/indicator/ny.gdp.mktp.cd. As noted by the World Bank, GDP is no longer used for classifying countries since it is subject to some distortion. It is increasingly criticized for use as an indicator of a country's standard of living.
13. Data | The World Bank, "GNI per capita, Atlas method (current US$) | Data | The World Bank," The World Bank (accessed June 5, 2010), http://data.worldbank.org/indicator/ny.gnp.pcap.cd.
14. Data | The World Bank, "GNI per capita, PPP (current international $) | Data | The World Bank," The World Bank (accessed June 5, 2010), http://data.worldbank.org/indicator/ny.gnp.pcap.pp.cd.
15. Data | The World Bank, "Foreign direct investment, net inflows (BoP, current US$) | Data | The World Bank," The World Bank (accessed June 5, 2010), http://data.worldbank.org/indicator/bx.klt.dinv.cd.wd.
16. Ibid.
17. For imports, see Data | The World Bank, "Imports of goods and services (% of GDP) | Data | The World Bank," The World Bank, accessed June 5, 2010, http://data.worldbank.org/indicator/ne.imp.gnfs.zs. For exports, see Data | The World Bank "Exports of goods and services (% of GDP) | Data | The World Bank, "The World Bank (accessed June 5, 2010), http://data.worldbank.org/indicator/ne.exp.gnfs.zs.
18. Data | The World Bank, "Military expenditure (% of GDP) | Data | The World Bank," The World Bank (accessed June 5, 2010), http://data.worldbank.org/indicator/ms.mil.xpnd.gd.zs.

19. Data | The World Bank, "Energy use (kg of oil equivalent per capita) | Data | The World Bank," The World Bank (accessed June 5, 2010), http://data.worldbank.org/indicator/eg.use.pcap.kg.oe.
20. Freedomhouse.org: Home, "freedomhouse.org: Methodology," Freedom House (accessed November 20, 2009), http://www.freedomhouse.org/template.cfm?page=35&ana_page=341&year=2008.
21. Ibid.
22. Ibid.
23. Data | The World Bank "Poverty headcount ratio at national poverty line (% of population) | Data | The World Bank," The World Bank (accessed November 20), 2009, http://data.worldbank.org/indicator/si.pov.nahc.
24. Variable codes are: GDP: Gross Domestic Product. FDI: Foreign Direct Investment. FOREX: Foreign Exchange Reserves. GNI: Gross National Income, Atlas method using current U.S. dollar. GNI, PPP, Gross National Income Purchasing Power Parity. GINI: Gini coefficient. POL: Political Rights Index. CIVIL: Civil Liberties Index. FREE: Freedom Status.
25. "Poverty headcount ratio at national poverty line (% of population) | Data | The World Bank."
26. China's political rights indicator moved from a 6 to a 7 in 1988 and remains static since. An increase in the rating indicates a decrease in rights. "freedomhouse.org: Methodology."
27. Ibid.
28. Both the purchase power parties (PPP) and the Atlas methods were employed. PPP conversion accounts for differences I the relative price of goods and services. The atlas method uses a three-year moving average smoothing fluctuations of the foreign exchange rates and a price-adjusted conversion factor. "GNI per capita, PPP (current international $) | Data | The World Bank."
29. With the exception of FDI and GNI, PPP for most countries. See Table 6.1 for detailed correlations.
30. The correlations for FDI and exports are .907 for China, significant at the .01 level; .823 for Poland, significant at the .01 level; .501 for Romania, significant at the .05 level; and a nonsignificant .053 for Ukraine.
31. China's political rights indicator moved from a 6 to a 7 in 1988 and remains static since. An increase in the rating indicates a decrease in rights. "freedomhouse.org: Methodology."
32. Model 2 standardized beta values for China are: exports 1.213, imports −.444, political rights .237, and civil liberties −.481.
33. Model 2 standardized beta values for Poland are: exports .067, imports .714, and civil liberties −.154.
34. Romania's standardized beta values are: exports −1.807, imports 1.907, political rights 1.429, and civil liberties −1.725.
35. Ukraine's' standardized beta values are: exports −3.295, imports 3.088, political rights .480, and civil liberties −1.145.

7 Successes

1. An Interview with Ling Lin 林凌, "Theory and Practice of China's Economic Reform 中國經濟改革的理論與實踐," *Wanfang Data*, 2007 (accessed July 27), 2010, http://d.wanfangdata.com/cn/periodical_ shkxyj200701033.aspx.
2. China's per capita income in 1980 was 463 Chinese yuan. A decade later, it was 1,644 yuan and by the end of the 20th century it reached 7,858 yuan per capita.
3. According to the World Bank estimate, by the end of 2009 China's GDP reached a new height of $4.9 trillion according to CNN, "China's GDP grows by 8.7 percent in 2009," CNN.com, January 20, 2010, http://www.cnn.com/2010/BUSINESS/01/20/china.GDP.annual/index.html. The exchange rate in December 2009 was 6.83 yuan to one U.S. dollar according to "China's population in 2009, China's GDP in 2009?" True Knowledge the Internet Answer Engine, http://www.trueknowledge.com/q/china's_ population_in_2009. China's GDP in 2009, therefore, approximated 33.5 trillion Yuan. China's population by then had grown to 1.345 billion., "Home—China Yuan Renminbi—CNY rate table," XE The World's favorite currency site, December 22, 2009, http://www.xe.com/ict/?basecur=CNY&historical=true&month=12&day=22&year=2009&sort_by=name&image.x=53&image.y=12.
4. Hongyan Yu, "China to invest 7t yuan for urban infrastructure in 2011–15," *ChinaDaily*, May 13, 2010, http://www.chinadaily.com.cn/business/2010-05/13/content_9845757.htm (accessed July 24, 2010).
5. "China Plans World's Largest Solar Power Plant," Popular Science, September 8, 2009 (accessed September 8, 2009), http://www.popsci.com/scitech/article/2009-09/biggest-solar-power-plant-set-china.
6. Jing Huang 黃靜 and Bingbing Su 蘇冰冰, eds., *China Center for National Accounting and Economic Growth* (Beijing: Being University, 2008), 31.
7. However, phased decentralization in time also carried with it extraneous burden for the millions of agricultural producers from the mid-1980s forward. Decentralization vested additional authority on local officials. Steeped in the widespread fever of "getting rich quickly," local officials began concocting imaginative schemes to exact fees and fines from farmers. Freed from the commune's repressive system, the farmers once again became victims of greed on the part of minor bureaucrats. Furthermore, decentralizing the pricing system also caused factor costs to rise on farm. Price liberalization, in conjunction with increased supply of farm produce, in turn translated into depressed prices for farm produce. Since demand for agricultural products is inelastic, the rise in real farm income decelerated. Growing income disparity between urban and rural producing kept widening.
8. Enterprise and financial reforms were difficult. They would involve bad credits being extended to loss-incurring SOEs and to borrowers with political connections. Those with political connections were known to be raiding the most competitive SOEs, buying them at disgracefully undervalued prices. Wen was either unable or unwilling to step on the toes of the political

elite who were publicly known to be deeply involved in such shady activities. The most cost-effective reform for Wen to focus on was the rural economy. Successes in rural reform would benefit the vast majority of China's rural population without risking the ire of corrupt high-level officials. Wen made known his intention to labor diligently for the improvement of living conditions in rural China.

9. Jiabao Wen 溫家寶, "The Central People's Government of the People's Republic of China 務府工作報告" (accessed March 19, 2009), http://www.gov.cn/test/200903/16/content_1260198.htm.
10. Ling Lin 林凌, "Theory and Practice of China's Economic Reform 中國經濟改革的理論與實踐," *Wanfang Data*, 2007 (accessed July 27, 2010), http://d.wanfangdata.com/cn/periodical_ shkxyj200701033.aspx.
11. Yongzbeng Yang, "SOE reform and private sector development in China," in *China's Third Economic Transformation: the Rise of the Private Sector*, Rose Garnaur and Ligang Song, eds. (New York: Routledge Curzon, 2004), 85.
12. Yifu Lin, *Analyzing China's Economy* (Taipei: Times Daily Cultural Publishing Co. Ltd., 2009), 249.
13. Wayne M. Morrison, "China's Economic Conditions," *CRS Issue for Congress*, July 15, 1998, http://www.fas.org/man/crs/980717CRSEconomic_Conditions.htm.
14. "The Economy of Poland," Wikipedia The Free Encyclopedia, last modified August 20, 2010 (accessed July 9, 2010), http://en.wikipedia.org/wiki/Economy_of_Poland.
15. The Economist: Pocket World in Figures, 2004 Edition, "Ukraine: Statistics and World Ranking of Ukraine," http://www.womenrussia.com/ukraine.htm.
16. CNN, "China's GDP grows by 8.7 percent in 2009."And, "China's 2009 GDP growth reaches 8.7%," CCTV, January 21, 2010, http://english.cctv.com/program/newshour/20100121/103664.shtml.
17. "List of Countries by Foreign Exchange Reserves, Wikipedia The Free Encyclopedia, Last modified August 21, 2010 (accessed July 31, 2010), http://en.wikipedia.org/wiki/List_of_countries_by_foreign_exchange_reserves.
18. "Economy Statistics, GDP (1979) by Country," NationMaster Statistics (accessed August 1, 2010), http://www.nationmaster.com/graph/eco_gdp-economy-gdp&date=1979.
19. Ibid.
20. Keiko Ujikane, "Japan's GDP Grows Less Than Forecast, Pressuring BOJ (Update2)," *Bloomberg Businessweek*, Business Exchange, May 20, 2010 (accessed August 2, 2010), http://www.businessweek.com/news/2010-05-20/japan-s-gdp-grows-less-than-forecast-pressuring-boj-update2-.html.
21. "China's GDP grows 11.1% in H1 2010," China.org.cn: Home, Business, Economy, July 15, 2010 (accessed August 2, 2010), http://www.china.org.cn/business/2010-07/15/content_20501801.htm.
22. Chinese President Jintao Hu, *Report to the 17th Congress of the People's Representatives*, Beijing, October 15, 2007.

8 Anomalies and Challenges

1. "Deng Xiaoping quotes," Quotesea Corporation, accessed August 3, 2010, http://www.quotesea.com/quotes/by/Deng+Xiaoping.
2. "GDP growth in China 1952–2009," Chinability.com, December 27, 2009 (accessed August 3, 2010), http://www.chinability.com/GDP.htm.
3. Daming Jia, "The Present State and Solution for Resolving the "Three-Rural' Problem," *China Reform*, April 2001, 43.
4. Passages of a Premier's annual report on a given year's government performance, as cited in this section, unless otherwise noted, may be accessed from this Internet source: Peng Li, "The Prime Minister's Annual Report in 1992," Gov.com 中央政府門戶網站 *(The Central People's Government of the People's Republic of China) 1992年國務院政府工作報告*, February 16, 2006 (accessed July 25, 2008), http://202.123.110.5/test/2006-02/16/content_200922.htm. For the passage cited in the text, cf. p. 13 ff of Li Peng's report on March 20, 1992, pp. 13 ff. see Li Peng, "The Prime Minister's Annual Report in 1993," Gov.com 中央政府門戶網站 *(The Central People's Government of the People's Republic of China) 1993年國務院政府工作報告*, February 16, 2006 (accessed July 25, 2008), http://202.123.110.3/test/2006-02/16/content_200926.htm.
5. Income disparity between farm and nonfarm sectors grew over time, owing largely to the persistent gap in productivity gains between the two sectors. Productivity gains in 1992 for agriculture, for instance, were 4 percent whereas for industry it was 21.1 percent; for 1994, the respective gains were 3.5 and 11.8 percent. Rapid income rises in the industrial and related sectors helped because general increases in price and cost, continually eroding purchasing power of farm producers. Peng Li, "The Prime Minister's Annual Report in 1993."
6. Peng Li, "The Prime Minister's Annual Report in 1996," Gov.com 中央政府門戶網站 *(The Central People's Government of the People's Republic of China) 1996 年國務院政府工作報告*, February 16, 2006 (accessed July 25, 2008), http://202.123.110.3/test/2006-02/16/content_201115.htm.
7. Report of government performance—March 5, 2008 政府工作報告—2008年3月5日在第十一屆全國人民代表大會第一次會議上國務院總理 Jiabao Wen 溫家寶, "The Prime Minister's Annual Report in 1998," People.com.cn, March 20, 2008 (accessed July 25, 2008), http://npc.people.com.cn/GB/28320/116286/116587/7021687.html.
8. "China's rural population to halve in 30 years: economist," *People's Daily Online*, February 24, 2010 (accessed July 30, 2010), http://english.peopledaily.com.cn/90001/90776/90882/6901672.html.
9. The taxes that were removed from the farmers were, as the premier reported, the "agricultural, livestock and special produce taxes." According to the estimate of researchers, other than fees assessed for social services, the "agricultural taxes" mentioned by the premier was 8.8 billion yuan in 1990 increased to 46.5 billion yuan in 2000. On the average, therefore, the farmer in 2000 paid 146 yuan in various taxes other than income taxes.

These various taxes for urban and rural township population in 2000 were 37 yuan. Furthermore, according to an interview granted by an agricultural expert from the School of the Communist Party in 2004, the main tax paid by urban and township population was income tax. Persons earning more than a monthly income of 800 yuan begin paying income taxes. That is, no tax on income was being paid if a person was making less than 9,600 yuan a year. Yet, irrespective of whether a farmer reaped a bumper crop or not, a fixed amount of taxes must be paid. Nearly 90 percent of farmers' annual income was significantly below that. According to the Prime Minister's Annual Report of 2008, farmers' annual income in 2007 was still only 4,140 yuan. The "agricultural taxes" that was eliminated was the excess taxes imposed on farmers that urban and township dwellers never had to pay, not taxes on the farmers' incomes. Xiwen Chen, "Reforming Tax Burdens in China's Rural Regions: The First time A Change That Took Place in 2600 Years," Hexun.com, August 5, 2008 (accessed August 10), 2010, http://news.hexun.com/2008-08-05/107924192.html and, Jiabao Wen 溫家寶, "The Prime Minister's Annual Report in 1998."

10. A Synthesis of the Prime Minister's Address at the 2nd Working Session of the State Council for Remedying Anomalies on Farm, Jiabao Wen 溫家寶, "Strengthen Supervisory System, Ensuring no Abuse of Authority," People's Net, April 9, 2009 (accessed August 25, 2009), http://politics.people.com.cn/GB/1024/9098050.htm1.

11. Some additional instances of odious practices by middle and lower level officials may be secured from the ensuing sources:

"*Times* Editorial: County Party Secretary General's 'Signing of' Document Imposing Labor Camp Education is an Abuse of Power 時評：縣委書記'簽發'勞教文件是濫用權力," China's new rural cooperative, June 24, 2010 (accessed July 28, 2010), http://www.xnchzs.com/zixun/ShowArticle.asp?ArticleID=7011; "Sixty Thousand Hainan Farmers' (Properties) Tragically Torn Down," *A Special Report' Open Magazine*, Issue 257, May 2008, 15–16; Li Jianhong, "The Precondition for Establishing Human Rights is to Circumscribe the Power of the Government on Various Levels," *Chinarural.org*, April 16, 2009 (accessed July 22, 2010), http://www.chinarural.org/newsinfo.asp?Newsid=26283;

Yunqing Zhou, May 15, 2009 comment on "A Social Commentary: How to Safeguard the Farmers' Lives, Property and Safety?" Yunqing Zhou's Blog (accessed July 15, 2010), http://blog.china.com.cn/zhouyunqing/art/671768.html; and Yang Chun, "Criticisms from a Professor at the School of the Communist Party Over Abuse of Power by Cadres," *Sina.com.cn*, April 22, 2010 (accessed July 27, 2010), http://news.sina.com.cn/c/2010-04-22/155320131100.shtml.

12. Will Hutton, *The Writing on the Wall: China and the West in the 21st Century* (Taipei: Yuan-Liou Publishing Co. Ltd., 2009), iii.

13. Industries such as steel, cement, and chemicals have already begun showing overcapacity. As in the past, government-directed investment often leads

to additional investment in industries already producing at below capacity. Waste of scarce resources and incurring high opportunity costs are some of the inauspicious consequences.
14. People's Republic of China State Statistical Bureau, *China's Statistical Yearbook, 2009* (Beijing: China Statistical Publishing House, 2009), 261,272; and People's Republic of China State Statistical Bureau, *China's Statistical Yearbook, 2007* (Beijing: China Statistical Publishing House, 2007), 298.
15. The six provinces are Hebei, Jiangsu, Shandong, Henan, Guangdong, and Sichuan, with respective population sizes of 69.9, 76.8, 94.2, 94.3, 95.4, and 81.4 million. *China Statistical Year Book 2009*, 91.
16. For statistics in the subsequent discussion, cf. Ibid., 91, 265, 268–269.
17. Yifu Lin, *Analyzing China's Economy* (Taipei: Times Daily Cultural Publishing Co. Ltd., 2009), 284.
18. Anne Tang, ed., "China's urban fixed-asset investment up 33.1% in first 10 months," *Chinaview.cn*, November 11, 2009 (accessed August 12, 2010), http://news.xinhuanet.com/english/2009-11/11/content_12430989.htm.
19. Shuang Mu, "China's Stock Market Mired in a Wild Frenzy," *Open Magazine,* June 2007, 74–75.
20. "China Housing," Geographic.com, March 27, 2005 (accessed July 27, 2010), http://www.photius.com/countries/china/geography/china_geography_housing.html.
21. "China's Developing Real Estate History 中國房地產發史," Baidu.com, April 23, 2010 (accessed August 15, 2010), http://hi.baidu.com/zhqs/blog/item/7402a91b8a2e8b158618bff8.html; and, "China Real Estate Development Group as a whole into China Communications Construction Group" Chinarealestatenews.com, Aug 6, 2010 (accessed August 15), 2010, http://www.chinarealestatenews.com/news/2010-08-06/22782/.
22. The original name for the current Real Estate Development Group was China Real Estate Development Company. See: "A Brief Introduction to China's 30 Candidate Primary Real Estate Companies in Beijing 中國品牌地產30強 北京候選企業簡介," Hexun.com, November 30, 2007 (accessed August 15, 2010), http://house.hexun.com/2007-11-30/101898031.html.
23. During early years of reform, market for new housing construction aimed mostly at enterprises that purchased units with employee benefits for their members of staff.
24. Zhqs's Blog, April 23, 2010 comment on "A Development History of China's Housing Industry," Safety?" Zhqs's Blog (accessed August 14, 2010), http://hi.baidu.com/zhqs/blog/item/7402a91b8a2e8b158618bff8.html
25. "China's Real Estate: Black-Hole Capital Trap," Oftwominds.com, July 14, 2010 (accessed August 14, 2010), http://www.oftwominds.com/blogjuly10/china-capital-trap07-10.html.
26. "China's Real Estate Development Annals," Credit Web Net, August 2, 2010 (accessed August 12, 2010), http://www.zhongyian.com/zhongyiandongtai/90/n-12690.html.

27. Zhqs's Blog, comment on "A Development History of China's Housing Industry," Safety?"
28. "China Mortgage," Economy Watch, May 28, 2005 (accessed August 14, 2010), http://www.economywatch.com/mortgage/china.html.
29. Haitao Wang, "Shanghai's Real Estate Alarms Zhong Nanhai," *Open Magazine,* May 2005, 16–17, "Zhong Nanhai" is China's seat of power as the White House in the U.S. *Open Magazine.*
30. Ibid.
31. "Asia China Housing Bubble China Miracles," Money Matters, July 23, 2010, http://www.minyanville.com/businessmarkets/articles/asia-china-housing-bubble-china-miracles.
32. Tyler Durden, "China Has Been Covertly Funding A Housing Bubble Five Times Larger Than That Of The US: 65 Million Vacant Homes Uncovered," Zerohedge.com, July 14, 2010, http://www.zerohedge.com/article/china-has-been-covertly-funding-housing-bubble-five-times-larger-us-65-million-vacant-homes-.
33. Jim Jubak, "Real Estate Sales Fall by 70% in Beijing and Shanghai on China Property Tax Fears," *Jubakpicks.com,* June 1, 2010 (accessed August 15, 2010), http://jubakpicks.com/2010/06/01/real-estate-sales-fall-by-70-in-beijing-and-shanghai-on-china property-tax-fearshtml.
34. Wang, 16–17.
35. The most serious unembellished instance of criminal–official association took place in Shanghai. The main character in the drama was Zhou Zhengyi who, among other business activities, was active in the housing development projects in Shanghai. *Forbes* listed him as number 90-something among the world's richest in 2002. The following year, he rose to be number eleventh as the world's richest. The central administration initiated an investigation. The process was derailed by the then party secretary general of Shanghai Liangyu Chen. "The Criminal Case of Zhou Zhengyi is one of Financial Deceptions周正毅案核心是金融詐騙," xs.gd.cn, October 30, 2009 (accessed August 15, 2010), http://www.xs.gd.cn/m/jr/23999.htm. In the end, Zhou was charged only with misrepresentation of registered capitalization. The sentence was three-year imprisonment. Jinbao Liu, on the other hand, was an associate of Zhou. He was charged with corruption, bribery, and unaccounted sources of mammoth wealth. The sentence was death. Though Zhou was rearrested and charged with the same crimes as Liu five months after his release from first imprisonment, one may wonder as to why he was faced with only a token charge during the first round of investigation.
36. David Barboza, "China Passes Japan as Second-Largest Economy," the *New York Times,* August 15, 2010 (accessed August 15, 2010), http://www.nytimes.com/2010/08/16/business/global/16yuan.html?_r=1&scp=1&sq=After%20three%20decades%20of%20spectacular%20growth,%20China%20has%20passed&st=cse.
37. Land resource for instance, a valuable asset, belongs to the state. No economic entity or individual owns title to a piece of land, although they may

have secured the right for its use. All mineral resources are also state-owned. That explains why commodity market does not exist in China. In addition, the capital assets in all the SOEs are owned by the state. The shares therein belong to the state. For SOEs whose shares are listed on the market, the majority of the shares are in the hands of the state and are not for trading, artificially pushing up the prices of the shares of these SOEs that are being traded.

38. Mu, 75.
39. *China Statistical Yearbook 2009*, 780.
40. "Where Can We Obtain a Birds View Perspective of China's Stock Market from the Beginning (1990)," Baidu.com, June 24, 2007 (accessed August 16, 2010), http://zhidao.baidu.com/question/30868148.
41. "Shanghai Stock Exchange," Wikipedia The Free Encyclopedia, last modified August 19, 2010 (accessed August 15, 2010), http://en.wikipedia.org/wiki/Shanghai_Stock_Exchange.
42. "China Stock Market Index," Trading Economics (accessed August 16, 2010), http://www.tradingeconomics.com/Economics/Stock-Market.aspx?Symbol=CNY.
43. *China Statistical Yearbook 2009*, 779.
44. Siwei Cheng, "Origin of the Bubbles Resides in Inferior Quality of the Listed Companies," *Finance.ce.c*n, 2007 (accessed August 16, 2010), http://finance.ce.cn/stock/gagdbd/200702/07/t20070207_10346950.shtm1.
45. Mu, 75.
46. "Shenzhen Stock Exchange," Wikipedia The Free Encyclopedia, last modified May 29, 2010 (accessed August 15, 2010), http://en.wikipedia.org/wiki/Shenzhen_stock_Exchange.
47. "An Analysis of 'The Changing Environment' Phenomenon and 'The Localization Trend' Characteristics During the Process of Our Economic Reform 轉型時期我國經濟改革中的 '淮桔成枳' 現象與 '本土化' 特徵分析," Lunwenda.com, April 15, 2008 (accessed August 14, 2010), http://www.lunwenda.com/jingjixue200804/4212/.
48. Jim Quinn, "Why the China Miracle Is Really a Debt-Financed Bubble," Minyanville.com, August 9, 2010 (accessed August 16, 2010), http://www.minyanville.com/businessmarkets/articles/asia-china-housing-bubble-china-mriacle/8/9/2010/id/29519.
49. "What Will Become of Our High Tech Products Consequent Upon WTO Membership 加入WTO中國高新技術產業怎麼辦？," MOST.gov.cn., May 29, 2002 (accessed August 10, 2007), http://www.most.gov.cn/gxjscykfq/dtxx/200205/t20020529_8990.htm.
50. "Industrial and Commercial Bank of China," Wikipedia The Free Encyclopedia, last modified August 16, 2010 (accessed August 17, 2010), http://en.wikipedia.org/wiki/Industrial_and_Commercial_Bank_of_China.
51. Ibid.
52. Ibid.
53. Other than the entry of foreign financial institutions into the Chinese markets, other foreign service industries such as entertainment, tourism and

restaurants will all pose compelling challenges to domestic concerns consequent upon China's entry into the WTO.
54. *China Statistical Yearbook 2009*, 91, 111.
55. Ibid., 111, 449.

9 Concluding Observations

1. Raphael Shen, *The Polish Economy: Legacies from the Past, Prospects for the Future*" (New York: Praeger Publishers, 1992), 3.
2. Raphael Shen, *The Restructuring of Romania's Economy: A Paradigm of Flexibility and Adaptability*" (New York: Praeger Publishers, 1997), 3.
3. The successful land reform program in Taiwan first placed a ceiling on the rent that landlords could collect from their tenants. The ceiling was 37.5 percent of the annual harvest. The next step was to oblige land owners to cede the land acreage that they themselves could not personally cultivate to the former tenants. The farmers were then to pay the landowners for the land granted to them on the basis of an installment plan. The former tenants did not have to pay the whole sum of the land worth. The government also assisted them. It sold publicly owned cultivable land to farmers at a price two and half times the value of annual yield. The acreage that a farmer could buy at this reduced rate was a function of available land to prospective buyers. Four years after the inception of the land reform program, the land owners were obliged to sell their land at the same price as the government-offered rate. The former tenants had ten years to pay off the liability. In time, they became land owners. Land-to-the-tiller program was a resounding success. Agricultural productivity soared. Success on farm began Taiwan's successful drive for economic revival and development.
4. "The lifting of martial law in Taiwan—proclaimed on July 14 by President Chiang Ching-kuo—is a welcome development for the 19 million people on the island. However, there was no dancing in the streets in Taipei or anywhere else on the island. The reason for the lack of public jubilation is that the Kuomintang regime still keeps a tight rein on Taiwan's political system: just a few days before the lifting of martial law, a new "National Security Law" was passed, which—while less harsh than the old martial law—still contains a significant number of restrictions on freedom of assembly and association, and on political rights. Other existing laws effectively limit freedom of speech and of the press. "Taiwan ends Martial Law after 38 Years but... *no dancing in the streets*," Taiwan Communiqué, September 1987 (accessed August 27, 2010), http://www.taiwandc.org/twcom/tc31-int.pdf.
5. Ibid.
6. "Park Chung Hee," Reference.com (accessed August 22, 2010), http://www.reference.com/browse/Park+Chung+Hee.
7. Wikipedia The Free Encyclopedia, "Vladimir Putin," last modified August 29, 2010 (accessed August 29, 2010), http://en.wikipedia.org/wiki/Vladimir_Putin.

8. "Mobutu Sese Seko," The Columbia Electronic Encyclopedia, 2007 (accessed August 27, 2010), http://www.infoplease.com/ce6/people/A0833515.html#ixzz0xirRumIH.
9. Joe Wein, "Zimbabwe history and politics" (accessed August 27, 2010), http://www.joewein.de/zw.html.
10. Ibid.
11. "History of Burma," Canadian Friends of Burma (accessed August 28, 2010), http://www.cfob.org/HistoryofBurma/historyOfBurma.shtml
12. The 1991 Nobel Peace Prize winner Aung San Suu Kyi, the daughter of Burma's founding father, was placed under house arrest for her prodemocracy stance. Large-scale demonstrations for democracy in 1987 and 1988 were ruthlessly suppressed by the military. Though still under house arrest, Aung won a multiparty election called by the military in 1990. She won 82 percent of the votes cast. The election results were ignored by the military and for most of the past twenty years, Aung San Suu Kyi has been under house arrest. Ibid.
13. "Myanmar," The Columbia Electronic Encyclopedia, 2007 (accessed August 27, 2010), http://www.infoplease.com/ipa/A0107808.html?pageno=3#axzz0xl10THHx
14. "The World Factbook: Burma," Central Intelligence Agency United States of America, last updated August 19, 2010 (accessed August 28, 2010), https://www.cia.gov/library/publications/the-world-factbook/geos/bm.html.
15. Stephen Young, "Special to the Nation." April 21, 2010 (accessed August 28, 2010), http://www.nationmultimedia.com/home/ 2010/04/21/opinion/Gini-Coefficient-30127515.html.

Bibliography

Baidu.com. "China's Developing Real Estate History 中國房地產發史." April 23, 2010. Accessed August 15, 2010. http://hi.baidu.com/zhqs/blog/item/7402a91b8a2e8b158618bff8.html.

Baidu.com. "Directives Over Some Questions Concerning Accelerating and Deepening the Structure of Foreign Trade 《關於加快和深化對外貿易體制改革若干問題的規定》." Accessed June 23, 2009. http://tieba.baidu.com/f?kz=151117887.

Baidu.com. "Where Can We Obtain a Birds View Perspective of China's Stock Market from the Beginning (1990)." June 24, 2007. Accessed August 16, 2010. http://zhidao.baidu.com/question/30868148.

Barboza, David. "China Passes Japan as Second-Largest Economy." *New York Times*, August 15, 2010. Accessed August 15, 2010. http://www.nytimes.com/2010/08/16/business/global/16yuan.html?_r=1&scp=1&sq=After%20three%20decades%20of%20spectacular%20growth,%20China%20has%20passed&st=cse.

Bill Brugger, and Steven Reglar. *Economy and Society in Contemporary China*. Stanford, CA: Stanford University Press, 1994.

Brussels. "EU requests WTO consultations on Chinese export restrictions on raw materials. *Europa Press Releases*, June 23, 2009. Accessed June 30, 2010. http://europa.eu/rapid/pressReleasesAction.do?reference=MEMO/09/287&format=HTML&aged=0&language=EN&guiLanguage=en.

Canadian Friends of Burma. "History of Burma." Accessed August 28, 2010. http://www.cfob.org/HistoryofBurma/historyOfBurma.shtml.

CCTV. "China's 2009 GDP growth reaches 8.7%." January 21, 2010. http://english.cctv.com/program/newshour/20100121/103664.shtml.

Central Intelligence Agency United States of America. "The World Factbook: Burma." Last updated August 19, 2010. Accessed August 28, 2010. https://www.cia.gov/library/publications/the-world-factbook/geos/bm.html.

Chai, Joseph C.H., ed. *The Economic Development of Modern China Volume 3: Reforms and Opening Up Since 1979*. Northampton: Edward Elgar Publishing Inc., 2000.

Chen, Pokong陳破空. Treading Russia's Path toward Russian Ascendancy: Mystery Solved for China's Frenetic Purchases of Western Enterprises 走蘇聯之路的俄式掘起：中國瘋狂收購西方公司解密. Hong Kong: N.H.K Books 吳興記書報社, 2005.

Chen, Xiwen. "Reforming Tax Burdens in China's Rural Regions: The First time A Change That Took Place in 2600 Years." Hexun.com, August 5, 2008. Accessed August 10, 2010. http://news.hexun.com/2008-08-05/107924192.html.

Chen, Yun 陳雲. *Selected Writings of Chen Yun*《陳雲文選》, Vol. 3 第3卷. Beijing: People's Publishing House人民出版社1995年版, 1995.

Cheng, Chu-Yuan. "Chinese Communists' Political Shift and Economic Readjustment." *Asian Outlook*, Vol. 21, No. 1, January 1986.

Cheng, Siwei. "Origin of the Bubbles Resides in Inferior Quality of the Listed Companies." Finance.ce.cn, 2007. Accessed August 16, 2010. http://finance.ce.cn/stock/gagdbd/200702/07/t20070207_10346950.shtml.

Chinability.com. "GDP growth in China 1952–2009." December 27, 2009. Accessed August 3, 2010. http://www.chinability.com/GDP.htm.

China.org.cn: Home, Business, Economy. "China's GDP grows 11.1% in H1 2010." July 15, 2010. Accessed August 2, 2010. http://www.china.org.cn/business/2010-07/15/content_20501801.htm.

China Infodoc Service China. Accessed Dececember 4, 2009. infodoc@online.be.

China Institute for Reform and Development, ed. *Illustrious Theory, Substantive Implementation*. Beijing: China Institute for Reform and Development, 2008.

China Institute for Reform and Development, ed. *The Path to a Stronger China: China's Reform Stepping into Its 30th Year*. Beijing: China Economic Publishing House, 2008.

China's National Bureau of Statistics 國家統計局. *Fifty Years of The People's Republic of China* 新中國五十年. Beijing: China Statistics Press 中國統計局出版社, 1999.

China's new rural cooperative. "Times Editorial: County Party Secretary General's 'Signing of' Document Imposing Labor Camp Education is an Abuse of Power 時評：縣委書記' 簽發' 勞教文件是濫用權力." June 24, 2010. Accessed July 28, 2010. http://www.xnchzs.com/zixun/ShowArticle.asp?ArticleID=7011.

"China Real Estate Development Group as a Whole into China Communications Construction Group." Chinarealestatenews.com, Aug 6, 2010. Accessed August 15, 2010. http://www.chinarealestatenews.com/news/2010-08-06/22782/.

"China's rural population to halve in 30 years: economist." *People's Daily Online*, February 24, 2010. Accessed July 30, 2010. http://english.peopledaily.com.cn/90001/90776/90882/6901672.html.

CNN. "China's GDP grows by 8.7 percent in 2009." CNN.com, January 20, 2010. http://www.cnn.com/2010/BUSINESS/01/20/china.GDP.annual/index.html.

Credit Web Net. "China's Real Estate Development Annals." August 2, 2010. Accessed August 12, 2010. http://www.zhongyian.com/zhongyiandongtai/90/n-12690.html.

Dan, Youwei但有為. "Astonishing Upsurge in Foreign Direct Investment (in China), A 353% increase During the First Quarter 我國FDI增速驚人，首季增長353%." May 12, 2008. http://www.sinotf.com/GB/ Tradedata/1141/2008-5-12/225938AFGBD.htm.

Data | The World Bank." Energy use (kg of oil equivalent per capita) | Data | The World Bank." The World Bank. Accessed June 5, 2010. http://data.worldbank.org/indicator/eg.use.pcap.kg.oe.

Data | The World Bank. "Exports of goods and services (% of GDP) | Data | The World Bank." The World Bank. Accessed June 5, 2010. http://data.worldbank.org/indicator/ne.exp.gnfs.zs.
Data | The World Bank. "Foreign direct investment, net inflows (BoP, current US$) | Data | The World Bank." The World Bank. Accessed June 5, 2010. http://data.worldbank.org/indicator/bx.klt.dinv.cd.wd.
Data | The World Bank. "GDP (current US$) | Data | The World Bank." The World Bank. Accessed April 12, 2010. http://data.worldbank.org/indicator/ny.gdp.mktp.cd.
Data | The World Bank. "GNI per capita, Atlas method (current US$) | Data | The World Bank." The World Bank. Accessed June 5, 2010. http://data.worldbank.org/indicator/ny.gnp.pcap.cd.
Data | The World Bank. "GNI per capita, PPP (current international $) | Data | The World Bank." The World Bank. Accessed June 5, 2010. http://data.worldbank.org/indicator/ny.gnp.pcap.pp.cd.
Data | The World Bank. "Imports of goods and services (% of GDP) | Data | The World Bank." The World Bank. Accessed June 5, 2010. http://data.worldbank.org/indicator/ne.imp.gnfs.zs.
Data | The World Bank. "Military expenditure (% of GDP) | Data | The World Bank." The World Bank. Accessed June 5, 2010. http://data.worldbank.org/indicator/ms.mil.xpnd.gd.zs.
Data | The World Bank. "Poverty headcount ratio at national poverty line (% of population) | Data | The World Bank." The World Bank. Accessed November 20, 2009. http://data.worldbank.org/indicator/si.pov.nahc.
Data | The World Bank. "World Development Indicators (WDI) | Data | The World Bank." The World Bank. Accessed June 6, 2010. http://data.worldbank.org/data-catalog/world-development-indicators.
Dempsy, Judy. "Economic Reform Lags in Ukraine." *New York Times*, July 25, 2005.
Deng, Xiaoping. 鄧小平, *Selected Writings of Deng Xiaoping*《鄧小平文選》, Vol. 2 第2卷. Beijing: People's Publishing House 人民出版社1993年版, 1994.
Ding, Qingfen. "China to see 'more trade disputes' this year." *China Daily*, March 6, 2010. Accessed June 27, 2010. http://www.chinadaily.com.cn/china/2010npc/2010-03/06/content_9546712.htm.
Du, Qunyang 杜群陽. "A Practical Analysis of Technological Externalities from FDIs' Research and Development 海外研發與FDI技術外溢的實證分析. 國際貿易問題." January 3, 2008. http://www.gjmy.com/Item /8873.aspx.
Durden, Tyler. "China Has Been Covertly Funding A Housing Bubble Five Times Larger Than That Of The US: 65 Million Vacant Homes Uncovered." Zerohedge.com, July 14, 2010. http://www.zerohedge.com/article/china-has-been-covertly-funding-housing-bubble-five-times-larger-us-65-million-vacant-homes-.
Economic Construction Institute. *An Evaluation of Economic Development Policy of the Chinese Communists*. ed. Taipei: Economic Research Division: Economic Construction Institute, 1990.
Economy Watch. "China Mortgage." May 28, 2005. Accessed August 14, 2010. http://www.economywatch.com/mortgage/china.html.

Fang, Weizhong房維中., ed. *Major Economic Events of the People's Republic of China, 1949–1980* 《中華人民共和國經濟大事記》(1949–1980). Beijing: China Social Sciences Press 中國社會科學出版社 1984年版, 1984.

Fureng, Dong and Peter Nolan, eds. The Chinese Economy and its Future Achievements and Problems of Post-Mao Reform. London: Polity Press, 1990.

Freedomhouse.org: Home. "freedomhouse.org: Freedom in the World Comparative and Historical Data." Freedom House. Accessed June 6, 2010. http://www.freedomhouse.org/template.cfm?page=439.

Freedomhouse.org: Home. "freedomhouse.org: Methodology." Freedom House. Accessed November 20, 2009. http://www.freedomhouse.org/template.cfm?page=35&ana_page=341&year=2008.

Freedomhouse.org. "freedomhouse.org: Freedom in the World 2010: Erosion of Freedom Intensifies." Freedom House. Accessed June 6, 2010. www.freedomhouse.org/uploads/fiw10/FIW_2010_Methodology_Summary.pdf.

Geographic.com. "China Housing." March 27, 2005. Accessed July 27, 2010. http://www.photius.com/countries/china/geography/china_geography_housing.html.

Haike 海克. "The Post Zhao Ziyang China 趙紫陽之後的中國." *Open Magazine*, Vol. 218, February 2005.

Halverson, Karen "Article address." February 27, 2006. Accessed June 17, 2010. http://www.bc.edu/schools/law/lawreviews/meta-elements/journals/bciclr/27_2/06_TXT.htm.

Harpaz, Marcia Don. "China and the WTO: New Kid in the Developing Bloc?" *Hebrew University International Law Research Paper*, No. 2-07, February 1, 2007. http://papers.ssrn.com/sol3/papers.cfm?abstract_id=961768.

Hexun.com. "A Brief Introduction to China's 30 Candidate Primary Real Estate Companies in Beijing 中國品牌地產30強 北京候選企業簡介." November 30, 2007. Accessed August 15, 2010. http://house.hexun.com/2007-11-30/101898031.html.

Hsu, Hsing, ed. *Chronicle of a Decade of Reform: 1978–1987*. 十年改革大事記: 1978-1987, Beijing: Hsing Hua Press, 1988.

Hu, Jintao, Chinese President. *Report to the 17th Congress of the People's Representatives*. Beijing, October 15, 2007.

Huang, Jing 黃靜., and Su, Bingbing 蘇冰冰., eds. *China Center for National Accounting and Economic Growth*. Beijing: Being University, 2008.

Hutton, Will. *The Writing on the Wall: China and the West in the 21st Century*. Taipei: Yuan-Liou Publishing Co. Ltd., 2009.

IMF, International Monetary Fund Home Page. "IMF World Economic Outlook (WEO)—Rebalancing Growth, April 2010—Table of Contents." Accessed June 10, 2010. http://www.imf.org/external/pubs/ft/weo/2010/01/weodata/index.aspx.

International Monetary Fund, Data and Statistics. "International Monetary Fund—Data and Statistics—BOP, DOT & IFS Data Browsers." Accessed June 10, 2010. http://www.imfstatistics.org/imf/.

Jia, Daming. "The Present State and Solution for Resolving the 'Three-Rural' Problem." *China Reform*, April 2001.

Jubak, Jim. "Real Estate Sales Fall by 70% in Beijing and Shanghai on China Property Tax Fears." Jubakpicks.com, June 1, 2010. Accessed August 15, 2010. http://jubakpicks.com/2010/06/01/real-estate-sales-fall-by-70-in-beijing-and-shanghai-on-china property-tax-fearshtm1.

Kong, Qingjiang. "EAI Background Brief No. 416," December 4, 2008. Accessed June 29, 2010. http://www.eai.nus.edu.sg/BB416.pdf.

Kuaijiren.com. "The Global Situation and Trend of Foreign Investment in China 中國吸引外資的國際地位及趨勢." Accessed July 30, 2007. http://www.kuaijiren.com/content/23555-0.html.

Li, Jianhong. "The Precondition for Establishing Human Rights is to Circumscribe the Power of the Government on Various Levels." *Chinarural.org*, April 16, 2009. Accessed July 22, 2010. http://www.chinarural.org/newsinfo.asp?Newsid=26283.

Li, Peng. "The Prime Minister's Annual Report in 1992, 1992年國務院政府工作報告." Gov.com 中央政府門戶網站 *(The Central People's Government of the People's Republic of China)*, February 16, 2006. Accessed July 25, 2008. http://202.123.110.5/test/2006-02/16/content_200922.htm.

Li, Peng. "The Prime Minister's Annual Report in 1993," 1993年國務院政府工作報告." Gov.com 中央政府門戶網站 *(The Central People's Government of the People's Republic of China)*, February 16, 2006. Accessed July 25, 2008. http://202.123.110.3/test/2006-02/16/content_200926.htm.

Li, Peng. "The Prime Minister's Annual Report in 1996," 1996年國務院政府工作報告." Gov.com 中央政府門戶網站 *(The Central People's Government of the People's Republic of China)*, February 16, 2006. Accessed July 25, 2008. http://202.123.110.3/test/2006-02/16/content_201115.htm.

Li, Xiannian 李先念. *Selected Writings of Li Xiannian 1935–1988《李先念文選》(1935–1988)*. Beijing: People's Publishing House 人民出版社1989年版, 1989.

Lin, Ling 林淩. "Theory and Practice of China's Economic Reform 中國經濟改革的理論與實踐." *Wanfang Data*, 2007. Accessed July 27, 2010. http://d.wanfangdata.com/cn/periodical_ shkxyj200701033.aspx.

Lin,Yifu. *Analyzing China's Economy*. Taipei: Times Daily Cultural Publishing Co. Ltd., 2009.

Long, Guoqiang 隆國強. "An Analysis for Improving the Quality and Level of Utilizing Foreign Capital 論新時期進一步提高利用外資質量與水平（上）. 國際貿易." December 20, 2007. 116–124. http://www.gjmy.com/Item/8860.aspx.

Lundin, Nannan et al. "FDI, Market Structure and R&D Investments in China." Örebro University & Research Institute of Industrial Economics, April 2007. Accessed January 17, 2010. http://magasinet.oru.se/oruupload/Institutioner/Ekonomi%20statistik%20och%20informatik/Dokument/NEK/Seminarier/wpICSEAD.pdf.

Luwenda.com. "An Analysis of 'The Changing Environment' Phenomenon and 'The Localization Trend' Characteristics During the Process of Our Economic Reform 轉型時期我國經濟改革中的 '准桔成枳' 現象與 '本土化' 特徵分析." April 15, 2008. Accessed August 14, 2010. http://www.lunwenda.com/jingjixue200804/4212/.

Ma, Guilan 馬桂蘭. "An Analysis of the Trend and the Factors of FDI in China 我國FDI獨資化趨勢的動因分析.當代經濟下半月." December 29, 2007. http://www.gjmy.com/Item/8857.aspx.

Money Matters. "Asia China Housing Bubble China Miracles." July 23, 2010. http://www.minyanville.com/businessmarkets/articles/asia-china-housing-bubble-china-miracles.

Morrison,Wayne M. "China's Economic Conditions." *CRS Issue for Congress,* July 15, 1998. http://www.fas.org/man/crs/980717CRSEconomic_Conditions.htm.

MOST.gove.cn. "What Will Become of Our High Tech Products Consequent Upon WTO Membership 加入WTO中國高新技術產業怎麼辦?," May 29, 2002. Accessed August 10, 2007. http://www.most.gov.cn/gxjscykfq/dtxx/200205/t20020529_8990.htm.

Mu, Shuang. "China's Stock Market Mired in a Wild Frenzy." *Open Magazine,* June 2007.

NationMaster Statistics. "Economy Statistics, GDP (1979) by Country." Accessed August 1, 2010. http://www.nationmaster.com/graph/eco_gdp-economy-gdp&date=1979.

National Bureau of Statistics of China 國家統計局. *Fifty Years of The People's Republic of China* 新中國五十年. Beijing: China Statistics Press 中國統計局出版社, 1999.

Oftwominds.com. "China's Real Estate: Black-Hole Capital Trap." July 14, 2010. Accessed August 14, 2010. http://www.oftwominds.com/blogjuly10/china-capital-trap07-10.html.

Open Magazine, Vol. 224, August, 2008, 22.

People's Republic of China State Statistical Bureau. *China's Statistical Yearbook 1996.* Beijing: China Statistical Publishing House, 1996.

People's Republic of China State Statistical Bureau. *China's Statistical Yearbook, 2007.* Beijing: China Statistical Publishing House, 2007.

People's Republic of China State Statistical Bureau. *China's Statistical Yearbook 2009.* Beijing: China Statistical Publishing House, 2009.

Popular Science. "China Plans World's Largest Solar Power Plant." September 8, 2009. Accessed September 8, 2009. http://www.popsci.com/scitech/article/2009-09/biggest-solar-power-plant-set-china.

Prybyla, Jans. *The Political Economy of Communist China.* Scranton, PA: International Text Book Company, 1970.

Quinn, Jim. "Why the China Miracle Is Really a Debt-Financed Bubble." Minyanville.com. August 9, 2010. Accessed August 16, 2010. http://www.minyanville.com/businessmarkets/articles/asia-china-housing-bubble-china-mriacle/8/9/2010/id/29519.

Quotesea Corporation. "Deng Xiaoping quotes." Accessed August 3, 2010. http://www.quotesea.com/quotes/by/Deng+Xiaoping.

Reference.com. "Park Chung Hee." Accessed August 22, 2010. http://www.reference.com/browse/Park+Chung+Hee.

Shao, Wangyu 邵望予. "A Cursory Analysis of the Transformation Process of China's Foreign Trade Increases 試論中國外貿增長方式的轉變.中國論文下載中心." 中國論

文下載中心, June 20, 2008. http://www.studa.net/china/080620/10073999-2. html.
Shen, Raphael. *China's Economic Reform: An Experiment in Pragmatic Socialism.* Westport, CT and London: Praeger Publishers, 2000.
"Sixty Thousand Hainan Farmers' (Properties) Tragically Torn Down." A Special Report. *Open Magazine*, Issue 257, May 2008.
Su, Xing 蘇星. *An Economic History of the New China* 新中國經濟史, revised edition 修訂本. Beijing: The Central Party School Publishing House.
Taiwan Communique. "Taiwan ends Martial Law after 38 Years but…*no dancing in the streets.*" September 1987. Accessed August 27, 2010. http://www.taiwandc.org/twcom/tc31-int.pdf.
Tang, Anne, ed., "China's urban fixed-asset investment up 33.1% in first 10 months." Chinaview.cn, November 11, 2009. Accessed August 12, 2010. http://news.xinhuanet.com/english/2009-11/11/content_12430989.htm.
"The 21 Concessionary Items China Made for Entry into the WTO, 2001 當代二十一條: 中國加入WTO的主要讓步清單," *Open Magazine*, November 12, 2001, 48-49, http://www.secretchina.com/b5/node/105849.
The Columbia Electronic Encyclopedia. "Mobutu Sese Seko." 2007. Accessed August 27, 2010. http://www.infoplease.com/ce6/people/A0833515.html#ixzz0xirRumIH.
The Columbia Electronic Encyclopedia. "Myanmar." 2007. Accessed August 27, 2010. http://www.infoplease.com/ipa/A0107808.html?pageno=3#axzz0xl10THHx.
The Economist: Pocket World in Figures, 2004 Edition, "Ukraine: Statistics and World Ranking of Ukraine," http://www.womenrussia.com/ukraine.htm.
"The latest news and statistics on China's business and economic climate." http://www.Chinability.Com/Reserve.htm.
The Standing Committee of the National People's Congress. *Foreign Trade Law of The People's Republic of China.* April 6, 2004. http://tradeinservices.mofcom.gov.cn/en/b/2004-04-06/8381.shtml.
"The State Council's Decision for Continuing Reform and Improvement of the Structure of Foreign Trade 《國務院關於進一步改革和完善對外貿易體制若干問題的決議》." January 1, 1991. http://www.chinalawedu.com/news/1200/22016/22037/22567/22570/2006/3/zh42711125197360028316-0.htm.
The World Bank. "World Databank." Accessed June 6, 2010. http://databank.worldbank.org.
The World Bank. "The World Bank." Accessed June 6, 2010. web.worldbank.org/wbsite/external/datastatistics/extdecstama.
Trading Economics "China Stock Market Index." Accessed August 16, 2010, http://www.tradingeconomics.com/Economics/Stock-Market. aspx?Symbol=CNY.
True Knowledge the Internet Answer Engine. "China's population in 2009, China's GDP in 2009?" http://www.trueknowledge.com/q/china's_population_in_2009.
Trumbull, Mark. "US–China trade dispute about more than tires" *The Christian Science Monitor*, September 14, 2009. Accessed July 2, 2010. http://www.csmonitor.com/Money/2009/0914/us-china-trade-dispute-about-more-than-tires.

Ujikane, Keiko. "Japan's GDP Grows Less Than Forecast, Pressuring BOJ (Update2)." *Bloomberg Businessweek*, May 20, 2010, Business Exchange, May 20, 2010. Accessed August 2, 2010. http://www.businessweek.com/news/2010-05-20/japan-s-gdp-grows-less-than-forecast-pressuring-boj-update2-.html.

Wang, Dominique T.C. 王泰銓, *China's Foreign Economic and Trade Law* 中共對外經濟貿易法. Taipei Wu-Nan Book Company Ltd 五南圖書出版公司,中華民國85年,1996.

Wang, Dominique T.C. 王泰銓., eds. A Compilation of the People's Republic of China's Most Current Laws and Decrees 最近中華人民共和國法律法規彙編. Taipei: Hanlu Book Company Ltd. 翰蘆圖書出版有限公司, 2002.

Wang, Haitao. "Shanghai's Real Estate Alarms Zhong Nanhai." *Open Magazine*, May 2005.

Wang, Mengkui 王夢奎. *China's Economic Development: Retrospect and Prospect* 中國經濟發展的回顧與前瞻 *(1979–2020)*. Beijing: China Financial and Economic Publishing House 中國財政經濟出版社, 1999.

Wang, Tsuo Tsien, ed. *China's Foreign Economic Relations*. Beijing: Foreign Economic Relations Educational Press, 1988.

WebNet of the Bureau of Statistics. "Foreign Trade 對外貿易." Accessed September 17, 2009. http://www.gov.cn/test/2009-09/17/content_1419657.htm.

Wein, Joe. "Zimbabwe history and politics." Accessed August 27, 2010. http://www.joewein.de/zw.html.

Wen, Jiabao 溫家寶. "Strengthen Supervisory System, Ensuring no Abuse of Authority." *People's Net,* April 9, 2009. Accessed August 25, 2009. http://politics.people.com.cn/GB/1024/9098050.html.

Wen, Jiabao 溫家寶. "The Central People's Government of the People's Republic of China 務府工作報告." Accessed March 19, 2009. http://www.gov.cn/test/200903/16/content_1260198.htm.

Wen, Jiabao 溫家寶. "The Prime Minister's Annual Report in 1998." People.com.cn, March 20, 2008. Accessed July 25, 2008. http://npc.people.com.cn/GB/28320/116286/116587/7021687.html.

Wikipedia, The Free Encyclopedia. "Chinese Economic Reform." Last modified August 22, 2010. Accessed August 19, 2010, http://en.wikipedia.org/wiki/Chinese_economic_reform.

Wikipedia, The Free Encyclopedia. "Industrial and Commercial Bank of China," last modified August 16, 2010. Accessed August 17, 2010. http://en.wikipedia.org/wiki/Industrial_and_Commercial_Bank_of_China.

Wikipedia, The Free Encyclopedia. "List of Countries by Foreign Exchange Reserves." Last modified August 21, 2010. Accessed July 31, 2010. http://en.wikipedia.org/wiki/List_of_countries_by_foreign_exchange_reserves.

Wikipedia, The Free Encyclopedia. "Shanghai Stock Exchange." Last modified August 19, 2010. Accessed August 15, 2010.http://en.wikipedia.org/wiki/Shanghai_Stock_Exchange.

Wikipedia, The Free Encyclopedia. "Shenzhen Stock Exchange." Last modified May 29, 2010. Accessed August 15, 2010. http://en.wikipedia.org/wiki/Shenzhen_stock_Exchange.

Wikipedia, The Free Encyclopedia. "Two Whatevers." Last modified July 24, 2010. Accessed July 9, 2010. http://en.wikipedia.org/wiki/Two_Whatevers.
Wikipedia, The Free Encyclopedia. "The Economy of Poland." Last modified August 20, 2010. Accessed July 9, 2010. http://en.wikipedia.org/wiki/Economy_of_Poland.
Wikipedia, The Free Encyclopedia. "Vladimir Putin." Last modified August 29, 2010. Accessed August 29, 2010. http://en.wikipedia.org/wiki/Vladimir_Putin.
"World Bank Report: A Study of the Prospect and Strategy of China's Utilization of Foreign Direct Investment (Abbreviated) 世界銀行報告: 中國利用外資的前景和戰略研究（摘要）, 世界銀行." Accessed December 15, 2007. http://www.gjmy.com/Item/8858.aspx.
"WTO successfully concludes negotiations on China's entry." *WTO News*, September 17, 2001. http://www.wto.org/english/news_e/pres01_e/pr243_e.htm.
XE The World's favorite currency site. "Home—China Yuan Renminbi—CNY rate table." December 22, 2009. http://www.xe.com/ict/?basecur=CNY&historical=true&month=12&day=22&year=2009&sort_by=name&image.x=53&image.y=12.
XS.gd.cn. "The Criminal Case of Zhou Zhengyi is one of Financial Deceptions 周正毅案核心是金融詐騙." October 30, 2009. Accessed August 15, 2010. http://www.xs.gd.cn/m/jr/23999.htm.
Xue, Muqiao. *Almanac of China's Economy 1981: With Economic Statistics for 1949–1980*. New York and Hong Kong: Modern Cultural Company in association with Eurasia Press, 1982.
Yang, Chun. "Criticisms from a Professor at the School of the Communist Party Over Abuse of Power by Cadres." Sina.com.cn, April 22, 2010. Accessed July 27, 2010. http://news.sina.com.cn/c/2010-04-22/155320131100.shtml.
Yao, Li姚莉. "Adjustment Strategy for Dealing with Transnational Corporations' Investments in China 如何應對跨國公司對華投資戰略調整." April 9, 2008. http://www.jjx.org.cn, http://www.gjmy.com/Item/ 7804_2.aspx.
Yang, Yongzbeng. "SOE reform and private sector development in China." In *China's Third Economic Transformation: the Rise of the Private Sector*, edited by Rose Garnaur and Ligang Song, 85. New York: Routledge Curzon, 2004.
Young, Steven. "Special to the Nation." April 21, 2010. Accessed August 28, 2010. http://www.nationmultimedia.com/home/ 2010/04/21/opinion/Gini-Coefficient-30127515.html1.
Yu, Hongyan. "China to invest 7t yuan for urban infrastructure in 2011–15." *ChinaDaily*, May 13, 2010. Accessed July 24, 2010. http://www.chinadaily.com.cn/business/2010-05/13/content_9845757.htm.
Zhang, Changwen,張昌文. "New Strategic Modification for Utilizing Foreign Investments 新時期國企利用外資的戰略調整." March 7, 2008. http://www.gjmy.com/Item/8877.aspx.
Zhou Yunqing's Blog. http://blog.china.com.cn/zhouyunqing/.
Zhqs's Blog. http://hi.baidu.com/zhqs/blog/item/7402a91b8a2e8b158618bff8.html.

Index

Africa, 76, 103–104, 107–108, 156
Agricultural Bank of China, 49, 186
Antonescu, 118
Asian Tigers, 20, 24, 34, 83, 194

Bank of China, 16, 49, 70, 153, 175, 179, 186
Bay of Pigs, 196
Burma, *see* Myanmar

Castro, Fidel, 196–197
Ceausescu, 118–119, 156, 158
Chen Yun, 9, 30, 37, 39, 52
Chiang Kai-shek, 1, 11
China Construction Bank, 179, 186
Chinese-Foreign cooperative Enterprise Law of 1988, 60
CMEA (Council for Mutual Economic Assistance), 17
COMECON (Council for Mutual Economic Assistance), 55
Communist Party, 11, 19–20, 22, 26, 46, 53, 112–116, 118–119, 121, 142, 157, 190–191
CPC (Central Planning Committee), 3–5, 35, 42, 121
Cuba, 196–197

Deng Xiaoping, 9, 11, 19–20, 112, 128, 163, 186

EU (European Union), 90, 92, 106, 109, 119, 158–160, 169, 186

FDI (Foreign Direct Investment), 56, 58–59, 65, 67, 70–71, 73–74, 76, 78–79, 97, 99, 124–125, 127–129, 133–140, 157, 159–161, 164, 192
Five Anti, 2–5
Foreign Capital Enterprise Law of 1986, 60
FOREX (Foreign Exchange Reserves), 124, 127, 129
Freedom House, 122, 125
Fujian, 30, 57
FYDP (Five Year Development Plan), 5, 8, 14, 18, 66, 75, 77, 82–83, 87, 110, 146, 149, 152

Gang of Four, 19
GATT (General Agreement on Tariffs and Trade), 89
GDP (Gross Domestic Product), 59, 88, 123–140, 143–144, 146, 148–149, 157–158, 161–162, 164, 168–169, 171, 184, 187, 191–192, 196
Gheorgiu-Dej, 118
Gierek, Edward, 116
Gini, 33, 74, 124, 126–127, 129–131, 201
GNI, 123–124, 127–128, 133–134, 138–140
GNP, *see* GNI
Gradualism Approach, 41, 52, 86, 109, 156
Great Helmsman, 1, 7, 9, 11

Great Leap Forward, 6–9, 12, 15, 20, 112
Guangdong, 27, 30, 57–58, 174

Hainan Dao, 58
Hu Jintao, 29, 114, 189
Hu Yaobang, 20, 23–24
Hua Guofeng, 19, 24, 35

ICBC (Industrial and Commercial Bank of China), 186–187
ICC (In Capital Construction), 14–15
IMF (International Monetary Fund), 90, 145, 162

JCV (Joint Capital Venture), 60–63, 66, 70
Joint Venture Enterprise Law of 1979, 60

Khrushchev, 17, 21, 55, 82
King Michael, 118

Land Reform, 2, 5, 7, 14, 193
Land Reform Act, 2
Li Peng, 27, 165
Li Xiannian, 38–39
Lin Biao, 10
Liu Shaoqi, 9, 11, 15, 45

Macro, 12, 17, 20, 25, 31–32, 34–38, 40, 44, 47–48, 53, 66, 111, 113–114, 140, 143–144, 154–157, 167–169, 171–172, 176, 184
Mao, 1–12, 14–17, 19–24, 30, 35–38, 42, 45, 55–59, 66, 82–83, 96, 107, 110, 112–113, 118, 141–142, 147, 154, 163, 168, 177, 190, 203
Mao Ze-dong, *see* Mao
Maytag, 77
Micro, 12, 14, 20, 25, 44, 47, 53, 66–67, 83–84, 88, 110, 150, 154–155, 172, 193, 201
MNE (Multinational Enterprises), 65
Mugabe, Robert, 196

Myanmar, 196

Nastase, Adrian, 160
Ne Win, 196
Nixon, Richard, 90
NSF (National Salvation Front), 119

OPC (Oceanic Petroleum Corporation, Ltd), 77
Open Region (Economic Development Zone), 59
Orange Revolution, 122

PBC (People's Bank of China), 16
Peng Dehuai, 11, 45
People's Bank, 16, 48–49
Petru Groza, 118
Planned Economy, 66, 117, 121
Poland, 60, 111, 115–117, 123, 125–141, 156–162, 192, 199
Politburo, 1, 3–4, 9, 11, 27, 30–31, 35, 37, 42, 52, 119, 121, 190
Pudong, 59
Putin, Vladimir, 193–195

Red Guard, 10, 19
Romania, 111, 118–120, 123, 125–140, 156–161, 192, 199

Sejm, 115, 117
Seko, 195
SEZ (Special Economic Zone), 57–59, 64, 66, 75, 97, 108, 126, 133, 156
Shantou, 57
Shenzhen, 27, 57–58, 178, 182, 184
Shock Therapy, 117, 141, 156, 195
Social Reform, 119, 125
Socialist Transformation, 4–6
SOEs (State Owned Enterprises), 16–17, 25, 28, 43, 47–49, 51–52, 60, 72–73, 83–86, 88, 92–93, 142, 150–153, 166, 176, 187, 199, 216
Solidarity, 116–117, 120
Soviet, 8, 22, 55, 81–82, 115–116, 118, 120

Stalin, 21, 115, 118, 120
Supreme Rada, 121

Taiwan, 36, 56, 64, 90, 102, 193
Three Anti, 2–5
Tiananmen Square, 23, 26–27, 70, 88

Ukraine, 111, 120–123, 125–136, 138–140, 156–161, 192–193, 199
UN (United Nations), 90, 155
UNCTAD (United Nations Conference on Trade and Development), 65
Unocal, 77
USSR, 3, 5, 7–8, 17, 26, 55, 81, 115, 118, 120–121, 157, 195

Vacaroiu, Nicolae, 119

Wen Jiabao, 29, 76, 108, 151, 166

World Bank, 90, 122–126, 145, 155, 162
World Economic Outlook Database, 123
WTO (World Trade Organization), 29, 72, 74, 88–93, 95–96, 99–100, 109, 128, 153, 185–188, 200–201

Xiamen, 57

Yeltsin, Boris, 194
Yushchenko, Viktor, 122, 157

Zaire, 195–196
Zhao Ziyang, 20, 23–25, 113
Zhou Enlai, 1, 9, 35, 82
Zhu De, 1
Zhu Rongji, 27–28, 151, 178
Zhuhai, 27, 57
Zimbabwe, 196

GPSR Compliance

The European Union's (EU) General Product Safety Regulation (GPSR) is a set of rules that requires consumer products to be safe and our obligations to ensure this.

If you have any concerns about our products, you can contact us on

ProductSafety@springernature.com

In case Publisher is established outside the EU, the EU authorized representative is:

Springer Nature Customer Service Center GmbH
Europaplatz 3
69115 Heidelberg, Germany

www.ingramcontent.com/pod-product-compliance
Lightning Source LLC
LaVergne TN
LVHW011813060526
838200LV00053B/3767